STUDIES IN AFRICAN HISTORY

Volume 7

I0091982

GHANA'S FIRST
REPUBLIC 1960–1966

GHANA'S FIRST REPUBLIC 1960–1966

The Pursuit of the Political Kingdom

TREVOR JONES

Routledge
Taylor & Francis Group

LONDON AND NEW YORK

First published in 1976 by Methuen & Co. Ltd.

This edition first published in 2024
by Routledge
4 Park Square, Milton Park, Abingdon, Oxon OX14 4RN

and by Routledge
605 Third Avenue, New York, NY 10158

Routledge is an imprint of the Taylor & Francis Group, an informa business

British Library Cataloguing in Publication Data
A catalogue record for this book is available from the British Library

ISBN: 978-1-032-62258-3 (Set)
ISBN: 978-1-032-62230-9 (Volume 7) (hbk)
ISBN: 978-1-032-62257-6 (Volume 7) (pbk)
ISBN: 978-1-032-62255-2 (Volume 7) (ebk)

DOI: 10.4324/9781032622552

Publisher's Note
The publisher has gone to great lengths to ensure the quality of this reprint but points out that some imperfections in the original copies may be apparent.

Disclaimer
The publisher has made every effort to trace copyright holders and would welcome correspondence from those they have been unable to trace.

Trevor Jones

Ghana's First Republic 1960-1966

The Pursuit of the
Political Kingdom

METHUEN & CO LTD
11 New Fetter Lane London EC4

First published 1976 by
Methuen & Co Ltd
© *1976 Trevor Jones*
Photoset by Red Lion Setters, Holborn
Printed in Great Britain by
Fletcher & Son Ltd, Norwich

ISBN 0 416 84430 8 hardback
ISBN 0 416 84440 5 paperback

Distributed in the USA by
HARPER & ROW PUBLISHERS, INC.
BARNES & NOBLE IMPORT DIVISION

Contents

Ghana and its Administrative Regions

Introduction

Ten years have passed since Nkrumah was overthrown in
Ghana — a decade which has been so eventful in Africa
that the lively, world-wide interest which Nkrumah's
activities once aroused has long since languished. Yet
Nkrumah is assured of a central place in the political
history of modern Africa. He pioneered a distinctive style
of African radicalism, even if he was not the author of its
principal ideas. Under his leadership Ghana between 1951
and 1957 set the pace and pattern for the winding-up of
Britain's African empire. Moreover, after Ghana became
independent in March 1957, Nkrumah succeeded in
holding the world's attention to a degree quite out of
proportion to his country's size and importance. If a 'wind
of change' blew throughout the continent in the early
sixties, he seemed to be largely responsible for its force and
direction. He claimed to have established in Ghana a
progressive political order which he hoped would be a
model for other African states and which would lay the
basis of continental unity. It is the failure of Nkrumah's
political order in Ghana which is the subject of this book.

Conservative observers sometimes regarded sceptically
the high hopes which initially attended African independence. Despotism of one kind or another seemed to them
the most likely form of rule which struggling, backward
states would adopt once they were left to make their own
way in the world. Hobbes rather than Mill or Marx would
be the unacknowledged guiding spirit of the new Africa.
Nkrumah's republic in its later stages therefore required no
special explanation. Had he not gathered all power into his

own hands and put down his opponents then, sooner or later, someone else would have done so. The ideological ornamentation of despotic power might then have been different — or it might not; it would not really matter.

Liberal sympathizers in the western world, on the other hand, have never enjoyed as much influence amongst African leaders as they did in the brief years of decolonization. They saw African independence as the successful outcome of a moral partnership between themselves and the African politicians. Reluctant to abandon their enthusiasm, they sought to excuse the alarming tendencies to personal dictatorship soon apparent in the new states by stressing the peculiar and formidable difficulties which African rulers faced — that is, until their hopes could no longer overcome their fears and they retreated into indifference or cynicism.

Ironically, it is the internationalist left which, in its view of modern Africa, has yet to undergo mental decolonization. The prescriptions it urges upon Africa and the 'third world' generally are as much derived from the worn-out intellectual capital of nineteenth-century Europe as was the idea of empire itself. Nkrumah sought and received advice and flattery from this quarter during his fifteen continuous years of power and it proved to be the source of some of his worst mistakes. The internationalist left was at first in no doubt about the causes of Nkrumah's downfall. Reactionary soldiers, aided and abetted by the sinister forces of capitalism, had conspired to overthrow him. Then, as irrefutable evidence began to mount about the shortcomings of his rule, the simple reasons for praising him dissolved and gave way to equally simple reasons for dismissing him. There had, after all, been no progressive revolution in Ghana. Nkrumah had merely been the mouthpiece of the 'national bourgeoisie', a greedy puppet of imperialism, mouthing revolutionary slogans whilst lining his own and his supporters' pockets at the expense of the masses.

Of course, the story is more complicated than this brief outline of diverse opinions allows. Nkrumah's republic has been regarded variously as a communist satellite state, as an exercise in African caesarism, an an example of 'social fascism', as a case-study of the tensions between modernization and traditional life, and as merely a crude device by which the leader and his followers screwed as much as possible from their subjects. All these elements were certainly present in the first republic — yet no single one of them was so overwhelmingly dominant as to endow it with an unmistakable political identity.

Is it possible to reach a neat conclusion about the political identity of Nkrumah's republic? Casting the analytic nets of western political science — whether liberal or marxist — into African waters can be a frustrating exercise. Their mesh is at once too coarse and too precise. Something will undoubtedly be fished up — details of party and administrative organizations, statistics of social class, the jostling of factions, and so on. From this catch tidy hypotheses about the nature of political action can be processed and consumed according to taste. But the vital substance in which these constructions alone possess life and motion — the dark waters of cultural confusion, ancestral pride, magic and superstition, memories of times past — will have drained away. If outside observers have judged the Nkrumah episode in terms of their own political presuppositions, however, it was partly because Nkrumah himself encouraged them to do so by building his 'political kingdom' upon forms and ideas imported from abroad and adorned by only the thinnest indigenous gilt.

Nkrumah and most of his followers without doubt thought of themselves as modern men charged with a special mission of regenerating negro greatness after the long night of empire. It was psychologically important for them that others outside Ghana should regard them so. Yet they were also the children of their own people, responsive to the inner, secret language of desires, fears and ambitions which they all possessed in common. Nkrumah, the marxist scientific socialist, was also the paramount chief, the consulter of soothsayers. Whilst he reproached his countrymen for their more venal activities, inappropriate to the revolutionary times he declared them to be living in, he also secretly shared in them. The political principles he proclaimed publicly had little connection with what went on in daily life. It all made for a difficult, sometimes tense, and always puzzling relationship between ruler and ruled — and yet it also had its moments of warmth and humour. Although immensely unpopular at the time of his overthrow, no subsequent ruler has succeeded in filling the place Nkrumah once occupied in the hearts of his people. He fell out of their affections not because he was a particularly brutal tyrant, but because in the long run his people did not share his extraordinary belief in the power of politics. They could not and would not be what he wanted them to be.

What can be said about the final years of Nkrumah's saga? Was it an aberration? — an unfortunate departure from a once-promising path towards representative democracy and prosperity for Ghana? Or was it indeed the prematurely strangled model of a future polity, not only for Ghana but for the rest of Africa? No easy answer ought to be expected. My object is not to pass a final judgment — which in any case is impossible — but to lay bare some of the complexities and ambiguities of an important episode in Africa's recent past. And if at times I appear to reproach Nkrumah's republic for straying too far from its British inheritance, let me add that a decade later the political life of Britain itself seems to be moving towards the standards and manners of Ghana's first republic. The consequences of laying down the imperial burden may yet prove to be quite as profound for Britain as for her former colonies. But that is another story.

1 The Redeemer

Nkrumah was born at some date between 1909 and 1912 in the village of Nkroful in the far south western corner of the Gold Coast. His people, the Nzima, were few in numbers, mainly farmers and fishermen, overshadowed by their Fanti neighbours of the western coastlands. Nkrumah's autobiography gives an account of his early years.[1] His family, although not rich, was sufficiently well off to pay for his education, and it was with the ambition of becoming a teacher himself that Nkrumah eventually entered the teacher training college at Achimota, close by the famous Gold Coast secondary school, in 1928.

There he began to feel the first incoherent stirrings of political passions. After leaving college he taught for a while in a Roman Catholic junior school in the small coastal town of Elmina. But school-teaching was unpalatable and after a few years Nkrumah decided to seek a university education overseas. He borrowed money from a distant relative, the chief of Nsaeum, and from a prosperous kinsman who had migrated years before to Lagos and set up a stevedoring business. In 1935, in his mid-twenties, he left the Gold Coast for the United States and an exile which was to last twelve years.

It was in the United States and later in Britain that the vital articulation of Nkrumah's political ideas took place. He moved largely amongst black American and African students living precariously on the fringes of powerful white societies largely indifferent to the opinions of Nkrumah and his peer group. On the verge of maturity Nkrumah felt himself intellectually and spiritually uprooted, his political passions unable to find a focus. Born into an obscure family from a small Gold Coast people, he could find no inspiration in a strong, indigenous tradition of politics. He had to become a modern man, but of what kind? The British system held little attraction for him because of his emotional aversion to colonialism. He found American politics 'too complicated' and alien. But politics of a revolutionary flavour began to fill the gap, encouraged by the small groups of black students, writers and journalists who were like himself searching for a personal and collective identity in a white dominated world. A number of these were moving steadily towards a fusion of racial assertiveness and revolutionary politics no less messianic in style than the varieties of black fundamentalism, but directed towards a secular rather than a heavenly redemption. For some communism appeared to offer a resolution of their problems. Stalin's Russia provided them with a spiritual homeland, whilst by contrast Italy's invasion of Ethiopia late in 1935 revealed their old enemy, white imperialism, once more engaged upon an assault upon their ancestral continent.

Significantly, Nkrumah revealed in his autobiography that the book which influenced him most during his student days in the United States was the *Philosophy and Opinions of Marcus Garvey*. Nkrumah never met Garvey who died in London in 1939, but he was captivated by the colourful Jamaican and his rambling, incoherent writings. Garvey's personality spoke volumes to the younger African who had yet to reveal to the world the traits he shared with him. Both men regarded themselves as messiahs, as men of destiny. Both regarded Africa almost as a spiritual entity, an injured mother to whom her sons would make reparation, and both shared the gift of inspiring uncritical popular support.

Nkrumah, however, did not share Garvey's dislike of

white men and of light-skinned blacks. Napoleon Bonaparte was the only white man whom Garvey admitted to be his equal, and he had quarrelled violently with the light-skinned Edward Burghardt Du Bois who had organized the first Pan-African Congress in 1919 as a sideshow to the Paris peace conference.[2] Nkrumah was an African and therefore psychologically sure of his identity, unlike so many of his black American and West Indian associates who were torn by conflicting emotions towards the white societies they so much wanted to enter and so vehemently rejected.

Nevertheless Nkrumah's racial assertiveness, although certainly not narrow and exclusive like Garvey's, became a central thread in his career. It is as a champion of black rights and the dignity of the 'African Personality' that he is principally remembered today.[3] Anti-colonialist feeling drew its real strength from this racial well. Arguments against colonial rule could always be countered by arguments in its favour, but the latter could never prevail on their merits. The issue was not one of reason but of will — of the powerful desire of the coloured peoples of empire to be ruled, whatever the risks, by their own kind.

After ten years in the United States Nkrumah arrived in London in 1945 and enrolled as a postgraduate student at University College. But his academic interests were marginal to what was now an all-consuming passion for politics. He quickly plunged into African student circles, making contact with sympathetic parliamentarians of the newly victorious Labour government. The Labour party's attitude to the colonial question and in particular to India raised hopes amongst African students that an end to colonial rule in Africa would soon follow. They were to be disappointed. Labour's most pressing problems lay closer to home and absorbed all its energies. Indeed, extending the war-time concept of 'partnership' between the colonies and Britain, the Labour government sought ways of using the vast British African territories to alleviate shortages of raw materials at home. To the impatient young Africans Labour's policy appeared to be an indefinite continuation of colonialism made even more sly than that of the Tories because of its profession of good intentions.

However, in the euphoria following Labour's unexpected victory in the general election, a group of West Indians resident in Britain took advantage of the temporary presence in London of a number of African trade unionists, invited there for a celebratory conference, to organize a Pan-African congress in Manchester in October 1945. This congress turned out to be a milestone in modern African political history. It was the first such congress dominated by African as distinct from West Indian and American negroes. With the young radical students forcing the pace — Nkrumah himself acted as rapporteur — it produced a series of militant, uncompromising demands which were to determine the style of the nascent nationalist movements in their homelands. To follow up the congress and maintain the momentum behind its demands, Nkrumah helped to set up the 'West African National Secretariat' in London to attract support for a rapid end to colonial rule in West Africa.

In London Nkrumah lived in a twilight world of cheap lodging houses, cold winters, grubby cafés and incessant political argument. As in the United States the company he kept was largely that of other African students. It was an atmosphere in which the demagogue and the café politician thrived, isolated from the mainstream of metropolitan life and seemingly unlikely ever to be called upon to match their actions to their words. It was in England that Nkrumah, making use of a letter of introduction from a West Indian trotskyite, C.L.R. James, first met the Trinidadian, George Padmore. Padmore was only three years older than Nkrumah but was to play an important part in the shaping of the African's still somewhat incoherent political ideas. Possessing a more vigorous intellect than Nkrumah and far more sophisticated, Padmore had travelled widely in pursuit of political enlightenment. Finishing his education in the United States, Padmore joined the American Communist Party and wrote for the New York *Daily Worker*. In 1929 he went to Russia to teach in Stalin's 'University of the Eastern Toilers', but soon left for Vienna and then Hamburg to work on colonial issues for the Comintern. In 1933, after the National Socialists came to power in Germany, he was deported to Britain and became friendly with Nancy Cunard, the radical, negrophile daughter of the shipping magnate. But in 1934, when Stalin began to soften his anti-colonial line because of his growing uneasiness over Hitler's Germany, Padmore quit the Comintern and renounced his links with Russia in disgust. His political thinking began to focus upon 'Pan-Africanism', as the only hope of salvation for the black man from the depredations of both western and Russian imperialism.

A warm friendship grew between the two men when they first met. There was even a curious physical resemblance between the older West Indian and Nkrumah. Padmore thought that Nkrumah was promising, malleable material from which he might fashion the instrument of his designs. He had previously held similar hopes of Nmandi Azikiwe, but the wily Nigerian had shown no disposition to swallow Padmore's lectures. Padmore, however, worked on Nkrumah's vanity, encouraging the latter's half-formed belief in himself as a man of destiny. Nkrumah in turn was impressed by Padmore's superior powers of articulation and his cosmopolitan, political experience. The West Indian's creed of pan-Africanism moreover helped to resolve the confusions which lay at the heart of Nkrumah's political ideas. Henceforth Padmore spent a great deal of time guiding and advising the fiery colonial. After Nkrumah's return to the Gold Coast, Padmore continued working in student circles and in 1951 was invited to attend Nkrumah's installation as leader of government business. But he believed himself to be at a dead-end in London, and in 1957 successfully prevailed upon his former protégé for a post in his newly independent government.[4]

The story of how Nkrumah and his party successfully led the Gold Coast to independence has already been fully and ably recorded and does not need elaboration here.[5] The British view of the end of empire in tropical Africa still awaits a definitive history, but it is at least clear that the British presence in the Gold Coast was not the principal obstacle facing the nationalist movement in the years between 1948 and 1957. The liquidation of Britain's African empire was determined at least as much by events and forces in London as by pressures in the colonies. By the late forties and early fifties Labour and Conservative governments alike had decided that once more the colonies were millstones around their necks. With the 'cold war' at its peak, British attention was riveted upon Berlin and the Far East where, in 1950, war loomed in Korea. The decision was taken in Whitehall to withdraw from Africa if only a decent formula could be found. What followed resembled nothing so much as a strange waltz in which the British government danced the female part, gliding gracefully backward in the embrace of its partner. As the nationalists moved forward, so the British withdrew — not so fast as to throw them off balance, but not so slow as to risk a collision. Despite an occasional, awkward stumble, the two moved together in reasonable harmony. But before the waltz could begin the British had to find acceptable partners.

Nkrumah's first start as a professional politician, the only career he ever followed, was given him by Dr Danquah in 1947.[6] Danquah, the chairman of the 'United Gold Coast Convention', the only important political association in the Gold Coast, needed a full-time general secretary for his working committee to inject much-needed energy into the rather sluggish Convention. Nkrumah, who was then in London, was suggested to him by Ako Adjei,[7] a young graduate recently returned from there. The Convention had as its aim self-government for the Gold Coast 'in the shortest possible time'. Its leading members were for the most part professional men of good family who regarded themselves as the natural heirs to power when the British acceded to self-rule. Although politics seemed almost to be a part-time activity for the Convention's working committee, it was unable to resist the temptation of exploiting the atmosphere of popular restlessness which affected the Gold Coast, as it did other West African territories, in the post-war years. The end of the war had not brought the immediate resumption of pre-war 'normalcy' in trade, and prices of imported goods were high. But it had brought about the return of thousands of ex-servicemen, dissatisfied with their gratuities and reluctant to sink back into the tedium of village life after the excitements of a great war. Before these springs of energy could be tapped and harnessed, however, the Convention needed new faces to inject life into it.

As things turned out, Nkrumah and the young men who joined with him — some like himself recently returned graduates, proved too much for the Convention to assimilate. An older pattern of Gold Coast life reappeared as tension built up between the conservative, rather staid Danquah and his friends, and the ebullient young lions gathered around the new general secretary. With the same energy he had displayed in London, Nkrumah set about broadening the popular base of the Convention and annexing its discontents to serve his political aims. Danquah, for his part, resented the manner in which Nkrumah built up his own personal following and used the Convention as if it were his own. He also feared, rightly as it turned out, that Nkrumah's forcefulness would bring about a confrontation with the government. Early in 1948 the Convention, acting largely upon the prompting of its general secretary, sought to exploit an outbreak of disorder in Accra. Danquah and his working committee were arrested and sent into exile in the north of the country.[8] The disturbances were eventually quelled, but they caused the Colonial Secretary to initiate an official enquiry which was to have a profound effect upon the colony's subsequent political evolution.[9]

To Danquah's astonishment, the report of the enquiry — the Watson Report — revealed to him for the first time the extent of Nkrumah's association whilst overseas with revolutionary circles. For Danquah, fear of the mob was as strong as his distaste for colonial government, and the revelation confirmed him in his suspicions of the man who had virtually taken over the Convention from him. However, he was by now tied to the wheels set in motion by Nkrumah. The road to self-government, far from being safe and comfortable, suddenly appeared to be both dangerous and unpredictable. A break between the two men seemed inevitable, but who would win?

The tension between the two men and their respective followers continued to build up during the year. Nkrumah had acquired his own newspaper, the *Evening News*, with the help of a businessman sympathetic to his cause, and its tone was both uncompromising and offensive.[10] He had also extended his personal empire by creating a 'Committee of Youth Organizations', bringing together existing youth associations in the colony behind his demand for immediate self-government. Early in September he was dismissed from his post.

Although Nkrumah remained within the Convention for a few months longer, he was already thinking of launching his own party, capitalizing upon the large popular following he had built up. Nkrumah had become the 'show boy', the most widely known and admired politician in the Gold Coast, cutting a path which every ambitious young man without money, education or good family connections could aspire to follow.[11] On 12 June 1949, Nkrumah announced the birth of his party — the Convention Peoples Party — bringing into it many of the younger, energetic men of Danquah's Convention. It was a gamble which paid off handsomely. Master of his own party, Nkrumah's restless energy and demagogic talents were given full rein. He undoubtedly possessed in those days an unerring popular touch, an ability to generate excitement amongst almost all sections of the community. Popular grievances over cocoa prices, the high prices of imported food, the lack of work in the towns, were married to the ambitions of traders, market women, and the younger, educated sections of the community and harnessed to his demand for 'self-government now'. Above all he succeeded in awakening a vague, inarticulate, yet powerful desire for movement — for *change.* It was a desire based not so much upon misery or oppression, but upon the simple, racial impulse of an African colonial community; of having their own way for once with the white man. It was a restlessness easily yet skilfully translated into a political formula: the villain was colonial rule, salvation lay in independence, and Nkrumah was its deliverer.

Nkrumah's accession to power was subsequently rapid. Invited by the Governor, Sir Charles Arden Clarke, to be 'leader of government business' early in 1951, at a time when he was serving a prison sentence imposed for an offence arising out of his political campaign, he became Prime Minister of an all-African cabinet in 1956. He and his party were successively endorsed by three general elections held under constitutions which progressively enlarged the area of local control in the Gold Coast. By the time independence arrived, in March 1957, the CPP held 71 seats out of the 104 in the National Assembly. With the British only too anxious to hand over power to a leader and a movement willing to acquire practical experience of government and able to command wide support, the end of colonial rule was no longer an issue.[12] Nkrumah's principal problems arose from within the Gold Coast, not from any external factors. The most serious problem was the rise of a sub-nationalism amongst the powerful Ashanti people, expressed in the 'National Liberation Movement' of the mid-fifties, which sought to delay the British withdrawal until a federal form of independence constitution could be introduced under which the centralizing power of Nkrumah's party might be diluted. But partly through skilful manoeuvring, partly through the ineptness of the opposition, Nkrumah was able to ride through the crisis in triumph. The road to the political kingdom lay open. With the removal of all external restraints, with undisputed control over his party, and with his party enjoying a secure majority in parliament, Nkrumah had little further use for the conciliatory tactics he had employed before independence and would henceforth be free to deal with opposition in his own way.

A strong streak of vanity is an essential part of the make-up of many ambitious politicians. The young Nkrumah had revealed such a streak even as an obscure, penniless student politician in London when he had demanded that his 'Circle' of revolutionary African students, dedicated to setting up a 'Union of African Socialist Republics', should swear a personal oath of allegiance to himself. In Ghana he showed every sign of enjoyment acting out his chosen part of 'show boy'. His followers had warmed in turn to the pleasure of their hero when he played to their gallery. By the early fifties, only a few years after returning home as a virtually unknown and undistinguished student, he found himself an internationally known figure, the leader of the first black African colony well on the road to independence and the symbol of a seemingly irresistible new wave in African or even world history. He never recovered his balance after this dizzy ascent. Once at the top, Nkrumah's vanity began to swell to grotesque proportions, untempered by the company of equals and encouraged by those who discovered that flattery could serve their own interests.

It could be argued that Ghana needed a strong, personal leader, well-known by sight and reputation to the illiterate masses; a focus of unity in a tribally-divided country. Moreover, as will be shown later, Nkrumah's hold over his movement depended to a great extent upon his ability to act as the supreme arbiter over its internal disputes. But the cult of personality with which Nkrumah surrounded himself in later years went far beyond deliberate calculations of policy. Naturally, as founder of the Republic, he had assumed all its grandest titles.[13] Ghanaians, however, like many other West African peoples, are sensitive about ancestry and family pedigree. The idea of equality does not particularly interest them, except in the context of relations between different races. As disenchantment set in it seemed to his many critics that his exalted rank and style was designed to compensate for his modest origins. Freed from overt public comment — protected even from the mild criticism uttered by one of his supporters, a university professor, of the atmosphere of 'unsober adulation' with which he allowed himself to be surrounded — the later Nkrumah began to show signs of megalomania corrosive to his political judgment.

Despite his inordinate vanity, which turned many of his old associates against him, Nkrumah continued to exercise his considerable charm over many of his admirers. He was not by nature a particularly cruel or vicious man. On the contrary he was made of rather softer, more sentimental material than many contemporary despots. Physical violence — of which he was the object several times in his career — repelled him and he shrank from political murder. The public executions now common in many parts of Africa had no place in his republic. The cruelties of his régime sprang as much from the activities of some of his subordinates, acting in his name and under his protection but usually without his knowledge, as it did from his own actions.

His personal charm was undeniable and his choice of friends transcended any ideological differences. Yet there was an element of capriciousness amounting to impru- dence in his selection of associates. Nkrumah was excessively loyal and generous towards those early political supporters who had accepted his authority without ques- tion. Many of them were later rewarded with posts of greater importance than their real talents merited. Others cynically used Nkrumah's partiality to flattery to advance them- selves. Tawia Adamafio, who rose in Nkrumah's esteem until he was widely and jealously regarded as his heir apparent, shamelessly exploited Nkrumah's trust and liking for him until his abrupt downfall in 1962. Yet Adamafio had been a bitter opponent of Nkrumah until a late date and had been welcomed into the party and favoured with all the generosity due to a repentant convert. Dr Danquah, on the other hand, who had given Nkrumah his start in political life, pioneered the independence movement after the war, and given his country its new name, died in one of Nkrumah's jails, an old, disappointed and sick man whose pleas went unheeded until it was too late. Characteristically his death brought a fit of belated remorse upon Nkrumah who had hitherto treated him with contempt and vindictiveness.[14]

In his later years of power Nkrumah's political ideas became both more precise and more incoherent. Moving away from the 'African socialism' based upon the 'African Personality' which he had favoured at the time of independence, Nkrumah arrived at 'scientific socialism' very similar to the kind officially propounded by the Soviet Union and its European satellites. He did not, however, reach this refinement by a systematic analysis of Ghana's position in the world. He was half-pushed, half-attracted towards it by the persuasions of his circle of foreign advisers, and by his own desire to recoup the ground he had lost as other African countries became independent. If he could no longer hope to be the architect of African continental union, then he could at least appear as Africa's philosopher king. His 'scientific socialism' had to be distinguished from other, rival brands by its title, 'Nkrumaism', which purported to be the only true 'ideology of the new Africa'. Various books outlining his position, not altogether consistently, appeared under his own name but drew largely upon the effort of other people who helped to give expression to his ideas.[15] Their message was emotional and apocalyptic; modern Africa was threatened by the sinister forces of world imperialism, and its only defence lay in embracing Nkrumah's formula of unity and socialism. Apart from this message, which, with its implication of Nkrumah's infallibility, did not commend itself to other African leaders, the books bore little consistent relationship either with the corpus of European marxist-leninism or with Nkrumah's activities as a politician. One Hungarian writer who taught for two years at Nkrumah's Ideological Institute considered that Nkrumah's political ideas 'should be studied geologically, for they consist of a number of successive layers of thought, almost hermetically sealed one from the other, and completely disconsonant both in style and matter'.[16]

The great importance attached by Nkrumah to ideological questions reflected in part the excessive intellectualism of an undistinguished student who had arrived at a position where he was able to impose his views upon others by all means short of persuasion. But it is likely that it represented in a contemporary form an old and deeply rooted West African obsession with 'book' — the secret of the white man's power. This had manifested itself earlier throughout colonial West Africa as a deep interest in Christianity. For their own purposes, European missionaries had been willing to represent their faith as the fountainhead of the powerful, alien culture to which they belonged. Nkrumah and other modern Africans had abandoned this particular Christian avenue in their search for the white man's philosopher's stone. It had after all yielded little of material value. But socialism — and 'scientific socialism' for Nkrumah in particular — with its invocation of the demonstrable power of modern science liberated another, more promising hare which they were eager to pursue. If 'scientific socialism' had apparently lifted Russia and China out of backwardness and made them mighty and respected powers, why should it not do the same for modern Africa?

Nkrumah's obsession with 'scientific socialism' stood in strange contrast with the almost universal beliefs in magic and the supernatural amongst his fellow countrymen. For them the world is peopled by benign and malignant spirits who take a lively interest in human affairs. They must be propitiated from time to time and their assistance can be invoked for one's own protection or to secure the downfall of an enemy. It is difficult for the European observer to gauge the importance of such beliefs in political life. For various reasons they have been ignored or suppressed, or dressed out in the more acceptable garments of folklore or traditional medicine, a quaint, picturesque expression of the 'African personality'. Colonial rule, popular education and independence have all had an impact upon such beliefs but have not succeeded in eradicating them. The CPP was a party committed to the ideals of modernity, science and progress. But underlying these public ideals superstition sometimes showed itself, not necessarily as a decisive spring of political action, but rather as an ancestral, subterranean influence even amongst the leadership of the party. At his trial in 1963, Ako Adjei, Nkrumah's early associate and an honorary doctor of philosophy, asserted in his defence that he had buried £25,000 taken from the Ghana Commercial Bank whilst he was Foreign Minister at the prompting of a spirit called 'Zebus', a visitor from the planet Uranus, who had promised to double the sum for him. Tawia Adamafio, a former general secretary of the party, admitted to consulting fetish priestesses for protection against his enemies. Kofi Baako, the leader of the party in the Assembly, publicly accused a cabinet colleague of using 'black juju' to destroy him. Even the head of the Kwame Nkrumah University of Science and Technology resorted to the use of an 'occult pendulum' to decide the guilt or innocence of students accused of fomenting a disturbance.[17] Other instances of magical practices occur from time to time in the story.

Nkrumah himself appeared to be affected by these widespread and deeply rooted superstitions. He recounted in his autobiography an incident which occurred in early childhood and which hinted at a belief in his own powers of second sight.[18] In later life he is known to have consulted the priestess of the reputedly powerful Akonedi shrine outside Accra on several occasions. One of his favoured countrymen, Ambrose Yankey, a distant relative who was in charge of the presidential bodyguard, was reputed to have discharged other, more occult duties from time to time in a special room reserved for such purposes within Flagstaff House. Yankey was certainly instrumental in securing for the President the services of a powerful fetish priest, a native of Guinea known as 'Kankan Nyame' or Alhaji Iwa, who was important enough to Nkrumah to be made a beneficiary of the latter's will to the amount of ten thousand pounds.[19] Seemingly more confident in the kind of magic practised by Muslims, Nkrumah also secured the services of another practitioner from Dakar in an attempt to rescue from its difficulties the OAU summit conference he wanted so much to stage in Accra in 1965.

This hidden and mysterious element in the lives of Ghana's public men does not, of course, account for all or even an important part of their political activities. But it makes an analysis of their political ideas, based upon the assumption that they thought exactly like European men in terms of European concepts — of which 'scientific socialism' is one — somewhat shallow. For many of them the use of English rather than their vernaculars for the expression of political ideas was not simply a matter of choosing the most suitable language in which to express themselves; it was a matter of choosing between different worlds of consciousness and experience, each with its own rules, conventions and insights, unrelated to and often inconsistent with each other. Using English, Nkrumah and his followers could claim with all seriousness to be 'scientific' and 'progressive'. In their vernacular world, however, they still lived amongst and respected the supernatural activities of good and bad spirits.[20]

By the early sixties Nkrumah had come to believe in the

legend he had created of himself as the man of destiny who alone possessed the key to Africa's future. He lacked a sense of irony which might handicap a visionary but is most useful for a statesman. He had set himself over and above other men, particularly those who had been closest to him in the early days of his movement, although he could not dispense with their services. As head of state, life chairman of his party and President, he jealously guarded his prerogatives. His suspicions of those old colleagues who might harbour hopes of the succession grew stronger. As for the others in his party, he grew indifferent to their squabbles, as if to emphasize the difference between his own Olympian position and the concerns of merely mortal men.

From his exalted but isolated position Nkrumah sought companions from outside the circle of his countrymen. He felt at ease with his cosmopolitan courtiers since they were aloof from local issues and utterly dependent upon his favour. The only price to be paid for their admission was to conceal their true feelings for their patron. Nkrumah never felt comfortable with those he suspected were cleverer than himself, or who he felt secretly despised him. Even before 1960 there had been a feeling in the party that too many outsiders — particularly West Indians and American blacks, who were on the whole not popular in Ghana — had been given jobs by Nkrumah. George Padmore's appointment especially, had annoyed the civil servants who resented his *ex-officio* influence, and it grated with Nkrumah's political chiefs who found Padmore's arrogance hard to take. Padmore died in 1959, but his posthumous monument, the Bureau of African Affairs set up in the following year, continued to keep Nkrumah's African policies beyond the reach of his cabinet colleagues.

So long as Ghana's course seemed set fair, however,

Nkrumah's followers grudgingly accepted the presence of the strangers. But when things began to go wrong they served as one focus of the party's unease. After Padmore's death the greatest influence wielded by an expatriate was that of Geoffrey Bing, a left-wing Ulsterman and a former Labour member of parliament in Britain. He served as Nkrumah's constitutional adviser for ten years and for a time acted as Attorney General. In these capacities he was widely regarded, perhaps somewhat unfairly, as the sinister architect of much of Nkrumah's repressive legislation.[21]

However, the cosmopolitan courtiers remained a carapace upon political life rather than a fount of power. They were a source of ideas and discussion, willing listeners to Nkrumah's political table talk. Nkrumah was particularly excited by their espousal of him as the apostle of African unity. Lacking much interest in domestic affairs they constantly encouraged him to look beyond Ghana's frontiers. But their enthusiams failed to strike any popular chords. Perhaps, in retrospect, Ghanaians got their independence too easily and were not disposed to make sacrifices in the pursuit of their leader's *ignis fatuus*. Perhaps, from another point of view, they showed practical common sense in preferring the concrete issue to the abstract ideal. Perhaps they felt that African unity would somehow follow automatically from Ghana's independence. It was an ideal with the power to excite, but not to move. In the darkening situation of 1965, one member of parliament expressed a common view when he spoke of the need for reform at home before unity abroad:

Many people cannot see our connections with Uganda, Kenya, Southern Rhodesia and other states far away. They know Bondoukou is in the Ivory Coast, that is, our immediate neighbour. We know that our people will support us physically and morally, but if they see something in a concrete form, they will be in a better

position to pray for unity to come quickly. If we tell
them that we are going to have unity with the UAR they
ask 'where is it?' If one speaks to them about Morocco
or Ethiopia, they ask 'are they in *Aburokyiri?* (Europe)
If one speaks about East Africa they think that is is a
far-away place, probably at the end of the world. When
our people think of Africa, they think of the man in
Bondoukou, Abidjan, Togo and other towns in neighbouring states.[22]

In curious contrast to his dream of binding Africa into one
great union, Nkrumah began in his later years to favour
men drawn from Nzimas and Fantis, with whom he shared
a vernacular, for both his private and public business. It
was not only the cosmopolitan court but also the charmed
circle of his kinsmen which made his lieutenants uneasy.
After the unsuccessful attempt on his life in 1962 Nkrumah
put his personal security in the hands of a 'special
intelligence unit' of two hundred and eighty men drawn
largely from the Fantis and Nzimas and headed by a Fanti,
Ambrose Yankey. Kwaw Swanzy became Minister of
Justice and then Attorney General. The energetic Kwesi
Armah was recalled from the High Commission in London
to take over the trade ministry. Ekow Ampah replaced
John Tettegah as head of the trade union movement.
Andrew Djin enjoyed a long career to the end as a
government minister. Nathaniel Welbeck increased his
hold over the party's central machinery, whilst other
Nzimas and Fantis were advanced to lesser positions. Their
rise to power, however, fell considerably short of a capture
of power by a tribal faction. It was nevertheless a tilt in a
direction which made other party stalwarts apprehensive
and increased their sense of isolation from their leader.

By 1965, in any case, most Ghanaians were engrossed by
the worsening economic situation. It was the manner in

which this was tackled by which they would judge their leaders. Every attempt at a spectacular breakthrough, or even a modest improvement, had come to nothing, and the people, weary of unfulfilled promises, were growing restive and cynical. Yet Nkrumah did not know what to do next. His advance in the past had largely been made possible by the opportunities opened up for him by others. He was a skilled political actor, but not so good at writing his own scripts. Padmore had inspired him to go on the stage and had showed him some exciting scripts. Danquah had provided him with his first real part in 1947 which Nkrumah had played so well that Danquah — himself an aspiring actor — found himself written out of the play altogether. Komla Gbedemah had given Nkrumah's party its first taste of power in 1951 and had been subsequently relegated to the wings. Thereafter the British provided Nkrumah with a part which, provided he played it with due respect to the stage instructions, left him in undisputed control of both audience and theatre.

After independence Nkrumah continued to play to the gallery, but with diminishing success as the parts written for him dried up. Henceforth he was thrown upon his own resources and was obliged to act out scenarios of his own composition. But the political actor turned playwright was not a success. Vanity and self-importance had blunted whatever originality he had once possessed. His new scripts cast himself as the father of his country and the Messiah of Africa. But in reality he was neither, and his audience, except a few uncritical admirers and paid hacks, dwindled steadily.

II The Republic

Soon after Ghana gained its independence in March 1957, Nkrumah, then the Prime Minister, announced that he would shortly introduce a republican form of government, although Ghana would seek to remain within the British Commonwealth. Ghana's position as a constitutional monarchy after independence was likely to cause misunderstanding amongst other African territories approaching independence. In the following year Guinea became independent as a republic with its leader, Sékou Touré, as first President. Other French African territories seemed certain in the near future to adopt a republican form of government with the passing of French rule. Nkrumah, in his pursuit of pan-Africanism, felt that he could not run the risk of being thought by his African peers as tied too closely to the British connection — of appearing to be rather less independent than they themselves were. Ghana, he announced, was to become a republic because the needs of the country would be best served in this new phase of her history by the adoption of a republican constitution. Ghana could best serve the interests of African unity with a constitution which made special and explicit provision for her union with other African states. The republic would be a symbolic departure, a final severance of the ties which bound the country to its colonial past.[1]

In March 1960, after many months' preparation, the government's draft constitutional proposals were published as a white paper.[2] In broad outline the new constitution bore a superficial resemblance to that of the

United States except, of course, that it was designed to provide a unitary not a federal structure. It nodded in the direction of the separation of the powers of government into its legislative, judicial and executive arms. The first part of the draft enunciated the doctrine that 'the powers of the State derive from the people'. The President, after his election and before taking office, was required to make a solemn declaration upholding the fundamental rights and liberties of the people he governed.

However the separation of powers explicit in the constitution hardly concealed its central feature — the augmentation of power in the hands of the President. Despite the widening of his executive powers as Prime Minster since 1957, Nkrumah was still constitutionally *primus inter pares* amongst his cabinet colleagues. He was still in theory at least subject to the possibility of upset or even removal in the event of a domestic crisis. His new constitution would insure himself against this contingency by providing for a chief executive and head of state, united in the person of the President, to be elected for a five year term of office. The constitutional proposals endowed him with exclusive powers of appointment and dismissal over judges, senior civil servants and officers of the armed forces. As Commander-in-Chief of the armed forces the President would be authorized to order them to engage in any operation he deemed 'expedient'.

Ostensibly parliament — that is, the National Assembly and the President acting jointly — possessed all the legislative powers of the state that were not specifically reserved by the constitution for the people. In practice, however, the National Assembly was to be the lesser, inferior half of parliament. The President was to be given power to refuse his assent to bills, either in part or as a whole, and a special section reserved the right for the first President to give directions by legislative instrument, with or without the assent of the Assembly, enabling him to alter all enactments other than the constitution itself. The former parliamentary practice of raising revenues on the basis of estimates submitted to the scrutiny and vote of the Assembly was retained, but the President was given a 'Contingency Fund' by a special provision of the constitution, giving him access to public money independently of the Assembly's control.

Written constitutions are part of the common furniture of the modern political world. Few of the new states feel that they can do without one, at least at the threshold of their careers. Yet written constitutions which guarantee the greatest degree of personal and collective liberty, only to whittle this down by subsequent regulation and non-observance, are only too familiar. Perhaps, as Joseph de Maistre once observed, the surest sign that a constitution is dead is when it comes to be written down, when it exists on ink and paper rather than in the hearts and spirit of those who govern and those who are governed by it. In Ghana's case, the 1960 constitution of the first republic proved not to be the political stage, deciding the nature of the game played upon it. It was rather a painted backdrop against which the political game was played with only an occasional nod in its direction.

Nkrumah himself moved the motion for the adoption of the new constitution in Churchillian language, referring to the 'sweat, blood, and sacrifice which have made possible the victory of Ghana we pronounce today'. But it was left to the opposition to inject a note of asperity into the self-congratulatory debate which followed. Simon Dombo, one of the leaders of the United Party, asserted that the draft constitution did not reflect the 'peculiar genius' of the Ghanaian people; it was the concoction of a group of expatriate lawyers working under Mr Bing, the Attorney General. Another United Party member, Victor Owusu, who had been with the CPP until the troubles of the mid-fifties, added his voice to the opposition's criticisms. He referred to the abuses of office which had occurred during the CPP's reign since 1951 and which were a cause of so much mistrust. As for the new constitution, Owusu concluded that 'a lot of humbug' could have been avoided if it has been written down in three lines, stating baldly that 'the President shall be responsible for the running of the government, for the dispensation of justice, and for the making of laws in Ghana'.[3]

Despite its misgivings the opposition was unable to delay the introduction of the new constitution, or to secure any substantial amendment to it. The National Assembly, which was elected in 1956, was due under the outgoing constitution for dissolution and re-election in 1961. To make sure of its majority in the new Assembly the government included in the legislation a provision converting the existing one into the first parliament of the Republic, extending its life until 1965. In March the Assembly converted itself into a constituent assembly 'to inform itself as to the wishes of the people on the form of the new Constitution'. Between the 19th and the 26th of the following month the draft proposals contained in the white paper were submitted to a popular referendum, together with the rival candidatures of Dr Nkrumah and Dr Danquah for election to the first presidency. The electors were asked two questions, 'do you accept the draft Republic Constitution as set out in the White Paper of 7 March?' and 'do you accept Kwame Nkrumah or Joseph Boakye Danquah as the first President?'

To the first question the voters gave their assent by 1,009,692 votes to 131,393. To the second they indicated their preference for Nkrumah by 1,015,740 votes to 124,623. But whereas the vote for the first President was regarded as definitive, the vote on the draft proposals did not prevent several interpolations being subsequently made so that the final bill giving force to the new constitution, enacted on 29 June, differed somewhat from the draft submitted to popular vote earlier. After their poor showing in the plebiscite, however, the opposition members were not inclined to put up much more resistance. There was little else for them to do except faintly welcome the few changes which they could regard as concessions to their earlier criticisms.

The power of Nkrumah's government to deal with political opposition by no means rested exclusively upon the provisions of the new constitution. It could be argued that the government of a newly independent state in which tribal and regional feelings run strongly is justified in restricting civil liberties to some degree in the interest of stability. Certainly there existed elements amongst the Ewe, Ashanti and Ga peoples of independent Ghana which were bitterly opposed to the rule of the CPP. A law against tribally-based political associations was passed in 1957 which brought about an alliance of opposition groups to form the United Party later in that year. Early in 1958 an alarming recrudescence of political violence in Ashanti took place which obliged the government to declare a local state of emergency. After this incident certain members of the government felt that stronger powers were needed to deal with malcontents. Krobo Edusei, then Minister of the Interior, was impressed by the news of a preventive detention law passed in the previous year by the Indian parliament. He rushed into the Assembly waving a newspaper containing a report of the Indian act and, without first consulting his cabinet colleagues, commended a similar measure for Ghana. At first the reaction in the cabinet was divided. Nkrumah and most of his colleagues were in favour, but Bing and Kofi Baako were lukewarm. However, they were induced to change their minds, and by mid-year a preventive detention bill lay before the Assembly.

The impact of the Preventive Detention act of 1958 upon the public was considerable. Under the war-time emergency regulations introduced by the colonial government a form of preventive detention was made available to the executive, but its use was strictly controlled by the courts and in fact it was scarcely used. These regulations were still in force and Nkrumah's government had inherited them at independence. Indeed, Nkrumah himself and a few of his close associates had been the principal victims of detention under the war-time regulations, an experience which they capitalized on by making a minor cult within the party of the 'prison graduates'.[4]

When the second reading of the new bill was moved by the Prime Minister on 14 July 1958, it was bitterly criticized by the opposition members. The government spokesmen tried to whip up the bogy of a foreign 'fifth column' at work in Ghana to subvert its independence. Even the war then raging in Algeria was adduced as a threat to Ghana. But opposition members pointed out that existing laws were adequate to deal with such a danger, if indeed it existed. To them it was clearly that the bill was aimed at establishing the supremacy of the CPP through the physical intimidation of its opponents and critics. J.A. Braimah commented bitterly that:

> having accused the British imperialists of oppression and suppression, it is unforgiveable for Dr Nkrumah himself to use worse methods of oppression in the administration of the people he is said to have delivered from imperialist oppression.[5]

But at the end of the debate the twelve opposition members could do little against the sixty-eight CPP members who voted in favour. Eleven of those opposition members —

and some of their successors — were soon to find themselves in preventive detention within the next few years, whilst several others escaped by the skin of their teeth.[6]

The first act of 1958 contained some safeguards for the rights of detainees.[7] Under its provisions they were to be served within five days of their arrest with a written notice stating the grounds for their detention, and these grounds were to be periodically reviewed by the authorities. Appeal against detention was to the cabinet, not to the courts. But the cabinet became increasingly careless about the operation of the act. After the 1966 coup the police chief, John Harlley, maintained that 'the act would not have been so bad if its terms of reference had been observed'. [8] Bing claimed that while he was still Attorney General he had insisted upon observing the proper procedures. But he left that post in 1961 and his successor, Kwaw Swanzy, said later by way of apology that 'nobody ever asked the Attorney General's office to have anything to do with the act'.[9]

The Preventive Detention act was challenged several times in the courts, but to no avail. Dr Danquah, himself later to be detained, appeared on behalf of a client, the chief linguist of the Asantehene, who together with several others had been detained late in 1959. The nub of his case was that the solemn declaration made by the President on taking office had the force of a 'bill of rights' which protected citizens from arbitrary arrest. The government's case, presented by Bing, was that the declaration had no force as a directive to the courts, but was merely a 'generalized policy guide' similar to the coronation oath taken by the Queen of England which had no power to bind the British parliament. The chief justice, Sir Arku Korsah, dismissed the appeal in 1961 on the grounds that the act vested full powers and discretion in the officials taking action under the act. As for the President's solemn declaration, Korsah declared that the people's remedy for any departure from that 'lay through the ballot box and not through the courts'. Other attempts to limit the operation of the act by invoking the British Habeas Corpus act of 1816, inherited by Ghana, were similarly unsuccessful. The Ghanaian Habeas Corpus act of 1864 simply removed the 1816 act from the laws of Ghana.

After the 1966 coup it became possible to get some idea of the numbers detained during the Republic. The *Ghanaian Times* estimated that about 908 were held at the time of the coup, 'although several hundred more were believed to have been held arbitrarily by the Nkrumah regime'. The vagueness of the estimate was not surprising. Originally designed to deal with subversion, the act became a device by which prominent party men got rid of small fry who for one reason or another stood in their way. Members of the opposition probably formed a small proportion of those detained. Many detainees were simply forgotten by the authorities. Many more were threatened with detention by their political masters who had, in the strict letter of the law, no power so to commit them. The result of this capricious abuse of the law was that cabinet ministers, even the Attorney General himself, did not know how many were detained, or upon what grounds.

After the coup Kweku Boateng was questioned closely by his old enemy, Krobo Edusei, the former minster who had inspired the act:

Edusei: How long were you Minister of the Interior?
Boateng: Two and a half years.
Edusei: Well, with your two years as Minister of the Interior, how many times did you inform the cabinet about the number of people being held under the Preventive Detention act?

Boateng: I never did.
Edusei: Why?
Boateng: Because I did not know the number.

With mock incredulity Edusei then said 'you didn't know the number as Minister of the Interior?' The court was convulsed with laughter.[10]

The first victim of the 1958 act was, ironically, Dzenkle Dzewu, one of Nkrumah's earliest associates. He had broken with the CPP in 1958 over an issue which affected the farmers and had gone over to the United Party. Released under the partial amnesty of 1962, he was called to Nkrumah's office. 'When we got there, Nkrumah said "Hello, DD" and I said "Hello, Kwame" and he shut the door. When we were alone in the room, he confessed to me he was so sorry to send me into detention, but certain people were the cause.'[11] Dzewu was fortunate. Nkrumah found him a car and a job in compensation for his four years imprisonment. Others were not so lucky. Conditions inside Ghana's hot tropical prisons were extremely disagreeable, but Boateng claimed that certain detainees were singled out for particularly harsh treatment. Danquah and Obetsebi Lamptey were put into solitary confinement in cells measuring six feet by nine, and although both were very sick men, no adequate medical treatment was provided.[12]

More than any other single measure adopted by Nkrumah's government, the preventive detention law was the most detested, and symbolized for many the true nature of the regime they were subjected to. Civil liberties under colonial rule had been wider and more secure than they were after independence. By introducing arbitrary arrest, Nkrumah and his party had betrayed the ideals of 'freedom and justice' in the name of which they had struggled to end colonial rule. By doing so they had destroyed their moral claim to respect in the eyes of many. It was not so much the necessity or utility of the law which was resented — many Ghanaians who were not warm supporters of the CPP were prepared to welcome firm measures against political terrorism from whatever source — it was the arbitrary, capricious, even offhand manner in which the law was exploited, often for petty ends, which aroused the most anger. No-one was safe; from the ordinary labourer to the most respected elder statesman: from the President's friends to his most inveterate critics.

After the emergency caused by the Takoradi strike in 1961 a fresh torrent of repressive legislation flowed through the National Assembly, although not without objections from some members of the ruling party. The Emergency Powers act gave the President the power to declare a state of emergency without reference to the Assembly or his cabinet. The Criminal Code amending act enabled the government to take action, retrospectively to March 1957, against 'citizens of Ghana who make false reports injuring the reputation... of the Government of Ghana', whether the offence was committed inside or outside the country. The same act also made it an offence to 'show disrespect to the person and dignity of the Head of State'. This act was followed by the Criminal Procedure amending act which provided for special courts, appointed by the President and empowered to pass the death sentence, to try political offenders. It was during the passage of this bill that one of the stalwarts of the CPP, Komla Gbedemah, decided that he had had enough and to break with Nkrumah. Victor Owusu's taunt of the previous year that the government of Ghana was a 'one man show' had for him become true.

The National Assembly invariably passed the bills submitted before it, although not without contentious debate at times. Under the constitution the Assembly consisted of the Speaker and not less than one hundred and four members, each elected by simple majority. Nkrumah as President no longer represented a constituency, but he was free to attend any sitting and was obliged to address the Assembly at the start of a new session. The composition of the Assembly remained remarkably stable throughout the lifetime of the Republic. When the newly enlarged second parliament met for the first time in 1965, eighty-two of its members had been returned at the last general election held in 1956. Between that date and 1963 thirty-three by-elections had taken place, thirteen of which were caused by the arrest or self-exile of members, one by the murder of a member, and the remainder by the natural deaths of the incumbents.

For the most part members of parliament were drawn from relatively modest backgrounds — farmers, store-keepers, clerks, elementary school teachers, building contractors and transport owners — a faithful reflection of the groups who had become politically active after the war and who had given Nkrumah's party its popular support. Nearly all had started their political careers as agents of one sort or another of the CPP. Some had been propaganda secretaries or secretaries of local party branches. Others had been district commissioners who had risen in the party's regional organization. For nearly all of them their election to parliament was the summit of their careers. By prevailing local standards their salaries were large and dependable. They were entitled to the perquisites of subsidized housing in the capital, transport and entertainment allowances as well as enjoying the esteem and influence which were attached to their status. Few of them possessed substantial private means or were conscious of representing great corporate interests within the country. During the elections of 1954 and 1956, which the CPP seemed set fair to win, the fruits of election tempted many enterprising but unauthorized candidates to stand on the CPP ticket. Their intervention embarrassed the party leadership and caused it to tighten up on the selection of candidates. The 1959 party constitution reposed the exclusive right of nominating candidates with the central committee and helped to give rise to the later dispute between CPP members — that members of parliament owed their loyalty to the party which had selected them rather than to their constituents who had elected them.

The CPP parliamentarians were not of the stuff of which rebels were made, although they might occasionally kick over the traces. There was no issue after independence upon which the party leaders would allow their parliamentary majority to be weakened to the point of defeat, even though the opposition was so numerically weak. Fear of presidential displeasure, fear of unemployment, fear of arrest and detention, these were the invisible but effective whips which kept the parliamentary ranks of the CPP under discipline.

When one surveys the general wreckage of parliamentary Africa since the end of empire it seems, in retrospect, that few institutional devices could have prevented the accumulation of power in Nkrumah's hands. The surprising thing is that parliamentary life in Ghana managed to retain as much vigour as it did right up to Nkrumah's downfall. A superficial resemblance to the parliamentary tradition as bequeathed by the British remained, but the game being played after independence was quite a different one. The CPP was born and nurtured in a mood of opposition to colonial rule which was of its nature an unrepresentative form of government. The colonial administration, however, was much more than the rule of a party representing a coalition of sectional interests. It was the creator of the political identity of the

Gold Coast itself, bringing together the territory's contrasting regions and peoples into a common political union. It was also the major source of non-rural employment and patronage. Long before the independence movement got under way the inhabitants of the Gold Coast had grown accustomed to crediting government with more resources, power and ingenuity than it really possessed.

All this prestige the CPP expected to acquire after the British departure. But although the colonial administration had been much more than a ruling party, it was nevertheless not totally sovereign but was accountable to the imperial government in London. Moreover its officers carried out their duties subject to the ethics and restraints of an imperial service. The CPP expected to inherit all the power of its predecessor but was indifferent to its glory — the invisible elements which controlled and tempered its exercise. The transition from empire to independence in Ghana, as in other parts of the former empires, exalted — or debased — politics into what a former adviser to Nkrumah compared to a 'zero-sum' game in which the winner took all and acknowledged few if any restraints upon his inheritance.[13] All the impressive paraphernalia of Ghana's republican constitution could not disguise this central fact of political life.

The principal link man between the party members in parliament and the party outside was Kofi Baako. He was appointed leader of the Assembly in July 1961, succeeding Kojo Botsio. Baako's job was to explain the party's policies to parliament, to ensure discipline amongst CPP members of parliament, and to report on the feelings of members to the party leadership. Throughout the life of the first Republic he was a key member of the central committee of the party and a member of the cabinet. One of Nkrumah's most trusted confidants, he had been a founder member of the 'Committee of Youth Organizations' which was virtually the nucleus from which the CPP had developed. Too young to stand in the 1951 election, he became general secretary of the CPP and in the 1954 general election represented his home town, Saltpond.

Baako was not an unsophisticated party bully whose task was to enforce the party line. He treated the rulings of the Speaker and the Clerk of the Assembly with considerable respect and relied more upon exhortation and persuasion than upon threats to keep discipline. On several occasions he looked into the grievances of individual members of parliament who felt that they had had a raw deal from the leadership. Nor was the Speaker of the first parliament of the Republic, Joseph Asiedu, afraid to stand up to the government front bench and defend the conventions and rights of the Assembly. But in 1965 he was replaced by a former Minister of Justice, K.A. Ofori Atta, who proved more pliable to the wishes of the government. In August that year, during a stormy debate, the new Speaker allowed Baako to usurp his right to rule upon a point of order, thus throwing doubt upon the effectiveness of the standing orders of the house.

Although the Assembly was submissive, it never became totally abject. It was tolerated by Nkrumah as a useful sounding board for grievances and it provided an arena in which the party's factions could openly brawl without damage to the leadership. The government, which had first intimidated and then abolished the opposition parties — turning the Assembly into a branch of the party — actually facilitated these functions. If the Assembly was far removed from the levers of power, what went on inside it did not really matter. Individual members disposed to rebel could do so without running the risk of being accused of jeopardizing the party's majority. Thus it was in the Assembly, not in the party machinery, that the last forum of vital public debate was preserved.[14]

In April 1961, members actually refused to approve a 'progress report' submitted to it by a government minister. The result of this open act of defiance; admittedly directed more against an unpopular minister than against the government as a whole, was that the progress reports were abruptly dropped. Henceforth members of parliament turned to other devices to interpellate their ministers. One which lay at hand was the private member's motion. From 1963 onwards more time was spent upon debates arising from private members' motions than upon debates arising from government motions. The leader of the House, Kofi Baako, regarded it as 'a most encouraging sign' that members were taking their duties seriously. Providing they took care to frame their motions under innocuous titles, backbenchers quickly found that they could force a debate on an issue of their choice without much interference from above.

However, despite the Assembly's development of the private members' motion against the executive arm, Baako made it clear that such motions had no compelling force against the government. He ruled that 'a private member's motion, even when accepted by the House, is in fact an advice to the government, and the government can take it or leave it'.[15]

Nevertheless such motions did exert considerable pressure upon the government. It was, for instance, a backbencher's motion on the distribution of essential foodstuffs which led in March 1965 to the public revelation of ministers' possession of pass-books for use in the wholesale trade of commodities in short supply. And the debate later in the year upon a motion calling for the implementation of the President's 'dawn broadcast' — a motion fiercely resisted by important party officials newly installed in parliament — revealed the extensive and dangerous loss of confidence within the ranks of the CPP in its leadership.[16]

Suleman Ibun Iddrissu, the member of the remote northern constituency of Gushiegu who had introduced the latter motion, was an outspoken, eccentric figure who attracted the wrath of the party leaders — and the covert admiration of many backbenchers — by his frequent attacks upon corruption in high places; attacks which eventually led him to question openly the integrity of the central committee itself. Iddrissu, however, did not have an irreproachable record of probity himself. Born in Kumasi of immigrant parents from the north, he had been an early supporter of the CPP and in 1958 rose to the rank of ministerial secretary. In 1954 he had been censured in the findings of a commission set up to enquire into allegations of corruption made against certain CPP politicians.[17] Iddrissu's later explanation of his dealings was that he had been obliged to adopt the methods of financial pliancy common in the south of the country in order to get a larger share of development funds for the north. Whilst he was a ministerial secretary he was suddenly expelled from the party altogether for being involved in a 'shady transaction' with Dr Emil Savundra when the latter was making a bid to acquire a monopoly of mining rights in Ghana.[18] Still in parliament as an independent, Iddrissu was eventually re-admitted to the CPP in 1961 after declaring that he 'had learned his lesson'.

But Iddrissu ruined his chances of further promotion by continually harrying ministers over corruption. He was determined to be the scourge of those who he considered had abused their public office. In his campaigns Iddrissu pioneered the use of the private member's motion, developing a technique he called 'tactical action' which consisted of praising Nkrumah fulsomely in order to damn his lieutenants. The party leadership was unsure of what it could do to silence him. To have put him into preventive detention would have seemed to vindicate all his accusations. Iddrissu was a lonely figure in the Assembly, regarded by his colleagues as a dangerously reckless, even lunatic, critic of the party and government. But he frequently said out aloud what many dared only think, and the debates on his motions always resulted in a packed house. Angered by the stormy debate of September 1965, sparked off by a motion of Iddrissu's, Nkrumah approached him through another northern member, Susanna Al-Hassan, with an offer of £2,000 to settle his debts if only he would keep silent.[19] Iddrissu accepted the money, but continued his scourging until Nkrumah secured his dismissal from the Assembly early in the new year. However, fortune smiled on Iddrissu, and when the coup took place a few days afterwards, he was one of only two members of parliament not to be arrested by the new regime.

In addition to the use of private members' motions, the National Assembly also retained a measure of independent initiative in its committees. The most vigorous of these was the public accounts committee, which had survived the change to a republican form of government. Like its Westminster counterpart, the public accounts committee was drawn from the backbenchers. Its function was to act as a watchdog over the financial activities of government departments, using material supplied to it by the public auditing service. It did not possess statutory powers to act upon its findings but was able to present them for the attention of the Assembly. Following the Westminster tradition, the chairman of the committee of twelve members was drawn from the opposition party, although a majority of members were of the ruling party. B.K. Adama, the United Party member for Wala South, was chairman until he was served with a detention order late in 1963. The Westminster convention was then broken when he was succeeded by J.D. Wireko who belonged to the CPP. Wireko had been a member of the banned National Liberation Movement and had 'crossed the carpet' to join the CPP ranks in 1960. Two other opposition members, Simon Dombo and A.W. Osei, survived the thinning-out of the opposition after the arrests of November 1961, and continued to sit on the committee for the duration of the first parliament.

The public accounts committee did much useful work in uncovering deficiencies of financial control, wastage of public money, and irregularities in the work of government departments. In 1961 the secretary to the cabinet, Enoch Okoh, arranged that the newly established Budget Secretariat at Flagstaff House should refer all cases of unauthorized expenditure by government departments to the committee. Okoh was appalled by the frequency and casualness with which ministries, departments, and secretariats exceeded their approved votes without seeking authorization from the National Assembly.

The usefulness of the committee's work, however, was curtailed by the fact that its findings were published on only a limited scale, and were never given a wider audience by the press or radio. Yet their reports between 1961 and 1964 give a detailed picture of abuses and mismanagement within government agencies and departments. The committee, which always met with the Auditor General or one of his deputies in attendance, consistently pressed for more effective action from the government to remedy these shortcomings. But although promises were given of more secretarial and accounting assistance, and of more vigorous government action to implement the law in respect of erring government departments, little was done. The Auditor General commented that 'after the detention of the Chairman of the Public Accounts Committee, the examination of the Accountant General's report by the new committee lost its usual vigour .... and .... no effective action was taken on the recommendations of the Committee'.[20] Indeed, it was risky for public servants to probe too deeply into the finances of certain departments. The Auditor General, Mr A. Osei, commented that a 'senior auditor in Accra was nearly sent into preventive detention when he attempted the inspection of the accounts of the Bureau of African Affairs, an assignment which had previously been authorized by the ex-President'.[21] Only the swift intercession of the secretary to the cabinet prevented this attempt at intimidation.

But these solitary islands of independence within the National Assembly were not sufficient to transform the legislative arm of the constitution into a centre of effective control over the activities of the executive. On the other hand, the overwhelming dominance of the CPP within the Assembly could not prevent outbreaks of squabbling within the semi-public forum; squabbles which were considered increasingly harmful and injurious to the facade of party unanimity thought desirable by the President. With the first parliament of the Republic due to conclude in 1965, signs were apparent that the second parliament was to have a new role prescribed for it by the party.

Shortly before the dissolution of the Republic's first parliament which took place in June 1965, an article appeared in *Spark* giving an authoritative exposition of the new role envisaged for the second parliament. This article stemmed from sources very close to the President. It was apparent that the dictum, 'The Party is Supreme', was, in future, going to be rigorously applied to the incoming parliament. *Spark* revealed that the government intended to put an end to the 'capitalist formula' of 'career parliamentarians' for whom it was alleged a seat in the

National Assembly was primarily a means of getting rich. Membership of parliament would henceforth be given only to those of proven loyalty to the party and its ideals.

> Members could be withdrawn from Parliament at any time on the discretion of the Central Committee of the Party .... it is proper that the Central Committee, the collective leadership of the Revolution, should exercise this power .... The selection of new members should be guided by a few rules .... foremost amongst such rules is ideological orientation. We have reached a stage where only such persons who are ideologically sound — the test to be made by the General Secretary himself — should be considered as MPs.[22]

The membership of the new National Assembly was going to be widened to take in members drawn from all wings of the party, from the Ideological Institute, the various stage boards and corporations, editors of the party newspapers, and the regional organizations of the party. In this way, Nkrumah hoped to end the antagonism between the representatives of the party in parliament and the party radicals outside it. Parliament was going to be transformed from an institution representing local and sectional interests within the nation into something vaguely resembling a corporate assembly, purporting to represent the entire nation and party in unity.

After the general election of July 1965 — which was in fact a non-election since all the candidates were picked by the central committee and declared to be returned unopposed — the second parliament was to enjoy a life of only a few months before it was cut short by the coup. It was too short-lived to judge whether the changes contained the seeds of a successful experiment in corporatism, or whether it represented a cynical attempt to dilute the ranks of the critics by swamping them with obedient placemen.

Under the new dispensation parliamentary time and the salaries and allowances paid to members were curtailed.[23] Many of the new men were political nominees drawn from the party machinery and the integral wings, ignorant of or indifferent to parliamentary conventions, but highly conscious of their debt to the central committee which had chosen them. Yet, notwithstanding its demotion, the second parliament was to enjoy a brief, unexpected autumn flowering as a centre of critical and pungent debate before its extinction.

Whilst the President and the National Assembly provided the public constitutional buttresses of the first republic, it was the senior civil service — particularly the small, group of permanent officials who were involved with the framing of policy — which was responsible for the running of the administration.

The civil service which Ghana inherited at independence was cast very much in a British mould. The recruitment and conditions of service of its senior ranks were governed by an independent civil service commission and, like their counterparts in Britain, Ghanaian civil servants enjoyed the career security and professional anonymity considered necessary for the proper discharge of their duties. There was no question of a different system at that time. As the last Governor observed, 'we had to give them the best that we had'. Any attempt by the British on the eve of their departure to set up a different kind of service specifically geared to Ghana's conditions would have been deeply resented. It would seem to imply that Ghanaians were not capable of running a British built machine.

Although Nkrumah, after his fall from power, singled out the 'colonial civil service' as one of the principal elements opposed to his rule, he resisted the demands from within his party to get rid of all white faces from the administration immediately after independence. The pace of Africanization — already rapid by 1957 — was stepped up,[24] but Nkrumah prudently avoided the risk of administrative upheaval. This policy was the cause of some embarrassment at first. African visitors to the newly independent country were struck by the number of white faces in the ministries and apt to conclude that not much had really changed.

Those Ghanaians who had entered the civil service before independence worked amicably with their British colleagues, but their relationship was at first essentially one of apprenticeship. The cadets were inducted into the work of framing policy, advising their political masters, and ensuring the smooth running of the administration. In time most of them developed a respect for their craft and a loyalty to the conventions of their service which were to persist when their apprenticeship was over. This professionalism was quickly to become a source of tension in their relationship with the CPP government. The civil servants, like elements in the judiciary, the universities and the armed forces, possessed something that their political masters did not have, and which they usually failed to understand when they came up against it — a professional, corporate ethic which regulated the way in which they discharged their duties. To the politicians and camp followers of the CPP in the days before independence the concept of a civil service above politics, serving masters of different and opposed convictions with equal loyalty, was a difficult one to grasp. They found it hard to understand how a Ghanaian civil servant could sympathize with their cause, and at the same time loyally serve the very government he wished to see depart. To the politicians it indicated either deep deceit or naked opportunism.

After independence the civil service succeeded in retaining its unrepresentative and protected status, much to the irritation of some ministers who grew resentful of what they considered to be, justly or unjustly, the superior and condescending attitudes of a bureaucratic mandarinate towards those who had secured election by going down amongst the people in the sweaty heat of the market places.[25] Nkrumah's injunction to seek the political kingdom above all else expressed the deepest convictions of many of his followers, and it was hard for them to reconcile this advice with the continued existence of a career civil service in the new Ghana.

Under the tough system of recruitment by competitive examination, nearly all the Ghanaians who entered the senior grades of the civil service had enjoyed secondary education and usually university education at home or overseas. Naturally enough, such recruits tended to be drawn from relatively well-off families able to afford the further education of their sons. The civil service staff lists reflect the predominantly middle-class background of the senior civil servants. Anglo-Ghanaian names, such as Mills, Bannerman, Hayford, Phillips, Nelson, abound drawn from the important Accra and Cape Coast families of the South. The sons of such families, together with the sons of successful merchants, chiefs and wealthy cocoa farmers, attended the long established secondary schools of the Gold Coast and then completed their education in the universities, medical schools and inns of court in Britain. Returning to the colony as lawyers, doctors, teachers and professional men, they had formed the largest reservoir of trained and energetic men to be found in any tropical African dependency. After the war the British government's aim of making the Gold Coast into the first self-governing country of her tropical African empire was greatly facilitated by the existence of this reservoir. Up to the present day a career in the public service is eagerly sought after by many able Ghanaian graduates. For the CPP government, which had in many cases paid for their university education after 1951, it seemed base ingratitude that so few of them sought to make a political career within the party.

Nearly all Ghanaian senior civil servants welcomed the advent of independence. They belonged to the class which had first inspired and then provided the leadership of the nationalist movement and were broadly in sympathy with its aims. Sentiment apart, the departure of the British promised an improvement in their own career prospects. Yet there was an ambiguity in their attitudes towards the CPP which by 1954 seemed certain to become the ruling party at independence. They admired Nkrumah's party for its energy in forcing the pace towards independence, but direct experience of working with the CPP after 1951 convinced many civil servants that the party was riddled with corrupt and untrustworthy men, unfit to hold public office. The Braimah affair and the revelations of the activities of the Cocoa Purchasing Company in the mid-fifties added to their suspicions. The United Party, which emerged in 1957 under the leadership of Dr Danquah and Dr Busia, seemed to some civil servants to represent a more attractive alternative to the CPP, although, unfortunately, with a rapidly diminishing chance of ever gaining office. Nevertheless with the same fidelity to the standing orders of their service which they had demonstrated by their co-operation with the British, the civil servants continued to co-operate with the CPP.

In 1951, after becoming leader of government business, Nkrumah made a first attempt to bring the Civil Service Commission under the control of his majority in the legislature. He failed at that time, but the later attacks on the civil service by his party for 'collaboration' with the British — a charge that might equally be levelled against the CPP in its own years of apprenticeship — were not forgotten. Until 1954 the civil service was responsible to the Governors not to the cabinet. It was thus part of the colonial establishment and, as such, out of the reach of the politicians. Nkrumah's inexperienced and enthusiastic ministers frequently found themselves and their plans cut down to size by their senior civil servants. There was usually little they could do except ungraciously accept their advice. When full independence finally arrived, however, the time seemed ripe for the government to try once again to secure full control of the civil service.

A few months before Ghana was to become a republic, the government set out its plans for the civil service in a white paper. It sought to end the independence of the Civil Service Commission over matters of recruitment, dismissal, conditions of service and discipline which had been one of the principal features of the old dispensation. The white paper stated that it was:

> quite inappropriate that the control of the Civil Service machine should not be in the hands of a government which relies on it for getting its work done.[26]

Nevertheless, the steps proposed fell far short of the transformation of the civil service into an 'integral wing' of the party. Civil servants were expected to remain above party politics, at least whilst opposition parties were still in existence.

> The Civil Service is a permanent service and members of it would not normally expect to take up or quit office on a change of government. The Civil Service must therefore be in a position to serve all governments of whatever complexion with equal loyalty, and to obtain the confidence of ministers irrespective of their political party. This can come about only if Civil Servants, particularly those in high ranks, exercise special restraint in political matters.[27]

The white paper tried hard to reconcile the independent and impartial tradition of the service with the personal control over public affairs which the new President seemed certain to exercise. Civil servants were advised to seek anonymity in the performance of their duties. They were not to become publicly identified with any political ideology or party. They were to do their duty without regard to personal or family interests. A 'healthy civil service tradition' would be fostered if the most effective sanction of good behaviour was the unwritten code of ethics of the service itself, transcending the written standing orders and reinforcing a high state of morale and spirit of self-criticism.

This appeal to the collective professional pride of the civil service, however, was not to last for long. The republican constitution and the Civil Service act of 1960 gave effect to most of the recommendations of the white paper, but introduced other charges strengthening the President's control over his public officers and diminishing the authority of the Civil Service Commission. The service was divided into four grades, from A to D. Grade A comprised all permanent secretaries and other officers 'of paramount importance'. These were appointed, dismissed and disciplined by the President himself — powers formerly exercised by the Commission. Over the inferior grades the Commission retained its powers, unless the President considered their exercise 'inexpedient'.

The troubles of 1961 brought in their wake further changes. During his long tour of the communist countries Nkrumah had impressed upon him by his hosts the critical importance of his bureaucracy, and he resolved to bring it even more closely under his control on his return. During the reorganization of the party's machinery early in 1962 he took the opportunity to attack the convention of political impartiality which had hitherto been central to the civil service. Dismissing the colonial civil service as 'an instrument of imperialist administration', Nkrumah spoke of impending changes in the standing orders of the service. In the past, he declared, the civil service had been guilty of obstruction and red-tapeism:

> Very often, sitting in my office at Flagstaff House, I threw out a number of ideas for the good of the nation. These have been worked out by some Ministry or Department. For a brief period....there seems to be some activity. After that one hears nothing and all action seems to cease. Suddenly I make an enquiry about the scheme only to find that the idea is buried in the files and covered with dust.[28]

Worse than obstruction, however, was the danger of subversion within the service:

> Our official secrets are the targets of the colonialists.... who are busy in our midst and who will pay fabulous sums to obtain information for our undoing. We must at all times ensure that we are alert to sabotage and subversion. Any civil servant who sells information concerning his work is worse than a traiter and incurs an eternal curse upon his head.[29]

In future, civil servants would be free to engage in politics, but only on behalf of the CPP:

> Every citizen has a right to full participation in the political affairs of this country, and it is my intention that civil servants of all ranks should have the freedom to exercise this right. That is why the CPP has actively supported the opening of branches in all departments. This is in accordance with our policy to establish a one party state in Ghana.[30]

The establishment of party branches within each government department was intended to give the party a lever within the civil service. It would be supplemented by the proposal announced at the same conference to establish 'expediters' within all ministries, whose job it would be 'to see that all decisions of the Government were carried out promptly'. The expediters would be drawn from the deputy ministers of each department and would be required to submit written reports to their chiefs on all obstructions and delays.

The effect of the Winneba address with its barely concealed hostility and hints of unwelcome change was a depressing one for most of the assembled civil servants. They were being lectured like naughty schoolboys. Many had worked side by side with British Civil servants before independence. Others had experience of public service abroad. Nearly all of them had a high regard for their British predecessors and for the traditions of their service. Their loyalty was to the state they served, not to a particular political party. Now they saw their careers in danger, at the mercy of any ill-disposed party activist who might report them for 'incorrect' ideological attitudes or suspected disloyalty to the party. They were being browbeaten by a man whom many suspected would himself have failed to qualify for a career in the service; by the leader of a party many of whose members they knew to be conspicuously lacking in efficiency or honesty.

In fact, as was so often the case, little was done to follow up Nkrumah's 1962 proposals which were soon swallowed up in the growing morass of more pressing problems. Nevertheless the party kept up its attacks on the civil service until the end. It had become a mute and convenient scapegoat for the depressing setbacks encountered by official policies. At the end of 1963 the *Evening News* called for a totally political civil service:

The question is: which is better? A highly loyal personnel with little professional technique and a lot of revolutionary experience — or a highly skilled intellectual group which continuously seeks new and covert ways of undermining State security?

The newspaper was in no doubt about the answer. The Civil Service Commission should be:

... stripped of all pretences to impartiality and become a genuine machine for the promotion of the Party's aims and objectives. (The civil service) is British in character and British bourgeois codes apply. The result of this class division is that a build-up of subversive lawyers, reactionaries and dark-coated intellectuals and friends of western diplomats hold sway and show little respect for the Party...[31]

Nkrumah did nothing to suppress such thunder from the left of his party. The Civil Service Commission, and in particular its chairman, Sir Charles Tachie Menson, who had accepted a knighthood from the British and had stood against the CPP unsuccessfully in the 1951 election, was a vulnerable target for the militants. In November 1965 the Commission was dissolved and replaced by the CPP 'civil service committee' run by Enoch Okoh, the secretary to the cabinet, and two of the 'socialist boys', Kweku Akwei and Kodwo Addison, but the final triumph of the party over the civil service proved to be very short-lived.

Although the existence of a civil service recruited by competitive examination was a standing affront to the ideologues of the party, Nkrumah had little confidence in the ability of revolutionary fervour alone to tackle the problems which taxed his civil service. Indeed, the logic of his policies was to make him more rather than less dependent upon the proven talents of his top civil servants.

A subtle shift in the balance of power was taking place in the last years of the Republic. Power was sliding out of the hands of the politicians and into those of the small group of civil servants around the President at Flagstaff House. Ministers became caretakers rather than active policy-makers and the party itself lost any vital political function.

Nkrumah did not have a high regard for the talents of many of his political associates.[32] To tighten up his overall control of public business he had at first appointed overseers directly responsible to himself, ministers of state for presidential affairs, drawn from men like Baako, Adamafio and Botsio whom he most trusted. But this arrangement proved unsatisfactory and caused resentment amongst their cabinet colleagues. Instead, he turned to 'state secretariats', super-ministries located in the Flagstaff House complex, which supervised from the highest level important areas of public business already ostensibly covered by the existing ministries.[33] The state secretariats were controlled by a handful of top civil servants who were in daily contact with Nkrumah and became, through him, the most powerful men in the administration of the country. In 1962 Enoch Okoh succeeded A.L. Adu as secretary to the cabinet and head of the civil service.[34] He, together with T.K. Impraim and Michael Dei Anang, controlled the highly centralized structure based at Flagstaff House. Despite Okoh's commanding position and his flirtation with some of Nkrumah's political ideas — he had been a member of the Socialist Club when at Cambridge and had attended some of Nkrumah's 'inner study group' meetings — he was faced with the difficulty of having to execute policies which he sometimes thought dangerous or ill-advised. It was in response to presidential pressures, not to the situation prevailing on the ground, that the state secretariats shaped their activities.

Senior civil servants could afford to ignore the attacks

made upon them from outside. They were indispensable and they knew it. The closer they were to the President's office the better they were protected. Nkrumah's hopes of converting his key civil servants to his enthusiasms met with only limited success. A few, such as Dei Anang, the permanent secretary of the Foreign Affairs ministry, and H.P. Nelson of the State Enterprises secretariat, went 'political' and threw themselves behind the leader and party. Most of their colleagues held back circumspectly, although one, J.H. Mensah of the Planning Commission, went so far as to argue against the drift of Nkrumah's economic policies in a published article.[35]

Although the top civil servants were safe because they were necessary, the antagonism displayed by the party led to a decline in morale amongst the lower and middle grades which were most open to the interference of party officials and ministers. The party could not destroy the best elements in the civil service, but it could corrupt the weakest. The public accounts committee drew attention to the state of affairs amongst the lowest grades late in 1964:

> We have observed with concern that the standards of efficiency and discipline in the lower grades of the civil service have deteriorated... Many officers were irregular in attendance at work. Those who attended regularly... put in very little effort into their work. Many leave their offices before closing time. We have learned that the deterioration is due to patronage and external inter-ference. We feel sure that (these factors) are embarras-sing and have a demoralizing effect on the officers responsible for ensuring efficiency and maintaining discipline within the service.[36]

A bureaucracy is only as strong as its weakest links. Whatever plans and projects were conceived and initiated at the highest levels stood in danger of being damaged by faulty execution at the lower levels.

The supply of trained and experienced civil servants could not meet the additional demands made upon them by the volume of work issuing from the President's office. Although the civil servants extended their control not only over the business of government but eventually even over Nkrumah's sickly party itself, it would be inaccurate to describe Nkrumah's republic as a government of bureaucrats. The civil servants were called in rather as the principal prop to shore up the increasingly ramshackle structure of the political kingdom. Nkrumah remained throughout the fountainhead of policy which the civil servants, true to the traditions of their service, did their best to execute. But the arrangement was neither happy nor fruitful. The politicians depended upon the civil servants but did not trust them. The civil servants carried the political system but were unable to alter it. It was a novel, unintended variation of the doctrine of the separation of powers which sustained the Republic in a paralysing stalemate only resolved by the intervention of the military.

III 'The Party is Supreme'

The Convention Peoples Party was the first political party in British colonial Africa to emerge after the war as a national, popular movement. It ruled Ghana continuously from its election victory in 1951 until its overthrow early in 1966, extending its hold to include a large proportion of the country's population through its youth movements, farmers associations, trade unions and co-operatives. At the time of its overthrow it possessed a size of membership and income, a variety of functions, and a sheer presence remarkable for a small, under-developed country. Yet the entropy within the party proved to be such that it became impossible for it to translate all these assets into effective political energy.

Like every political movement, the CPP was forged out of a coalition of interests. But the departure of the British in 1957 removed at one stroke the only external principle of unity common to the party as a whole. Thereafter Nkrumah faced a dilemma which proved impossible for him to resolve. He could keep the open, popular character of his movement, using it to prod from outside the existing machinery of government into new directions. Or he could convert it into a party of revolutionary transformation run by a small, disciplined, authoritarian group entirely under the control of himself and his central committee — a political force designed to dominate and then supplant the state machine. In the event he followed both courses and fell between two stools. He could not resist the temptation to bring all aspects of the nation's life under the control of the party. His attempts to create a a dedicated party 'vanguard' came to nothing. His periodic attempts to revive a spirit of purposefulness within the party as a whole by exhortation fell on deaf ears. The exact relationship between party and state was never constitutionally or effectively defined, even after the introduction of the single party state in 1964. Eventually Nkrumah drifted away from his creation, losing confidence in its powers of self-repair, but refusing to yield his supremacy over it. He had little difficulty, however, in maintaining at least an external facade of party unity. The patronage at the disposal of the party was sufficient to ensure a steady flow of supporters, whilst the threat of expulsion was enough to bring most malcontents to heel.

As the CPP extended its empire it stood in danger of absorbing all the myriad tensions, frictions and rivalries within the community without really resolving them. The supremacy of the party was bought at the cost of diluting its identity. It had always attracted 'carpet-crossers' — those attracted more by the fact of its success than by the content of its policies. One of the principal causes of the malaise from which the party was suffering was singled out in 1962 as the presence within it of lately arrived opportunists:

> Our experience has been that just before the general elections of 1951, 1954 and 1956, many new people rushed into the Party and organized and gained admission into executive offices of the Party. Most of these people were later discovered to have formed opposition in the Party and caused considerable trouble... and put a wedge in the Party's solidarity.[1]

The factions which grew up within the party were only prevented from open warfare against each other by their mutual acceptance of Nkrumah's leadership. But if they were held together by him, he in turn was obliged to maintain some kind of balance between them. The cult of personality which surrounded Nkrumah stemmed partly from his personal vanity, but it was none the less an essential part of the equipment he needed to bind his movement together.

For the most part his followers welcomed Nkrumah in his role as supreme arbiter of their disputes. A few strong-minded men might harbour secret thoughts about the succession, but for most a CPP without Nkrumah was inconceivable. Under his paramountcy, moreover, each faction came to understand that it would survive its rivals' attacks to fight another day. Nkrumah's balancing act was an insurance against total rout, and this realization gave the protagonists of each faction a continuing stake in the system infinitely preferable to hazards they might have to face if their leader were to be abruptly removed.

Nkrumah, however, never totally abandoned his efforts to create a 'vanguard' of party activists who, he hoped, would be imbued with revolutionary enthusiasm and socialist purity. In 1959 he had the party's education college at Winneba, a pleasant coastal town forty miles to the west of Accra, converted into an 'ideological institute'. Its purpose was 'to train socialist Ghanaians capable of taking into their hands the key posts of all sectors of the apparatus of the state and the economy'. In 1961 the Kwame Nkrumah Ideological Institute was opened and in the following years several million pounds were spent on the construction of a campus. It was the party's 'anti-university', a reproach to the University of Ghana, most students of which stood aloof from the party. Giving a two-year course in 'marxism' and 'leninism' in addition to instruction in 'Nkrumaism', its teaching staff was a cosmopolitan collection of communist writers and teachers.[2] The first director, Kwodwo Addison, was a former trade union official who had been expelled from the CPP in the fifties for his communist affiliations. Three years afterwards, sponsored by his fellow trade unionist, John Tettegah, Addison was re-admitted to political life and by 1960 was a member of the central committee.[3]

However, the Winneba experiment was to prove a disappointing failure. The quality of students was generally poor. Few young Ghanaians possessing entrance qualifications for the universities or the professions thought of Winneba and a career with the party as a serious alternative. The Institute therefore had to keep its admission standards modest to attract sufficient numbers of students. It had difficulty even in attracting established party workers to its courses and in 1964 was obliged to advertise in the newspapers inviting minor party officials and workers in the integral wings to attend courses without loss of salary. Moreover few of its graduates later displayed the qualities expected of them. Late in 1965 the *Evening News* commented sadly that:

> in every region of the country, the general membership of the CPP are questioning the attitude of most of the graduates from the Institute and are wondering what went wrong... Why are most of the graduates asking how much they must first be paid before thinking of the work they are going to do? Why are some in a hurry to enter Parliament or to be Regional Commissioners, or enter the highest positions just after two years at Winneba, and without wishing to start from below with the masses of people?[4]

It was never made clear what the most important component of the ideological training given at Winneba was — whether it was Nkrumah's eponymous brand of socialism over which he exercised papal powers of interpretation — or 'scientific socialism's, independent of Osagyefo's ideas and to which even he must conform. For the great majority of Winneba students Nkrumah's authority was the clear and indisputable central fact of Ghana's political life — a certainty which they clung to and preferred to the sophisms and traps of intellectual debate, for which in any case they were ill-prepared. In these circumstances it was not surprising that their ambitions emerged unscathed from their ideological training. The Institute apparently offered them a short-cut to important posts in the party and the state corporations. But those who had already established themselves in the upper reaches without the benefit of a Winneba training showed no inclination to make way for the new graduates.

The CPP self-consciously cultivated the image of a highly ideological party. Certainly, a very left-wing variety of socialism flavoured its official statements and publications, particularly in its last years. In his first public statement on becoming leader of government business, in February 1951, Nkrumah described himself as 'a marxian socialist and an undenominational Christian'. Ten years later his policies had veered sharply towards closer relations with the communist countries. He began to denounce the 'African socialism' of other African leaders, particularly that of Julius Nyerere, as a deviation from the 'correct' road of 'scientific socialism'. By the time of his downfall he had committed his régime deeply, but not irrevocably, to both the Russian and Chinese communist camps. East German advisers helped to strengthen his security services. He frequently took advice on world developments from M. Rodianov, Russia's ambassador in Accra, and Chinese and Russian experts were invited to Ghana to run the training camps for exiled African revolutionaries. As Ghana's financial indebtedness to the western world increased, so Nkrumah's ideological hostility towards the west became more open and strident.

Yet it is questionable whether he carried his party with

him far along this road. There were those who were always prepared to shout the President's ideas louder than he did himself. A few did so because they retained to the end a belief in their leader's overpowering genius. More did so because it served their private purposes. But the body of his party was a much more substantial thing than the buzzing of its ideologically-minded flies. Its composition and its leading personalities had remained remarkably unchanged throughout its fifteen years of power. It was relatively easy for Nkrumah to launch new diplomatic initiatives on African and world issues corresponding to his changing political ideas. It was far harder for him to change Ghanaian society, or even to carry his party with him along his chosen road.

Nkrumah himself defined 'Nkrumaism' as 'scientific socialism' applied to countries emerging from colonialism.[5] There seems no doubt that by 1965 there was little to distinguish Nkrumah's idea of socialism from the Russian brand of orthodoxy. He was nevertheless careful to keep his links with the Chinese. Ghana, like other tropical countries, was being actively wooed by both of the rival communist papacies and Nkrumah saw advantage in keeping in with both. Nkrumah did not, however, regard Ghana as having arrived at socialism under his rule. Not until complete industrialization had been achieved, not until all agriculture had been collectivized and mechanized, not until the state had acquired total control over all the means of production and distribution, could Ghana in his view be within reach of socialism. There was indeed little that was original in his position; it was the common stuff of leftist dictatorships. For their part the Russians looked with favour upon the general direction of his policies, although their industrious ideologists grudgingly admitted Ghana to be on the right road only in the most general terms.[6]

But what did 'Nkrumaism' and 'scientific socialism' signify to the main body of the CPP? How strong was its apparent addiction to ideology? Considerable attention was paid in the sixties to the official ideologies of ostensibly radical African parties. In some cases this arose out of a sympathetic identification by foreign observers of their own political tendencies with the stated aims of ostensibly leftist African parties. Thomas Hodgkin, for instance, claimed in 1951 that the 'spiritual ancestors of the CPP are Rousseau and Tom Paine'. The CPP, he declared, 'interprets democracy in the more traditional sense — the rule of the common people, the poor, and the illiterate'.[7] Ten years later, when he had become director of the Institute of African Studies in the University of Ghana, he could still perceive a 'strong strain of Rousseau-esque revolutionary democracy running through the ideologies of most African radical nationalist parties'. He saw amongst them a desire 'to push forward the frontiers of liberty against the repression of authority and legitimacy', sparked by an urge 'to remind the world of the possibilities of human happiness in the face of the prophets of doom'.[8] Hodgkin's evangelical optimism was shared by many foreign socialists and liberals in the early sixties who were inclined to take the public statements of African leaders at their face value. It was an attitude which confused rather than clarified the admittedly complicated question of what relationship an official, political ideology has with a living community's other activities.[9]

English is the family language of a tiny minority of Ghanaians. Since colonial days, however, it has been the language of the highest levels of administration, education and politics and is, in limited and debased forms, the principal auxiliary tongue in a country whose inhabitants lack a common vernacular. Many Ghanaians, including the bulk of those in the middle and lower ranks of the CPP acquired an uncertain grasp of English in primary and middle schools from teachers whose own command of the language was often weak. School English was strongly influenced by the English classical writers with a strong biblical strain added by the many mission schools. The result was a peculiar yet robust English, filled with literary and scriptural allusions, very evident for instance in the debates of the National Assembly. One member once produced before his fellows an adaptation of the Nicene Creed in praise of the President:

> I believe in politics, the big game of patriotism, mother of philosophy and love, and in Kwame Nkrumah, her only genius, our leader, who was chosen from amongst the hosts of the Ghanaian bulwark (*sic*) of the vigilant masses, who suffered under perturbating powers, was arrested, tried and imprisoned. He deigned himself into cell. After a few months he came out of prison, and with truth and victory, he is able to make powers sublime, indicating right and justice.[10]

From the beginning Nkrumah and the CPP leadership used English to put across their ideas and policies to the country at large. But the party faced an in-built problem of communication as it sought to establish itself as a popular, national movement amongst peoples whose grasp of English was weak and uncertain. Inevitably it became a party of the half-literate, and it was in this shadowy area where native thoughts struggled to understand the modern world through the medium of an alien tongue that the dangers of confusion lay. The many vernaculars used by the great majority deal with the concrete experiences of work, family life and traditional affairs. Such languages relate words to things in a vivid, direct fashion immediately apprehensible to those who use them. The chances of verbal or conceptual misunderstanding are small. English, however, is the means of access to ideas, knowledge and experience over and above the quotidian level. The connection between words and things begins to break down — particularly when the words relate to political abstractions. It was through English that the ideas of 'anti-colonialism' and 'socialism' entered Ghanaian consciousness. But whereas the first idea was easily grasped by a black population well aware that they were ruled by white men, the second idea had no such universally comprehended meaning. It lacked a perceived applicability in a country which, unlike so much of the rest of the third world, was not faced by the massive problems of a landless peasantry or vast, swollen cities.

The importation of a marxist-leninist vocabulary, with its ideas drawn from a tradition even more alien than that imposed by the departed British — yet expressed in their language — compounded the confusion. The very remoteness of Marx and Lenin from anything African was an asset rather than a handicap for those still very close to a magical view of the world.[11] Amongst those partial to it, political rhetoric soared like an escaping balloon, swelling with each moment of ascent above the plains of common sense, imposing in size but filled with nothing but gas. The Minister of Agriculture, F.A. Januah, for instance, once made an attempt to wrestle with the arcane socialist 'theorems' contained in the President's book *Consciencism*. 'It seems to me, Sir', he began, 'that it would be superfluous to say that Osagyefo, the President, is a man who is endowed with the wisdom of Ulysses, the courage of a Hercules, and the Platonic vision of a clairvoyant.' He continued, 'the next thing I want to touch on hinges on the question of criticism, Sir, it is quite clear that in philosophy, in the dialectical method, the essence of social development is criticism. The idea of the thesis is the existence of a given situation, then the coming into conflict of forces to uproot the given situation, and the checking of those elements which have come into conflict with the existing situation, which is the antithesis used, which is the essence of social development.'[12] He was heard in astonished silence.

Bemused by these new and unfamiliar ideas, which enjoyed the added sanction of their leader's patronage, the political language employed by the middle ranges of the party — and sometimes by its leaders — expressed not so much an intention to act in a particular way, but an enhancement of feeling accompanied by a kind of mental dissociation. At one level passionate affirmations of 'scientific socialism' held sway. But they barely covered up the older beliefs in magic and in the omnipresent world of ghosts. As neither level was strong enough to overcome and purge the other, both co-existed uneasily, often in the same individuals. Perhaps it was hoped that the constant invocation of an ideology ostensibly based upon science and progress would drive out superstition. But all too often the old superstitions succeeded in contaminating the ideology. 'Socialism' became itself a world-magic, a conjuration which would change the world into the desired shape; a weapon against the inescapable stubbornness of reality.

The institutional structure of the CPP in its last years is by now only of interest to political archaeologists.[13] All power in the party derived from Nkrumah himself, the life chairman, and his circle of intimates who might not even belong to it. The function of the party machinery was to endorse and transmit downwards its leader's decisions — a task, however, which it did with only partial success. The party's supreme organ was the central committee of which Nkrumah was the permanent chairman. In the last years few people knew the exact composition of the central committee at any one time. The highest plenary meeting of the CPP was the annual delegates' conference. In theory, this was the supreme legislature of the CPP, charged with laying down the 'broad basic policy and programme of the party for the ensuing year'. But it showed no independence and meekly endorsed the life chairman's general line. At no time during the last six years of the party's life did any of its upper reaches display any initiative. It was only in the lower reaches — at branch, district, constituency and regional levels, where the authority of headquarters was diluted by distance — that traces of independence survived, although not always of a kind welcomed either by the leadership or the local peoples.

The CPP was acutely aware that its early success had in part been due to its nation-wide organization. Once in power it took steps to build up an elaborate though informal party organization covering the country's eight regions. Before independence the CPP had regarded the colonial district officers with great suspicion. They appeared to epitomize the arbitrary and unrepresentative nature of colonial rule and the CPP had demanded their abolition. After the 1951 election the party modified its previous attitude and demanded changes which would introduce an element of representation into the selection of district officers. This was resisted by the Governor who retitled the officers 'government agents' to make it clear that they were exclusively under the control of the executive. In a countryside of poor communications and high illiteracy government agents were indispensable for explaining the central government's policies to local chiefs and headmen, and were able to give Accra an accurate picture of rural problems free from local pressures and influences.

After independence the CPP perceived advantages in the system and was unwilling to discard it completely. But the new 'district commissioners' it proposed to introduce were to be party functionaries, not agents of the government.

Inheriting some of the functions of their colonial predecessors, the district commissioners were also intended to raise the level of political consciousness in rural areas of forming and supervising local party branches. Not unnaturally, the opposition parties viewed this arrangement with great suspicion, seeing in it a first step towards the establishment of a permanent CPP presence throughout Ghana which would undermine the very representative principle the CPP had espoused only a short time before.

The apex of the party in the regions was made up of the eight regional commissioners who were appointed by the central committee and ranked as ministers in the Assembly. When the Assembly was not in session the regional commissioners resided in the principal towns of their regions. Reports on the state of the party in the various districts were forwarded to them by their district commissioners and other local party officials. The regional commissioners ran a party organization parallel to but dominant over the institutions of local government. They provided a vital link between the cabinet, the party headquarters and the party in the countryside. In theory the appointment of district commissioners and other local officials rested with the central committee, but the regional commissioner's voice in these matters was an important one. Commanding a salary of £4,350 — reduced in 1965 to £4,150 — plus allowances, theirs was one of the party's highest paid posts.

During the first republic there were thirteen tenants of the eight posts of regional commissioner. They were drawn from the most forceful of the party's lower ranks. Seven of the thirteen had begun their careers as teachers. The four northern regional commissioners — Ebenezer Adam, Ayeebo Asumda, E.A. Mahama (later Minister of Animal Husbandry) and Mawumia Bawumia (later Minister of

Local Government) had all been primary school teachers, but their upward advance into political life had really begun with their service as clerks and treasurers with the Native Authority councils — as was also the case with many district commissioners. Despite being commoners for the most part, their connections with traditional circles brought them great prestige in their areas.[14]

The regional commissioners were in effect the party's 'bossmen' in the regions. Answerable only to the President's office, they could afford to ignore local government and the strictures of the cabinet. Since they rarely communicated directly with the President's office, however, they sometimes ignored even the latter's authority and interfered with the activities of other state secretariats in their regions. One of their functions was to maintain security in their regions. After the Kulungugu assassination attempt in 1962, the commissioner for the Upper Region, Asumda, and for the Volta Region, Hans Kofi Boni, were instrumental in organizing mass arrests of 'political undesirables'. Boni later described the 'normal procedure' for dealing with such people:

> ... when the activities of people believed to be indulging in subversive activities were reported to him, he asked the police to investigate the matter... afterwards the regional security committee of which he was a member, usually met and submitted minutes on the alleged (subversives) to the Minister of the Interior.[15]

The other members of the security committee were the assistant commissioner of police, the local army commander, and the secretary of the regional commissioner.[16] But it was usually the regional commissioner's decision which was final at such meetings.

Unhindered by local government and close to the centre of power, some commissioners made themselves highly unpopular amongst their subjects by dispensing favours to their friends and maintaining an extravagant way of life. One, for instance, was discovered after the coup to have acquired amongst other things sixteen houses and ten cars. Having four wives and sixteen children he was, no doubt, under some domestic pressure. Finding life rather dull in his remote outpost he imported a dance band from Accra to brighten things up. His view of his duties was a simple one. He 'settled disputes between various chiefs to maintain party unity and also saw to it on election days that nobody stood against the official candidates.'[17] He was not alone in his dubious activities. Several commissioners were the subjects of some sharp comments from the Auditor General and in the National Assembly, but they were virtually irremoveable and disinclined to mend their ways.[18]

The district commissioners, working under their regional bosses, were expected to keep the leadership of the party in touch with local opinion. They were also expected to keep the local party machinery in good repair. Much of their time was spent trekking through their districts, gathering material for their reports and patching up quarrels within local party branches, or between party officials and local men of influence. In most cases the district commissioners were natives of the localities they served. An attempt was made to secure a degree of impartiality by appointing men with few ties with their areas, but this was not successful. In the Akan societies of southern Ghana a man's allegiance is reckoned to rest upon his place of birth. Consequently, outsiders and 'strangers' tended to come up against a blank wall of local suspicions and their effectiveness was severely circumscribed. As the number of district commissioners was increased, the party once again found itself obliged to accommodate itself to ancient prejudices and appoint men who had proved their enthusiasm in party work.

The number of district commissioners rose from 45 in 1960 to 117 in 1962 and to 160 in 1964. These increases reduced the size of individual districts, giving the party a denser network of control over the countryside, but at the cost of weakening the supervision over the commissioners. Potential district commissioners usually came to the notice of the regional commissioners through reports by party agents of their activities in junior capacities on behalf of the party. There was no shortage of applicants. The post carried a salary of £1,200 a year, plus a bungalow and the use of a car. In theory district commissioners were elected by the district conferences of the party every two years and their election endorsed by the central committee. But in practice the influence of the regional commissioners was usually sufficient for them to get their nominees appointed. However, it sometimes proved a totally different matter for them to control the activities of the district commissioners once they were safely installed.

District commissioners, if they were ambitious, hoped to graduate to more senior positions in the party or to a seat in the National Assembly. Their quality varied widely.[19] Few had had a secondary education although at least one possessed a university degree.[20] Some succeeded in reaching higher things. One became Ghana's ambassador to Japan. But a few fell by the wayside, including the egregiously named E.K. Powerful Bulley, the district commissioner for Accra. Between 1958 and 1963 fourteen were sacked, some, like Cofie Crabbe and Amadu Seidu, because they had strayed to the wrong side in metropolitan politics, others because they succumbed to the temptations of their office too blatantly for the public peace. The district commissioner for Amansie, for instance, was himself detained for accepting £200 for deleting a man's name from a list of those ordered to be arrested in 1962.[21]

Close as the district commissioners were to local pressures of village life, many inevitably became bound up with disputes arising out of chieftancy and traditional affairs. Their help was frequently sought to assist one faction or another against its rivals. The Winneba conference in 1963 warned that 'destoolment affairs have tended to disturb party unity', but two years later the problem of involvement in stool quarrels had not been solved. A member of parliament warned that district commissioners should steer clear of traditional disputes, 'because once he supports one side in the dispute, the trouble becomes very bad indeed. If people are determined to destool a chief, and the District Commissioner goes to the side of a chief, there can be any amount of chaos.'[22]

The absence of a clear definition of the district commissioner's function and status within his local area and outside was a perpetual source of irritation. In one sense the local machinery of the party became a familiar part of the everyday life of the countryside. One study of the small town of Larteh has shown in detail how little traditional rules of precedence in a community only thirty miles from the capital were upset by the new offices introduced by the CPP.[23] Far from politicizing the countryside, the countryside often succeeded in traditionalizing the party. Yet by creating a new, external source of power and patronage the CPP introduced a divisive element into rural life which a backbench member of parliament described in 1964:

In the villages...the chairman of the Party branch considers himself the leader of the people...The headman also considers himself the leader of the people and equal or superior to the Party branch chairman. When these two persons are unable to compromise, there is always friction. Until a way is found to make it quite clear that the headman deals in traditional matters, and when it comes to Party matters, he must come under the branch chairman... the problem will remain.[24]

Party members of parliament and district commissioners were both the nominees of the central committee. But this did not stop a considerable amount of bickering between the two careers. The district commissioners, resident within their districts had their ears closer to the ground than the members of parliament obliged to spend a great deal of time in Accra. Members of parliament for their part resented the influence of the district commissioners within their constituencies whom they regarded as party functionaries having no claim to be representative of the people they served. It was, naturally, even worse for the opposition members. Joe Appiah complained to the Assembly before his arrest that the press and radio gave far more prominence to the activities of the district commissioners than to those of members of parliament. When a member addressed his constituents, Appiah said, 'you hear people in the community saying, "Has the District Commissioner allowed him to come and talk here?"'[25] Even within the CPP members of parliament and district commissioners were as sensitive and touchy as old world ambassadors over questions of placement and precedence in their local districts. By 1962 the bickering between the two careers had grown so bad that the party's study groups conference held at Winneba later in the year paid special attention to this problem, noting that 'some District Commissioners, in trying to do their duty in their districts, rather create confusion and misunderstanding, thereby disrupting the party organization'. The conference recommended that in future members of parliament should be consulted in the nomination of candidates for the post of district commissioner and should receive copies of the commissioners' political reports. The difficulties had arisen, the conference contended, because 'the Regional Commissioners and District Commissioners have tended to ignore Members of Parliament in many directions.[26]

Apart from interference in local issues within their districts, some district commissioners made themselves locally unpopular by shamelessly exploiting their office to their own advantage in a variety of ways. A letter published in the *Ghanaian Times* from an officer of the Young Pioneer movement gave voice to some of these grievances:

> Those of us Party members who have been alive to the activities of some of our District Commissioners are more often than not at a loss to believe whether some of them are really aware of the purposes which made the Party appoint them their posts... some of the District Commissioners by their very actions lend support to the subversive activities of the detractors of the Party. There are District Commissioners who on account of women and other petty squabbles, intimidate loyal Party members, ... and at times exchange blows with people in bars or other public places. The worst of it all is how some of them are making the work of the Young Pioneers very difficult because of their lust for school girls.[27]

Maxwell Owusu's detailed study of local politics in Swedru,[28] a busy market town forty miles west of Accra, has revealed how the local district commissioner operated within his locality. The district commissioner, R.K. Appiah, was the nominee of Swedru's member of parliament, E.K. Bensah, at the time when Bensah was a minister.[29] Appiah exercised power over his local community 'almost without limit', forming a cabal with a small group of cronies drawn from his former classmates, one of whom was chairman of the town council, to run the town. Despite a government circular of 1960 which stressed the need to avoid conflicts between local councillors and district commissioners which were apt to 'hamper smooth and progressive local government administration', local councillors were sometimes reduced to impotence by the activities of the local party bosses. In Swedru Appiah and his cabal took over police duties, settled disputes which should have gone before the courts, and decided issues which properly belonged to the urban council. The district commissioner was, by virtue of his office, also an *ex officio* member of the local council, empowered to countersign all cheques paid out of local council funds. This gave Appiah ample opportunity to direct the award of contracts to his friends for work undertaken on behalf of the local council in Swedru.

Locally elected councillors rarely offered opposition to the district and regional commissioners. The result, despite the long tradition of local self-help in the Ghana countryside, was a growing demoralization within local government. In many areas development funds found their way into the wrong pockets, contracts were awarded to the friends and patrons of the commissioners. The threat of being reported by the district commissioner to the regional security committee, entailing the risk of arbitrary arrest and detention, effectively overcame any misgivings of local government officers. A few district commissioners, however, did succeed in maintaining some sort of harmony in their districts. T.K. Danso, the district commissioner for Asamankese in the Eastern Region, showed considerable skill in bringing to an end a quarrel which had broken out between the local member of parliament, Sintim Aboagye, and the local constituency secretary of the CPP, S.W.K. Yankson. Their argument began over the acquisition of land for a petrol station in the small town of Asamankese. Danso patched up a compromise and saved the party headquarters in Accra from further embarrassment. For this service to the party Danso was himself chosen by the central committee for a seat in the second parliament in 1965.[30]

The CPP never succeeded in securing the total obedience of the countryside to its central control. The regional organization of the party was intended to be the spearhead of Ghana's modernization outside the capital, but it succeeded only to a minor degree. Traditional group and territorial loyalties remained largely intact. Unlike the colonial district officers whose activities were controlled and directed by the rules and ethics of an imperial service transcending not only local areas but also the boundaries of particular colonies, the new district and regional commissioners, remote from Accra and party headquarters, acted increasingly as autonomous agents. The directives and policies of the party's leadership were frequently transformed beyond recognition by the resilient yet tough fibre of life in the countryside. The party not only failed to break up the crust of rural conservatism, but on the contrary, became absorbed into it and added to its strength. Party branches and agencies of the party in the countryside became transformed into local institutions, appropriately deferential to local customs and personages. Unmoved by the radical froth emanating from the upper reaches of the party in Accra, the farmers passively accepted the fact of the party's national power, but remained absorbed in such local issues as the provision of water supplies, the repair of roads, disputes between chiefly families and the ownership of land. At its local level, the party was obliged to adapt to these preoccupations to survive at all. Its regional network of commissioners became a strange parody of the old colonial system of indirect rule — a new collection of officially favoured petty and paramount chiefs, the objects of petitioners and supplicants, whose principal function was to keep the peace in the countryside.

The CPP could not with accuracy be described as a totalitarian party in the sense in which this term is understood in Europe. Nkrumah, sometimes acting alone, sometimes on the promptings of individuals and groups close to him, did take arbitrary decisions which affected the everyday lives of everyone within Ghana. He was, when all is said and done, a despot. But his party never developed effective means of exercising comprehensive control over all aspects of the people's activities. Its domination over the press and radio services, its use of preventive detention, the network of spies and informers it set up, were all crude instruments of political control. The party's very nature as an uneasy coalition of mutually hostile elements prevented it from becoming a ruthless engine of repression. A reign of terror could conceivably come about only with the total triumph of one faction over its rivals, and Nkrumah was well aware of the risks to himself of such an occurrence.

The alliance between party and government which was the heart of the political system was more apparent than real. It was not an alliance between equals. Only in Nkrumah's own person — as Head of State and life chairman of the party — were party and government truly united. In theory the party was supposed to be the political power house from which members of the government drew their energies and inspiration. But at all levels below the leader, party and government viewed each other with reserve and sometimes hostility. Cabinet ministers found their scope for independent initiatives whittled down by the growing concentration of power in the President's 'state secretariats' at Flagstaff House. Power flowed, not from the ministers in the cabinet, but through them from above. Deprived of great importance, ministers became adept at cutting corners off presidential directives, implementing them just sufficiently to ensure their survival, but often ignoring their spirit and purpose.

Ministers depended upon the civil servants for the efficient running of their departments. They could hope for little assistance from the rank and file of the party — and frequently smarted under the attacks upon them in the party's press. However, the party was no substitute for the civil service, no alternative reservoir of talent or administrative experience. Increasingly, the party was not regarded by the ministers, the civil servants, or even its life chairman as an essential — or even particularly desirable — partner in government. And in time it found itself relegated to the position of an honorary partner, ignored on all important issues and left to occupy itself with its own internal wranglings.

The smart modern building in Accra which housed the party headquarters barely concealed the confusion within. Fifteen bureaux and committees lay at the party's heart, none with a clearly defined area of responsibility and with no clear chain of command. In its later years it was kept from complete administrative breakdown by one man, Nathaniel Welbeck,[31] the executive secretary of the party. Welbeck took more and more of the headquarters business upon himself, showing scant regard for the procedures and rules laid down in the standing orders. He acted as a strong man, sorting out inter-departmental quarrels and cutting various Gordian knots — a task which the headquarters staff were only too willing to leave to him. As a result a great deal of business was left undone.

Large numbers of letters and petitions flowed into party

headquarters. The bulkiest files were those dealing with complaints about the behaviour of officials or those containing appeals for headquarters arbitration in local and often trivial disputes. Grievances, real and imaginary, were referred increasingly to headquarters, by-passing the district and regional commissioners in whose impartiality or competence the plaintiffs had little faith. Petitioners felt that their only hope of redress was to contact personally some 'big man' at headquarters, preferably a kinsman, who could act on their behalf. Late in 1964 it proved necessary to set up a permanent committee of six officials to sift complaints to see which warranted action. Malicious reports from individuals seeking to discredit their enemies appeared to be a staple item. The Winneba conference of 1962 had urged that 'anonymous letters should be thrown into the waste paper basket', and warned that 'people who rush to headquarters with wild stories should not be entertained. They should be redirected to their districts for comradely efforts to be made to resolve their differences.' The conference felt that this was 'a most serious question on which the Central Committee should issue a firm ruling', but the situation failed to improve despite these resolutions.

Even the handsome building which housed the headquarters was falling into dilapidation. The two lifts were frequently out of order and important officials would sometimes spend an uncomfortably hot time inside them when they jammed. Office discipline was lax. Files were not kept up to date and were sometimes mislaid. In one room party membership cards lay in disorder on the floor, decaying in Accra's humid heat. Sanitary facilities for staff and visitors alike deteriorated to everyone's discomfort.

By 1964 Nkrumah spent little time at party headquarters, preferring the cooler, wooded environs of Flagstaff House or the breezier aspect of Christiansborg Castle. The party's organization bureau was run by Suleman Tandoh, a former storekeeper who had worked his way up through the Ashanti regional organization. But the state of the party's machinery proved too much for him, and Nkrumah summoned the organization and methods unit of Flagstaff House to overhaul the party's machinery. Much to the disgust of some of his colleagues, it was a senior civil servant, I.K. Impraim, who produced a plan in mid-1964 to rescue the party from imminent administrative breakdown. The plethora of bureaux and committees at headquarters was reduced to three new bureaux under the control of three secretaries who, although nominally responsible to the executive secretary of the party, were given more initiative. The 'general administrative bureau' was put under another senior civil servant, D.K. Ntosuoh, the 'party organization bureau' remained under Tandoh, and the 'education and information bureau' went to Kweku Akwei.

In January 1965, as part of yet another attempt to revivify the party Nkrumah ordered that the party's weekly newsletter to party branches should be incorporated with the *Evening News* to try and bring it before a wider readership. Regional party secretaries were instructed to send a copy of their weekly reports to headquarters to the editorial offices of the *Evening News*, the 'organ of the central committee'. None of these reports was ever published by the newspaper, however, and in fact few were received. It was a makeshift arrangement, indicative of the state of decay into which the inner lines of communication within the party had fallen.

There was little time left to judge whether these organization changes would have had much of an effect. The last major overhaul of the party early in 1962 had failed to rescue it from decline. Certainly, the streamlining of the bureaux was long overdue; but the irony of calling

on the help of the senior civil service to come to the rescue
of the party which had so much distrusted them was not
lost to local observers. As one local writer succintly put it:

> ... and so the formidable CPP, once the effective voice
> of the Ghanaian people, settled into honourable
> retirement as a kind of minor government department
> ruled over by a civil servant... the triumph of bureau-
> cracy over political enthusiasm was complete.[32]

The introduction of the single party state was not of itself
an event of great significance. Since independence it had
become clear that the CPP had no intention of allowing
itself to be voted out of office and it had equipped itself
with extra-parliamentary means of sustaining its power.
The constitutional change involved in abolishing the
opposition parties and entrenching the CPP with a legal
monopoly of political power merely added a *de jure*
embellishment to what had been for some years a *de facto*
situation.

The notion of creating a one party state had been widely
canvassed for some time but the events of 1962 forced the
pace. At the party's eleventh congress at Kumasi in August
of that year a resolution was proposed and adopted calling
for the introduction of a single party form of government.
Shortly afterwards, as Nkrumah embarked upon a tour of
northern Ghana, the Kulungugu incident took place. On 11
September, whilst the passions aroused by the attempt on
the President's life were fully aroused, Suleman Ibun
Iddrissu, the member for Gushiegu, moved a private
member's motion in the Assembly calling for the
introduction of the single party state. Individuals from all
sides of the party spoke in support of his motion —
although their reasons for welcoming the change was
different and somewhat opposed. The party's radicals saw
the single party state as the means by which the total

control of the CPP over all aspects of the national life — particularly the remaining commercial and business interests — could finally be enforced. Some conservatives believed that a single national party was more congruent with Ghanaian traditional polity under which a community's decisions emerged after much argument between its members and were unanimously adopted by the community as a whole. Iddrissu's own hope was that the single party state would somehow end the hatred and bickering within the movement and enable it to set its own house in order.

The arguments advanced in favour of the single party state as the form of government most suited to the needs of a new tropical African country received much sympathetic attention abroad in the early sixties. The former British ambassador to Senegal, for instance, saw the single party as 'a surgical clamp which holds each territory together while the different economic and political parts knit themselves into a nation'.[33] An American writer commented that 'the single party state provides a mechanism whereby the majority of the population can have some regular meaningful connection with, and influence upon, the governmental process and vice versa.'[34]

The advent of independence in tropical Africa in the early sixties attracted a great deal of interest overseas, particularly in the United States where for many years Africa had virtually been an unknown continent. Many of the first writers attracted to independent Africa were young Americans, combining a sympathy with black emancipation at home with a desire to exploit an untapped rich field for doctoral dissertations. Like travellers in a strange land they first sought out the few familiar landmarks. American political life is dominated by the two main political parties. In post-colonial Africa the travellers perceived in the political parties existing there a ready point of reference. Conveniently for them, the majority of African parties conducted their public business in French or English, so that the illusion of familiarity was deepened. The radical vocabulary and style of some of these parties further appealed to the travellers and led them into a generally sympathetic and occasionally uncritical examination of political life largely in terms of the visible features of the parties rather than towards investigating who was doing what to whom. 'Emancipated' Africa appeared to have discovered the secret of combining progressive ideals with the urge to experiment which constantly eluded the older, tired, white world from which the travellers came.[35]

Yet in essence the movement towards one party rule, soon evident after independence, was no more than a movement towards the concentration of power in the hands of individuals. Parties do not rule as much as they reign. Power resides in the hands of those who control the party. Single party rule was little more than a mask for personal dictatorship — an indication that tropical Africa's brief experience of representative government was breaking down. Those who regarded the single party state as a new form of polity uniquely suited to Africa's needs neglected the central problem — one which has always concerned political commentators in every age — namely, how those who acquire power can be made or induced by those over whom they rule to exercise it wisely and moderately. The excess of sympathy for the new states amongst many foreign observers led them to credit their rulers with qualities of altruism and energy which they could rarely discover in their own political leaders.[36]

The debate on Iddrissu's motion gave Kofi Baako, the leader of the House, an opportunity to enlarge on the merits of the single party state. Although Iddrissu's motion failed, the government had already decided, in fact, to give the CPP in the near future a legal and constitutional political monopoly. This would require a constitutional amendment and subsequent amending legislation, and, at the time Iddrissu introduced his motion, the necessary drafting work had not been completed. Baako explained that the 'supremacy of the party' meant nothing more or less than what he called 'democratic centralism' — 'By which', he said, 'is meant the submission of the individual view to the overriding majority view... that is the principle which governs our Party'.[37] He went on to explain that 'there must be one central forum which the people can use without fear or favour to express their support for or distaste against various aspects of national policies or measures taken by the Government... an all-embracing political movement of party which will serve as the principal guide for the people's leaders and representatives in their Government duties.'

Baako rejected the notion that the ends of progress and liberty are better secured in a multi-party state. The degree of democracy in a country was not proportional to the numbers of political parties in it. Nor did he believe that a strong united opposition was essential to a democracy. Such an opposition only thrives in a country where the government was failing in its duties. Government in a multi-party state was obliged, in Baako's view, to make 'deliberate mistakes', solely in order to ensure the survival of an official opposition.

Baako refuted the view that the CPP was 'in alliance' or in some kind of confederation with its integral wings. 'All these organizations are committees or platforms of the party', he stated bluntly. They could not represent groups or interests in isolation or in opposition to the party. All their members were party members, and it was because they accepted the overall supremacy of the party that the party was 'in a position to relate their interests and desires to the overall interests of the nation'.

The apotheosis of the CPP — that is, its conversion from a political party in the western sense whose mandate was subject, in theory at least, to mortality at the hands of the electorate, into the only legally permitted political association in Ghana — followed the results of the national referendum on the single party state which was held late in January 1964. Voters were asked to say 'yes' or 'no' to the government's proposals for constitutional amendment necessary to give the CPP a permanent monopoly of power.

Because of the difficulties of organizing a national referendum in an under-developed country, the voting days varied between different parts of the country. Accra and the north voted on 24 January, Ashanti and the Volta Region on the 28th, and the remainder of the country on 31 January. The results — published as soon as they were received — were an apparently overwhelming triumph for the CPP. Out of a total registered electorate numbering 2,877,464, some 96.5% cast their vote; a far larger proportion than had voted during any previous general election. Of these, 2,773,920 voted 'yes' and only 2,452, or 0.1% of the total, voted 'no'.

It soon became apparent, however, that this massive endorsement was more indicative of the party's unscrupulous manipulation of the referendum than it was of the true state of public opinion. It was remarkable that the whole of the Ashanti Region, for instance, which was one of the main centres of resistance to the CPP nine or ten years previously, did not record a single 'no' vote. Two British newspaper correspondents sent to Ghana to cover the referendum reported on the 'mixture of intimidation and ballot-rigging which ranged from the brutal to the farcical'. On the instructions of the government, the

Christmas vacation of the universities and training colleges was extended over the period of the referendum, ostensibly so that students could serve in country districts as assistants to returning officers, but in reality to avoid the possibility of hostile demonstrations. Students returning to the University of Ghana after the referendum reported that in some areas boxes containing the 'no' votes had simply been emptied into the 'yes' boxes. Boxes for the 'no' votes had been placed in inaccessible positions, or had been placed in full view of the returning officer and his party helpers. In one area the 'no' boxes had simply not been provided with slits through which to put the voting papers.

There was also a strong element of intimidation. The *Ghanaian Times* of 24 January, the day when Accra went to the polls warned that:

> In this referendum we have mounted our vigilance to find out those who are with us and those that are against us. Those who think they can hide under the so-called 'secrecy' of the polling booth to fool us must know that the days when we could be fooled are gone. And those fence-sitters who prefer to stay at home must likewise know that the people's wrath is apt to descend without mercy on those who are not with us.[38]

The conditions under which voting took place were not consistent with a secret ballot. Voters were given slips numbered according to their numbers on the electoral roll and were required to put their slips in one of two boxes labelled 'yes' or 'no'. Under these conditions, a voter was well aware that his identity could be traced by local party officials.

Indeed, it is a wonder why the exercise was undertaken at all. If it was to impress foreign opinion then it was clumsily stage-managed. Referenda yielding such massive majorities have been such a common feature of European totalitarian régimes that they actually excite suspicions of ballot-rigging. The whole operation appeared to be designed to give the party a renewed sense of its own authority and presence within the country at a time when it was growing acutely conscious first, of its own internal strains, and secondly of a mood of popular disillusion with its lack of achievement.

Amending legislation to the constitution was required in order to give effect to the introduction of the single party state. In May 1965, the Minister of Justice, K.O. Ofori Atta, introduced two bills touching those provisions of the constitution regulating electoral procedures. During their second readings on 18 May latent confusions emerged, stemming from the muddle between the idea of a single, all-embracing national party on one side, and the idea of popular representation on the other. Neither bill appeared to have been drafted with much care and both were severely mauled from the floor of the Assembly. The first bill sought to restrict candidates for future presidential elections to members of the 'national' party. It required a change to article eleven of the constitution which regulated the election of a President in the event of that election being contested. Article eleven in its unamended form gave members of parliament the right to determine a contested presidential election in certain circumstances by secret ballot. But the new bill provided for only one nominee to stand for a presidential election. 'The person who is going to be president will be elected by the National party. So there will be only one person, and it will not be contested.'[39] In plain words the CPP had no intention of allowing even rival presidential candidates from *within* the party to stand. Presidential elections in future were to be a one-horse race; simply formal endorsements of the party's choice candidate. Members of parliament were unhappy with this further derogation of their powers, but another tricky question had emerged; who was a member of the 'national' party?

To Kofi Baako the answer was simple: 'anybody who is a member of the CPP has a party card'. Benjamin Kusi, who had been lately deprived of his membership of the CPP demurred on the grounds that if the CPP was to be a truly national party, then everyone by virtue of his citizenship should be regarded as a member. Otherwise the amendment was discriminatory against that large section of the country not holding party cards. 'Why should the Constitution say one cannot form one's own political party and at the same time cannot be allowed to bring to the CPP CPP?'[40] 'As it is', he continued, 'things look as if we have two constitutions for the country. The constitution of the Party on the one hand, and the constitution of the country on the other'. Baako did his best to turn aside Kusi's disingenuous remarks, but could not explain satisfactorily how, in the single party state, those who were not card-carrying members of the ruling party could be regarded otherwise than disenfranchised for the purposes of presidential election. It seemed as if the single party state, far from absorbing the opposition in a national movement, simply created, rendered all those outside the party, or expelled from it, into an opposition group, denied a choice in the election of their own President.

On the same day a second bill — the Electoral Provisions bill — implementing the single party state was brought before the Assembly. A further lacuna appeared. No provisions had been made to ensure that only members of the national party stood for parliamentary elections. This led Iddrissu to enquire what would happen if a general election returned a majority of independent members to the Assembly. Baako, growing confused, took refuge by asserting that 'so much is the confidence' of the country in the CPP that no independent member could hope to enter parliament. Iddrissu drove his point home by asking why, in the case of a presidential election, it was necessary to exclude an independent candidate, but not in the case of parliamentary elections? '... If we have no fear, then all should be the same. Democracy is democracy, whenever it is practised.'[41]

But notwithstanding these irritating pinpricks which were brushed aside by the government, Nkrumah's party became supreme — the only constitutionally recognized and legally permitted political association in the country. Under the new dispensation the first general election — or non-election — was held in July 1965. Since all the candidates belonged to the CPP, and since the central committee picked the candidates, allowing no others to stand, all were declared to be returned unopposed without even the formality of a vote. But the party's final triumph was shortlived. The fiction of the CPP as a united, monolithic union could not be sustained and its quarrels were shortly to burst out into the open.

How is the CPP best described in its last years? The usual European categories of 'left' and 'right' cannot be fruitfully applied to it. Fleeting resemblance to forms found at both ends of this spectrum can be found, but they were will o' the wisps. It is difficult to find much trace of the 'mobilizing agency', having as its purpose the modernization of a traditional society, as perceived by one writer on the earlier CPP.[42] Traditional forces had a stronger, more insidious hold over the party than innovatory pressures. It is equally hard to regard the CPP as 'a case of socialism badly manqué' as described by another writer.[43] The gap between the party's public ideology and the private activities of its members had for a long time been too large, too obvious, for its 'socialism' to be taken seriously — even if it is allowed that socialism in any of its contemporary modes can find expression in a tropical African community. Nor does it make much sense to dismiss the CPP as a tool of the 'national bourgeoisie', an obstacle despite its professions to true revolution, as some marxists have subsequently maintained to rescue themselves from embarrassment.[44] Although it was never a party exclusively of the poor, it had always embraced a large and important element drawn from the unemployed, the town workers and the farmers. But their instincts tended to be even more conservative than those of the journalists and former teachers who provided so much of the party's ideological gloss.

The CPP has also been described by others as a ghost party in its final years, possessing an impressive, elaborate organization but lacking any inner driving spirit or sense of purpose. John Tettegah told his interrogators after the coup that 'the banned party never existed for some years since Nkrumah took direct personal control, so it didn't matter whether you were a member of the party or not'.[45] There is some truth in this assertion. Nkrumah's supremacy stifled all independent life within his party, even as he drifted steadily away from his creation, an indecisive Hamlet rather than a ruthless Lenin, unable to discard it or subject it to major surgery.

Yet the fact remains that the CPP retained a formidable presence feared by some, admired by others, right up to the moment of its extinction. Cast at first in a European mould, it became in time a thoroughly African institution, resembling a great clan structure under a paramount chief and reflecting the feuds and preoccupations of its members. It was a giant self-perpetuating machine for the benefit of its members and as such presented a massive obstacle to securing the progress and reform which it proclaimed were the ends for which it existed.

IV The Divided House

The crowning embellishment that the CPP bestowed upon itself in 1964 — the introduction of the single party state — was hailed by its sympathizers as a new, progressive form of political organization and dismissed by its opponents as a lurch towards totalitarianism. In reality it was neither; it was a makeshift attempt to paper over the cracks which had existed within the ruling party before independence and which had subsequently widened further.

The early months of 1961 saw a renewal of disquiet when Nkrumah took a sudden leftward turn in his foreign policy. His frustration over events in the Congo came to a head with the murder of Lumumba in February. Later in the month Leonid Brezhnev, the Russian party leader, arrived in Accra to review the Congo crisis with Nkrumah. He was followed shortly afterwards by President Tito. Nkrumah was by now firmly convinced that the failure of his Congo policy was the work of western imperialism. Early in March he announced that he would take over the general secretaryship of his party from Tawia Adamafio, a move which he claimed had been urged upon him by his central committee in the interest of promoting the kind of decisive action required in a rapidly changing African scene. Adamafio, widely regarded as the rising new man under Nkrumah, was amply compensated by a seat in parliament and a new job as minister of state for presidential affairs. These developments, fanned by a virulent, anti-western tone in the party's press, brought out into the open the fears of the party's old guard, the loyalists and the foundation members, for whom the sudden move to the left was unwelcome.

Much of the quarrelling between the factions within the party over the next years was couched in the familiar political language of 'left' versus 'right'. But the division between conservative and radical groups was not a simple one. Certainly it did not rest upon a division between the 'haves' and the 'have-nots'. Some CPP conservatives were businessmen, a few of them operating on a considerable scale. They had backed the CPP as the winning horse in its early days, hoping that its victory would put a larger share of Ghana's trade into their hands. Others, however, were conservative by instinct rather than by material interest, suspicious of innovation and close to village life and the farmers from whom they had recently come. Rewarded for their loyal support of the party by seats in parliament, they had remained on the backbenches and regarded the rapid ascent of lately-arrived radicals in their movement's ranks with lively resentment. Throughout the conservatives' quarrels with their rivals there was a constant effort by both sides to capture the President's ear and gain his favour. An element of caprice, rarely absent from the politics of court favouritism, was thus introduced, which blurs any attempt to distinguish between the factions purely in terms of differences over policies.

The conservative faction was faced with a dilemma as Nkrumah lurched to the left. Some, like Kojo Botsio, were prepared despite secret misgivings to back Nkrumah unconditionally. His errors, they reasoned, were not his own but those of Adamafio and his radical friends under whose influence he had apparently fallen. Others in the government, like Gbedemah and Patrick Quaidoo, were less sure that such an excusing distinction could be made. But their unease at Nkrumah's growing powers and the direction of his policies was swamped by their dislike of the party radicals — the new men associated with Adamafio.

These the conservative suspected of being more royalist than the king, cloaking their relentless ambitions with adulation of the leader. Yet with the fortunes of the Adamafio group so strongly in the ascendant early in 1961, the conservatives were forced in spite of their misgivings to look to Nkrumah as the only effective barrier against the total triumph of their opponents. They were reluctant therefore to hand over to their opponents their strongest weapon — their loyalty to Nkrumah — by openly criticizing him. The President's ideology was for them a matter of fashion which they were willing to embrace if he so wished, providing that it did not endanger their own position. Thinking of themselves as practical men, indifferent to the theoretical questions which so excited their leader, the conservatives' scorn was directed upon the radicals whom they regarded as rabble rousers having no competence in business or administration.

The conservatives' principal spokesmen in the government were Komla Agbeli Gbedemah, the able minister of finance who had been the architect of the party's crucial election victory of 1951, and Krobo Edusei, linch-pin of the party's support amongst the powerful Ashanti. As a group, their stronghold lay within the National Assembly. Their opposition to the new men gradually took the form of defending the authority of parliament and the principle of elective representation against the party's claims to unlimited supremacy. In the days before independence the parliamentary wing of the CPP had been the spearhead of the movement as a whole. But afterwards, in the drift towards Nkrumah's personal rule, the parliamentary wing of the party suffered a loss of authority. By 1961 Adamafio and his men had acquired control over the party's central machinery, the trade unions, the press and publicity services, and other 'integral wings' of the CPP. Worse still, these men appeared to have the President's ear. Few of the conservatives seemed any longer to enjoy an easy social relationship with Nkrumah or even had access to him. It seemed as if Adamafio and his associates had succeeded in keeping them out in the cold.

Tawia Adamafio was born into a well-connected Ga household early in the 1920's. Christened Joseph Tawia Adams, he changed his name to a Ga form as a defiant gesture in 1946 when working as a clerk in the supreme court. Adamafio had not enjoyed a secondary education, but despite recurrent eye trouble he had improved his qualifications with determination, teaching himself stenography and the rudiments of journalism. He belonged to the politically restless post-war generation and showed an interest in the UGCC at the time of its formation. But he remained aloof from the CPP when it broke away from Danquah's organization. Indeed, he shared the resentment of many of the Ga people of the capital against the influx of settlers from other parts of the country for whom the CPP was the natural political home. A part-time journalist working for the now defunct *National Times*, Adamafio referred to the CPP on one occasion as 'the party of fooling and thieving'. In 1952 he took part in a raid on the offices of Nkrumah's own newspaper, the *Evening News*, and was alleged to have assaulted Kofi Baako who was then the editor. Later Adamafio became assistant general secretary of the short-lived Ghana Congress Party which was merged with other opposition parties to form the United Party in October 1957. However, before this union took place Adamafio had decided that his chances of a political career with the successful CPP would be greater than with the ineffectual opposition, and he 'crossed the carpet', bringing with him into the CPP, two Ga associates, Ako Adjei and Cofie Crabbe.

Adamafio had first been invited to join the CPP by Kofi

Baako in 1953. Baako had forgiven the incident of the previous year and had struck up some kind of friendship with Adamafio. In Adamafio's words: 'Mr Kofi Baako was a writer as I was. We were taking beer together and arguing in the streets.'[1] But it was Edmund Nee Ocansey[2], a Ga businessman and a friend of Adamafio's, who actually inducted him into the CPP. Adamafio shortly afterwards began to write a daily column entitled 'Tawia's Daily Notes' for the *Evening News*. The carpet-crossers were made welcome in the party by Nkrumah. They shared with the CPP a common opposition to colonial rule, and Nkrumah was anxious to heal the scars of political opposition, especially amongst the suspicious Ga people of the capital. Moreover Adamafio and Ako Adjei were very much the kind of men Nkrumah wanted within his party. Adjei came from a notable Ga family, was much travelled, had attended universities in the United States and London, and was a member of the Inner Temple. Adamafio was much less polished, but after showing considerable flair as assistant general secretary of the CPP — a position to which he was elevated after the general election of June 1954 — he prevailed on Nkrumah early in 1956 for a Cocoa Marketing Board scholarship to enable him to study law in England. Nkrumah, attracted by Adamafio's forceful, crude energy, agreed on condition that Adamafio undertook the task of bringing the large Ghanaian student population in London into the CPP's fold.

In London Adamafio found division amongst the Ghanaian students, reflecting the emnity back home between the CPP and the National Liberation Movement. Nevertheless, he set about the task of 'cipipification' with the same energy he had displayed in Accra. Acting on the advice of George Padmore, who was then living in London, Adamafio set up the National Association of Socialist Students Organizations — NASSO — in preference to setting up a London branch of the CPP.[3] Padmore had warned that the latter step would simply lead to a rival NLM branch being set up, thus widening the breach between the students. In essence, however, NASSO was controlled and financed by the CPP. Adamafio became chairman of the organization and Kwesi Armah, a young Fanti law student, became his deputy. Under their direction NASSO soon became the most vocal and active of African student organizations in London.

Adamafio's success abroad greatly pleased Nkrumah who had, of course, started his own political career in student circles. With the enthusiastic support of Kofi Baako and Nathaniel Welbeck, and with the decidedly cool assent of Botsio and Gbedemah, Nkrumah appointed Adamafio general secretary of the CPP in January 1960, although Adamafio remained in London until October, concluding his law studies and putting the finishing touches to his student organization.

As general secretary of the party Adamafio was, of course, in a very influential position, although his day to day decisions on the running of the party could be over-ruled by Nkrumah and the central committee. From the luxurious presidential suite at headquarters Adamafio kept in close touch with the Ga population of the capital. He secured for two of his kinsmen, Boi Doku and Kwatelai Quartey — who were not even members of the CPP until 1960 — the important party jobs of national propaganda secretary and his deputy. Adamafio also remained on good terms with Ako Adjei who had with equal swiftness risen to the position of Ghana's Foreign Minister, and Cofie Crabbe, who had been made executive secretary of the CPP. But despite the fact that Adjei and Crabbe enjoyed more popular esteem amongst the Ga people on account of their education and membership of respected families, both lacked the drive and determination of Adamafio and began to fade as political figures.

The CPP had never felt itself totally secure in Accra. In the mid-fifties there had been outbreaks of sporadic violence between the followers of the CPP and the 'Tokyo Joes' — supporters of the Ga Shifimo Kpee. The latter organization had been driven underground in October 1957, refusing to merge with the United Party. But it continued to exist as a secret society, its members bound together by oath-taking and the ritual slaughter of goats. Nkrumah hoped that the appointment of Adamafio as party boss would go some way to reconciling the Ga people to the CPP much as Krobo Edusei's position in the government had helped to maintain a popular following for the party amongst the Ashanti.

Adamafio was certainly in a key position to dispense or withhold favours to his countrymen. He proceeded to build up a network of spies and informers in the capital, reporting not only on popular feeling but also on the movements and contacts of other members of the government. Adamafio was well aware of the importance of the market women of Accra who were great repositories of gossip and information. The CPP had organized the 'National Council of Ghana Women' as one of its integral wings in 1960 under the chairmanship of the formidable Mrs Margaret Martei. Its ostensible function was to provide mass support for official rallies from amongst the many women traders. Covertly, it was the eyes and ears of the party in the markets and in return the Council exercised great powers over the issue of stall and trading licences. The 1961 budget, however, upset many women traders. Two rival factions emerged, both seeking an alleviation of the new taxes. The 'double action' group, led by Madam Lydia Addo, looked to Gbedemah as their champion. The other group was led by Madam Koshie Lamptey. She was related to Emmanuel Obetsebi Lamptey, one of the United Party leaders, and was the sister of Kwatelai Quartey, the recently appointed propaganda secretary of the CPP. Through kinship ties with Adamafio — himself distantly related to Obetsebi Lamptey — Madam Lamptey's group naturally looked to the new minister of state as their patron.[4]

The Lamptey faction quickly became known as 'emashie nonn' — meaning in Ga, 'it is still there' because it included many unrepentant supporters of the banned Ga Shifimo Kpee. By the end of 1961 quarrelling and brawling between the two groups was proving such an embarrassment to the party that Nkrumah called a meeting of a central committee to see if the two women leaders could be reconciled. A settlement was eventually patched up, with the party recognizing both groups on condition that they behaved themselves in public. This compromise was interpreted by many in the party who had wished to see the Lamptey faction quashed as a victory for Adamafio, and his enemies were quick to turn the gossip linking 'emashie nonn' with the Ga Shifimo Kpee against him. Those party members who resented Adamafio's rapid rise said little in public for fear of offending Nkrumah. But they quickly formed the opinion that Adamafio was out to create for himself a strong tribal base of power at the centre of things in the capital. From this opinion it was but a short step for them to conclude that he was actively preparing to remove Nkrumah should a favourable moment occur.

Adamafio, however, cared little for these murmurings. His position appeared to be impregnable so long as he held Nkrumah's confidence, and so long as he enjoyed daily access to him there seemed no reason to worry. His hold over the press and radio services gave him the means of publicly denouncing his enemies and critics, and he had built up a formidable following in the party machinery and the integral wings. Above all he had a towering contempt for most of his opponents and some of his followers, reflecting an excessive confidence in his own abilities. Unlike Krobo Edusei who made money in order to spend it, Adamafio was a shrewd political operator interested only in power. He did not use his position to accumulate wealth,[5] preferring to leave this activity to others and use it as an additional lever over them. Adamafio's championship of socialism was just as tactical, stemming from the self-made man's hatred of his country's former colonial masters and a contempt for the timid indigenous business community, rather than from any profound ideological convictions. As Nkrumah moved to the left, so Adamafio went with him, leaving the conservatives and loyalists in the party isolated from the President and open to attack. Undoubtedly Adamafio enjoyed some kind of hold over the President who admired and valued his forcefulness and energy. He lost no opportunity of presenting himself publicly on every possible occasion as Nkrumah's principal confidante and heir apparent.[6] Nkrumah's notorious vanity was put to good use by Adamafio, who was largely responsible for the cult of personality around the President which began to reach absurd proportions after the inauguration of the Republic.

Even when Adamafio ceased to be general secretary of the party, yielding the post to Nkrumah in May 1961, he remained to a great extent responsible for the direction of the party's affairs. Nkrumah was content to leave the day to day running of the CPP in Adamafio's hands, pleading that foreign and African affairs took up too much of his time. Nkrumah's assumption of the general secretaryship had been prompted more by pressures from other party stalwarts jealous of Adamafio than from any doubts on Nkrumah's part of his lieutenant's loyalty. On the same day on which Adamafio yielded up the post, Cofie Crabbe took over as the party's chief administrative officer, keeping Adamafio fully informed of the working of the CPP machinery.

Early in June 1961, when Adamafio took over the post of Minister of Presidential Affairs, his portfolio included supervision over the Establishments and the Scholarship Secretariat; responsibilities which brought him an office within Flagstaff House itself. One of his most important functions in this post was 'to see that undesirable elements did not enter the President's office'.[7] He admitted that the selection of petitioners for audience with Nkrumah rested largely with himself and the President's English secretary, Miss Erica Powell. But although Adamafio did not remain long in this ministry, taking over responsibility for the information and broadcasting services in October 1961, he managed to carry with him some of the duties from his previous position, in particular his job of filtering access to Nkrumah. He was not asked to leave Flagstaff House and the presidential ante-room until a week before his arrest in August 1962.

Shortly after Adamafio's return to Ghana to take up the general secretaryship of the party, Nkrumah ordered the abolition of NASSO. In its place party study groups were set up, ostensibly to raise the level of ideological consciousness within the party, reaching out beyond the students to include party workers, academics and civil servants. One of these study groups, assembled originally by Kweku Akwei and Kwasi Amoaka Atta, quickly fell under Adamafio's dominance. He later described how the group developed:

> We examined problems as they came in. We held four meetings in the Ministry of Kojo Botsio... but he became disinterested (sic) in the group and Mr Kweku Akwei transferred the meetings to my house.[8]

The composition of this 'inner party study group' varied from time to time. It was attended by Kwaku Boateng, John Tettegah, Kofi Baako, Alfred Dowouna Hammond, then Minister of Education, and several young ambitious civil servants, such as H.P. Nelson and E.N. Omaboe, together with sundry other followers of Adamafio from the party headquarters and press and information services. But the most important occasional attender was Nkrumah himself, who had never lost the taste for political table talk acquired during his student days.

The inner party study group quickly became an object of the deepest suspicion amongst the conservatives. It confirmed their fears that the direction of the party — indeed of the government — had fallen into the hands of a secret cabal, a kitchen cabinet, dominated by Adamafio and enjoying direct access to the President. Adamafio himself, although disclaiming any sinister purposes behind the group, later admitted that 'when we arrive at our conclusions, we meet the President and discuss our points with him'.[9] Indifferent to these suspicions, Nkrumah was already moving away from the regular machinery of his party as a forum for hammering out his thoughts on policy. Other members of the study group attended for a variety of motives. For the earnest socialists, the ideological purists, and those civil servants who were increasingly disillusioned by the condition of the party, the inner study group offered an opportunity to bring their ideas for reform and future policies directly to the President's attention. To others, for whom ambition was more important than principle, attendance was a useful means of commending their talents or their loyalty directly to Nkrumah.

The growing resentments of the conservatives at these developments were brought out into the open during the 'progress report' submitted to the National Assembly by the Minister of Labour in February 1961. Charles Baah[10], the member for Eastern Gomoa and a businessman with interests in building and contracting, spoke out against the growing political influence of the Ghana Trades Union Congress under its secretary general, John Tettegah.[11] Baah complained about the growing tendency of the TUC spokesmen to make statements directed against private enterprise. A few days previously one of Tettegah's men at TUC headquarters in Accra had called for increased union participation in private business. Editorials in the party's press had called for government purchase of foreign-owned goldmines which were about to close because they were uneconomic. Yet it was rumoured that the Industrial Development Corporation was unhappy at the losses made by a furniture factory it had handed over to the TUC to run. Baah thought the time was ripe to raise the whole issue of the political position of the TUC in the country at large:

> It seems to me that the TUC is being organized to such an extent that the Party which is in power is in danger of losing its identity. I say this because we have seen one union alone has been able to register 275,000 members. If we compare the membership of one union of the TUC with the total population — which is only seven million — we see clearly that in the future we shall have a 'labour' government, instead of a CPP government.[12]

Baah went on to complain that the TUC which was formed '... to support the CPP government, is now trying to make itself the centre of final authority'. They already had, he said, their own journal and their own president. 'Now, who is going to be the next President? Is it the head of the TUC, or is it going to be the head of the CPP?'[13] The leader of the House attempted to smooth things over when it became apparent that Baah had substantial backbench support. The TUC, he asserted, was one of the integral wings of the party and could not be greater than the party itself. Only the party was supreme; the magic wand, or *bodua*, 'with which Osagyefo works his political, economic and social miracles'.

The riposte of the Adamafio group to Baah's complaints was not long in coming. A few days afterwards, at a trade union rally in Accra, John Tettegah denounced the MPs who had criticized the TUC and the co-operative organizations, referring to them as the 'Tshombes' of Ghana:

> 'Our enemies should be warned here and now that the country is getting fed-up with their intrigues.'[14]

The report of this meeting was accompanied by a vitriolic editorial in the *Ghanaian Times* attacking Baah:

> Take C.C.K. Baah, for instance, after making a laughing stock of himself with several childish arguments and uniformed presentations, Baah asked if the Government was Socialist or Capitalist! What nonsense! The MP asked this foolish question with the tongue of an individual with a personal selfish interest. He was quarrelling with the Government because the Party organization, the Industrial Co-operative Corporation, has established a stone crushing plant which he finds a threat to his own business in Messrs. Baah Ltd.[15]

On the same day on which this editorial blast appeared, Baah was joined by the Minister of State for parliamentary affairs, A.S.A. Abban. Abban also had business interests, but had risen from lowlier origins and had started his career as a teacher. By publicly siding with the conservative malcontents Abban was to lose his ministerial post, but kept his seat in parliament. He made the point that, for all their talk of the 'masses' and 'democracy', the activists of the party had achieved their positions of influence through the manipulation of patronage, and could not claim to be the elected representatives of the people.

Abban was close to raising an important question which was to occur often in the assembly — indeed in most parliamentary institutions — whether an MPs first loyalty was to his constituents, or to the party on whose ticket he had been elected. From the ministerial bench he condemned the increasingly aggressive tone which had crept recently into the party newspapers against certain parliamentarians:

> I was horrified when I afterwards read in the *Ghanaian Times* — published by the Guinea Press — which has not made a profit of even one penny since it was established — how Government members and backbenchers of this House were critized and threatened.
>
> If we come into this House to vote moneys for the TUC and other organizations, and we find that they are not doing what we expect of them, it is our right to criticize them in this House. The personnel of the TUC are not better than hon. members in this House; their Ministers and Ambassadors were not elected by the people as Members of this House were (Hear, Hear). After all, we are also members of the CPP and have been in this House at least four years. In fact, we consider ourselves even more CPP than the leaders of the TUC and all the rest of them. (Interruption.) [16]

Kojo Botsio, the leader of the House, once again tried to calm down the angry backbenchers. He appealed to the Speaker not to allow these acrimonious public exchanges which damaged the party's unity. The Speaker, however, did not feel obliged to regulate debates solely with the object of saving the party's face. The article which had appeared in the *Ghanaian Times*, he ruled, constituted a 'complete threat to the freedom of speech of a parliamentarian'.[17] He warned the press and 'all members of whatever party' that threats made against members because of their contributions to the debates of the House would in future be severely dealt with. After the Clerk of the House, on the Speaker's instructions, had read out the relevant part of the National Assembly act of 1959 dealing with contempt of parliament, the Speaker warned the House that:

> If I happen to hear that after this admonition, and after the representations made by the Leader of the House.... any Member of Parliament is being threatened anywhere because of his contributions to a debate in this House, I shall bring the law into full force. (Hear, Hear.)[18]

Disturbed by the continued acrimony within his party Nkrumah addressed the nation by radio early in April at dawn — the traditional Akan time for the announcement of important decisions. Nkrumah expressed concern about reports of quarrelling between integral wings of the party which he had received since arriving home from the Commonwealth Prime Ministers' conference in London. He reproached those backbenchers who, he asserted, were more concerned with protecting and furthering their business interests than with the task of promoting development, and also the trade union officials who had 'indulged in loose, and reprehensible statements which do no good to the party, to the government, or to the nation. This is not the time for unbridled militant trade unionism in our country'. Nkrumah also condemned the atmosphere of rumour-mongering which was prevalent and which damaged public confidence in their politicians.

> Day after day, night after night, all types of wild allegations and rumours were circulated and they are always well sprinkled with, they say, they say, wo see, wo see, akee, akee. I have directed in future' he continued 'that

any allegations or rumours so circulated against any person must immediately be brought before the Central Committee of the party for investigation.

But the full blast of the President's ire was reserved for those members of the party who combined business interests with a political career. It was amongst the old guard, however, amongst Gbedemah, Edusei, Wiafe and others, that knowledge of Nkrumah's own dealings was most detailed. None of these dared to stand up to the President with counter-accusations of their own, without risking their liberty and the positions they had built up for themselves. Nkrumah felt secure enough with the support of the radicals of the party, who had their own reasons for distrusting the conservatives, to put all the blame for the whispers of corruption on the latters' shoulders:

They are tending by virtue of their function and position to become a new ruling class of self seekers and careerists. This tendency is working to alienate the masses and bring the National Assembly into isolation.

Nkrumah then came down heavily on the side of the radicals on the question of whether a member of parliament owed his first duty to the CPP, which nominated him, or to the constituents who elected him:

Members must remember at all times that they are representatives of their constituencies only by virtue of their Party membership and that on no account should they regard constituency representation as belonging to them in their own right. In other words, constituencies are not the property of MPs. It is the Party that sends them there and fights for them to become MPs.

He went on to stress that any party member who wished could take up a career in business, but if he did so, he would in future be expected to give up his political posts and his seat in parliament.

As a follow-up to the dawn broadcast, the President's office sent out a letter requesting all ministers, members of parliament and party officials to submit details of their business interests and personal assets by the end of the month. In addition, an *ad hoc* committee of three public officers was set up to investigate the manner of acquisition of these assets. But the committee did not turn out to be the instrument of a purge which the radical wing hoped it would be. Its composition reflected Nkrumah's tactic of balancing one faction against another.[19] Evidence heard before it was not given on oath and several of those summoned to appear proved uncooperative. Emmanuel Ayeh Kumi, the President's financial adviser, simply refused to appear at all. The committee's findings were never made public and the events of the following months were to rob it of much significance.

The dawn broadcast did little to assuage the seething passions within the party. The one-sided manner in which it was reported by the press and radio angered the conservatives even more by suggesting that it was only members of parliament who were being censured. A further incident was to upset them. A report appeared in the *Evening News* that Komla Gbedemah had engaged in the diamond smuggling racket whilst on official business in the United States. This was later admitted by Nathaniel Welbeck, the executive secretary of the party, to be an unfounded accusation, and the offending copies of the newspaper were withdrawn.

In this atmosphere of suspicion and recrimination a quarrel blew up in the National Assembly during the 'progress report' submitted by Kweku Boateng on behalf of his ministry. W.K. Aduhene, then ministerial secretary to the Development Secretariat, read out the full text of the

President's letter to members of parliament and party functionaries. Aduhene complained that Boateng's ministry, responsible for disseminating official information, had given the impression that the President's strictures had applied only to members of parliament. Aduhene, supported by several other members, wanted to know 'about Party officials who own numerous cars and houses'. Why, he asked, were these not referred to by the radio service and the press? Boateng could not answer these charges properly. He received a very rough handling and the motion accepting his progress report was rejected by a vote of the House. This was the first and only time that a motion sponsored by the government was ever thrown out by the National Assembly and it caused Nkrumah to direct that the progress report system, which had been introduced only the year before to ginger up his ministers' performances, should be abandoned. He was not prepared to risk another public rejection of the work of one of his ministries, which would sooner or later raise the contentious issue of parliamentary sovereignty versus presidential authority.

But the full fury of the conversatives was to break over the heads of Boateng and Adamafio a few days later during the debate on the President's address to the National Assembly. Abban, stripped of his ministerial secretaryship after his attacks in February on the Guinea Press, referred to Boateng's failure to resign after the defeat of his progress report:

….As elected representatives of the people, if a Minister's motion is defeated it seems he has totally failed and that no grant should be given to him to run his Ministry.... he is a liability to the nation. Everybody in this House was expecting that as the House said no to his progress report, he would resign.[20]

These remarks brought about a widespread outcry from the floor of the House for Boateng's resignation. Despite the efforts of Kofi Baako, the newly appointed Leader of the House, to keep the temperature down, the backbenchers brought out all the dirty linen they could find of the Guinea Press and the Adamafio group for resentful inspection. There had recently been a court case in which an employee of the Guinea Press had been convicted of using the printing equipment to make counterfeit currency notes. Despite Baako's assertion that the directors of the Guinea Press were in no way implicated in this bit of private enterprise, several members made it clear by their interjections that they did not believe the whole story had been made public. 'What did the *Evening News* say about that matter?' asked Abban. 'Nothing', several other members shouted. Abban went on:

> The editor of the *Evening News*.... thinks it is quite wrong for an elected MP to talk about the evil deeds of an official of an organ of the Party. The same editor now thinks it is fitting for himself to publish things about MPs.[21]

He went on to attack John Tettegah, the general secretary of the TUC, for owning three cars: 'But what has been said about him in the Press?' he asked, 'Nothing!' Reproached by the deputy Speaker, Alhaji Yakubu Tali, for attacking someone who was not present to defend himself[22], Abban was not in the least disconcerted. He went on to attack Adamafio directly:

> Then there is someone who is not a Minister but who receives a Minister's salary, and at the same time enjoys a salary of £1,500 as a member of the Law Chambers when, in fact, he has never practised in court before. Is this not capitalism? He is the General Secretary of

the CPP. What has been said about that?[23]

The debate continued on the following day with no lessening of the tension and bitterness. Patrick Quaidoo, the Minister of Social Welfare, now joined in the conservatives' attack from the front bench, bravely terminating any hope of a continued ministerial career. Quaidoo, although a Ga, was totally hostile to Adamafio and his followers. His speech evoked the shade of an African Edmund Burke. It was members of parliament, Quaidoo insisted, who had built up the party in the constituencies, not the other way around — and certainly not the loud-mouthed ideologists and journalists of Adamafio's clique. These people, Quaidoo claimed, had gone too far:

> Now... those who did not play any part in the setting up of this organization (the Party)... now tell us 'it is the Party who put you there'... What are the fundamentals? What do they mean by the Party? Some people think that the CPP which is the ruling Party is in Accra. It is not! The Party is within the country. No group of people sitting in Accra can speak for the CPP (*Gbedemah*: Unless they are authorized). Yes, unless they are authorized. But what is happening today is that because they want to attack parliament, they have started by discrediting members and they have touched on the fundamental thing — the representation. If they succeed in discrediting your representation, where are you?[24]

Quaidoo was bitter about the campaign waged against Krobo Edusei and Komla Gbedemah, the two stalwarts of the conservative wing of the party, by the new men, the 'small boys', gathered around John Tettegah and Tawia Adamafio.

People who have no foundation in either religion or philosophy, who have no faith, who have no principles on which to build their lives, have read what a certain gentleman called Karl Marx wrote. The late Karl Marx was a perpetual wanderer. If there had been an association of wanderers in his time he would have qualified for chairmanship.[25]

As for the party study groups, and those who had attended NASSO meetings, Quaidoo expressed his disgust for their opportunism and sycophancy:

If people find a man like myself standing and I fail to join in while others are clapping, they say I am a reactionary, bourgeois, saboteur, revisionist, and so on. What sort of state do these people want to import into Ghana?... they will tell us that the Leader never dies, Sir, you will remember... what the poet Dryden said —
 'All human beings are subject to decay
 And, when fate summons, monarchs must obey'

Why then should these people come and fool us with this idea of immortality? they are the people who should be rooted out of the Party.[26]

Quaidoo defended the authority of chiefs and elders as a bulwark against what he considered to be the dangerous and subversive nonsense of the militants. Reminded at one stage by the Speaker that his time was running out, the other members, fascinated by his audacity, called out to the Speaker to allow him to go on. He went on to defend the 'rich social custom' of Ghanaian life against those who spoke glibly of creating a new society. The great strength of Ghanaian life rested on the family, which in turn rested upon respect for authority and custom. The new socialists, with no credible alternative of their own, were tampering with these mainsprings of Ghanaian life to everybody's peril, including their own. The climate they were busy creating was fatal to traditional life and to intellectual integrity; their techniques resembled those of the Nazis. Quaidoo finally wound up his powerful and spontaneous peroration with a plea for parliament to safeguard its rights and position on behalf of the nation:

> We must cast aside all these ideas of Leninism and Marxism and come down to Ghana to build our own culture and that of Africa; because there is far more in our society and culture than Karl Marx or Lenin or anybody could possibly have thought of ... Mr Speaker, I think I have sufficiently exposed some of the things which are going to undermine us so as to enable this House to take a firm decision as to how best we can preserve the integrity of Ghana by asserting its Parliamentary supremacy.[27]

Amidst loud cries of 'Hear, Hear' from the floor of the House, Quaidoo sat down, his ministerial career almost at an end. His speech was not forgotten by Adamafio. Three weeks later Quaidoo was dismissed from the government although he kept his seat in parliament. By the end of the year he was in prison, together with opposition MPs of the United Party, victims of the opportunity for revenge which the September troubles offered.[28]

Although the substance of Quaidoo's speech was not reported in the press or by the radio, Adamafio lost no time in making a savage counter-attack. In the *Ghanaian Times* two days later, he denounced Quaidoo as:

> The Tshombe-faced nincompoop who stands out as one of the biggest buffoons who ever walked the floor of free Ghana's parliament... This is the man — the chaff-brained myopic man — who stood in Parliament on Tuesday and challenged the immortality of Osagyefo Dr

> Kwame Nkrumah, the Great Emancipator who delivered
> Ghana from the bondage of imperialism... the States-
> man to whom the world looks with reverence and hope,
> the man who sent Quaidoo to Parliament... Why must
> our Parliament be allowed to become an institution
> with which to battle against the very Party which put
> them in Parliament? An Institution with which to violate
> the constitution of the Party and country?[29]

Adamafio's level of argument rarely rose higher than
abuse when dealing with criticisms from members of
parliament. He singled out Quaidoo, Abban and Aduhene
in his insulting editorial without giving the curious public
any indication of what they had actually said. But he did
not feel confident enough to attack Krobo Edusei who had
followed Quaidoo in the same debate.

Edusei made several pointed references to the fact that
many of the party's activists and radicals, including
Adamafio himself, were 'carpet crossers' who had opposed
Nkrumah and his party in the past. They who now spoke in
the name of the CPP needed reminding that the party was
a national movement and was in important respects the
creation of parliament:

> The fact that Parliament elects the President of the State
> shows clearly the supreme power of Parliament. It is a
> pity that some people in the country fail to realize this...
> We are the pioneers of the struggle... it was we who
> called on our leader... People have been going about
> making unfounded allegations in order to impress the
> public that Parliament has no power. They are doing
> this with a view to forcing us out of Parliament so that
> they can come and take the very place they want to
> make unpopular. Are we small boys? (Members
> 'No'.)[30]

Edusei had made himself a target for the radicals by his unabashed fondness for luxury. But his extravagance merely underlined to his followers his political importance. His standing with Nkrumah was less strong than that of Adamafio at this time, but the President was aware that Edusei had risen as far as he expected to in political life and lacked further ambitions so long as he was left alone to make money.

But the most formidable figure amongst the conservatives was the finance minister, Komla Gbedemah. Born in 1912 in the small, decaying town of Keta near the estuary of the Volta, he came from a family wealthy enough to pay for his secondary education at Adisadel school. After finishing his education Gbedemah had a wartime spell as a science master at the Accra Academy before entering the family business. Like so many Ghanaians at that time he became interested in politics after the war, at first supporting Danquah's Convention. Tiring of its slow approach to the independence issue, he became one of the founders of the Convention Peoples Party in 1949 and was largely responsible for the party's sweeping victory in the Accra municipal elections in the following year. When Nkrumah and other leaders of the CPP were imprisoned in 1950-51 for their part in organizing the civil disobedience campaign, Gbedemah was chosen as the party's acting chairman. As such he was responsible for getting the CPP into fighting trim for the impending elections. Under his stewardship the party won the victory which was to put it into office for the following fifteen years. Ironically his achievement proved to be the ladder, not of his own, but of Nkrumah's ascent, denying Gbedemah the opportunity of grasping the leadership.

Gbedemah had little doubt about his own fitness to lead the CPP His talents for organization were amply demonstrated in later years. He proved an able minister of finance between 1954 and 1961, combining a natural charm with an ability to win the confidence of hard-headed foreign bankers. With characteristic energy Gbedemah made twenty-three visits to the United States in seven years 'to argue about, negotiate for, and finally procure the finance necessary for the Volta project'.[31] He regarded the Volta project as much of his own achievement as it was Nkrumah's and he had been deeply disturbed by Nkrumah's willingness to be wooed by the communist states late in 1960, knowing that this would cause acute American nervousness.

Gbedemah was an ambitious man. His appetite for power was whetted by what he considered to be the weakness and mediocrity of the men with whom Nkrumah surrounded himself. If Adamafio played Mark Antony to Nkrumah's Caesar, Gbedemah played Cassius, jealous of the success and power of the man he had helped to office.

As an Ewe, however, Gbedemah's political career was handicapped by the circumspect attitude which most other peoples in Ghana evinced towards his countrymen. The Ewe people were divided by the frontier between Ghana and the French-speaking state of Togo. Although their numbers within Ghana were relatively small, the Ewes were an energetic people widely thought by others to be a close-knit, clannish group. Certain areas of their homeland in Ghana, including Gbedemah's home district of Anlo South, were bastions of anti-CPP sentiment and their inhabitants suspected by many within the party of harbouring a secret desire for re-unification with their kinsmen across the frontier.

Gbedemah's jealousy of Nkrumah was mixed with growing unease about the general drift of the party after independence. But clear-cut choices did not come easily to him. Although he was still a member of the party's central committee — as he had been since its earliest years —

Gbedemah had come to realize that he had risen as far as he could go under his master. Resignation in protest against the political tendencies in evidence after 1957 would simply have meant the sacrifice of his own ambitions to no effect. His growing estrangement with Nkrumah began to come to a head early in 1961 over three issues. The first and least important was over Nkrumah's desire to have his own effigy printed on Ghana's new republican banknotes. Gbedemah threatened to resign over this, but Nkrumah capitulated and persuaded him to stay in view of the delicate stage reached over the Volta negotiations.

The other and more serious bones of contention arose out of responsibility for the control of the budget and a projected increase in the presidential Contingency Fund. In March 1961, whilst Gbedemah was preparing the budget for submission in July, Nkrumah asked him to increase the fund to £2 million. When Gbedemah objected Nkrumah revealed his plans to remove control of the budget from the Ministry of Finance and place it in the hands of a new Budget Secretariat at Flagstaff House. This decision had been made earlier, unknown to Gbedemah, after Geoffrey Bing and Enoch Okoh, soon to become secretary to the cabinet, had prevailed upon Nkrumah to invite Dr Nicholas Kaldor, the left-wing Cambridge economist, to become temporary economic adviser to the government. After seven successful years in control of finance, during which he had almost completed the negotiations for the Volta project, Gbedemah could not agree to having control of the budget taken from his hands. This was almost the final humiliation. He angrily demanded another portfolio and was given, symbolically, that of the Ministry of Health — the same ministry in which he had started his career in political service ten years before. The final break was not far off and the popular unrest which followed the introduction of the new budget was to participate it.

The revised budget proposals were eventually introduced before the National Assembly on 7 July by F.D. Goka, Gbedemah's successor at the Ministry of Finance.[32] Two days later Nkrumah and some of his ministers and senior party officials including Adamafio, embarked upon an extended tour of the communist states, leaving the government in the hands of a presidential commission of which, as a gesture of conciliation, Gbedemah was made a member. Not unexpectedly the budget proposals were greeted with gloom by most of the CPP members and with outright indignation by the opposition. In essence the purpose of the budget was to maintain a rising level of public spending upon development at a time of falling cocoa prices and diminishing reserves. A general income tax on all incomes over £120 per year was introduced, together with contributions to a 'national development fund'. Although levied compulsorily at the flat rate of five per cent on all incomes over the tax threshold, the bonds were in theory redeemable at a future date.

But the most unwelcome feature was the shift of the burden of taxation from direct on to indirect taxes, notwithstanding these innovations. The new taxes fell heaviest upon imported items, such as tinned meat and fish, canvas shoes, tea, lard, sugar, beer, kerosene, flour and cotton goods, all of which the Ghanaians had come to regard as necessities. However, a gesture was made towards making the budget politically more acceptable by increasing steeply the rates of imported luxury items, such as cars, refrigerators, air-conditioners and cosmetics. Whatever might be said in economic justification of these new and unpopular taxes, the government's presentation of the budget was clumsily stage-managed from the start.[33] The *Ghanaian Times* carried a headline stating 'Taxes on Luxuries increased'. A few days later the newspaper referred to 'a flood of telegrams' which had poured into Flagstaff House and the headquarters of the CPP congratulating the government and party on its budget. In fact, frantic instructions had been sent out over the week-end to local officials of the party and its integral wings ordering them to send enthusiastic telegrams back to party headquarters.

Listening to Goka's outline of the budget, members of parliament were despondent. Even ministerial speeches in support of it lacked conviction. H.S.T. Provencal claimed that the budget was the work of Osagyefo himself who was 'well aware' of the hardships it imposed. But he then provoked uproar by claiming that some traders had got wind of the proposals before they were announced and were taking the opportunity to raise prices all round. Provencal started a hare to which the activists of the press gratefully gave chase, hoping to draw public attention from the new taxes to the iniquitous activities of the as yet unsocialized traders. The *Ghanaian Times* opened up against the 'vicious profiteering racket' operated by private traders, and in the National Assembly, Kofi Baako offered a crumb of comfort by announcing that the party's inner study group would study price control measures and report to the President.

But the party's critics of the budget had their say, although as usual the press and radio services failed to report their deliberations. S.I. Iddrissu expressed the feelings of many backbench members in the Assembly when he asked:

Now, who is going to suffer? The people in the rural areas, not the Ministers, the Ministerial Secretaries and the MPs. I do not feel that we who are the students of Nkrumaism based on marxist socialism should stand here and introduce these tax proposals which will benefit only a few and impose hardship on the majority.[34]

The opposition members also refused to pull their punches. Owusu called upon the House to reject the proposals altogether:

> We owe a duty to those who brought us here to protect them against these harsh proposals and I trust... I shall see in this House a concrete and practical demonstration of this responsibility by all members of this House.

Owusu saw the budget as just one more step along the road to despotism taken by Ghana since independence:

> Slowly but surely... by means of threats, arrests, preventive detention, discrimination in dispensing patronage, and other such agencies, the masses have been cowed into submission, and have surrendered without a fight their freedom of speech, freedom of association and freedom of conscience. It now seems that their last remaining freedom — that of the right to a decent standard of living — is about to be taken away from them.[35]

Owusu's call for the rejection of the budget proposals was not, of course, followed. He and other members were intensely irritated by the *Ghanaian Times* report of the debate, headlined 'Budget Proposals are Progressive, say MPs', which failed completely to mention any of the criticisms made by opposition and CPP members. But when the vote on the proposals were taken, forty-three members voted in favour and six — all the opposition members — voted against. A large number of the CPP members had wandered disconsolately out of the chamber before the vote was taken, unhappy and anxious about the possible repercussions of the government's measures which seemed to vindicate their fears of the new trends evident in

Ghana's policies. Few foresaw that within a few months Komla Gbedemah would denounce the government in terms very similar to those just used by Victor Owusu.

In the face of widespread public scepticism the government kept its efforts to defend the budget. The line taken was that sacrifices would have to be made as the price of future prosperity. A health service and a free education system within three years were promised as the eventual fruits of the budget proposals. Adamafio, who had left Nkrumah's entourage in Russia, told a party rally on 24 August that only 'capitalists' could find fault with the budget. Edusei, also recently returned from Russia, went on a two-week tour of his native Ashanti to scotch the wild rumours circulating there. Before he left he made a public statement asking Ghanaians:

> to take no notice of the stories being spread by those traitors and enemies of Nkrumaism that the government is going to seize private properties or confiscate their private savings.[36]

Despite these attempts to mollify the public, by the end of August the impact of the new duties was felt in every household. The cost of living rose sharply. Early in September, on Monday the 4th, a strike broke out amongst the railway and dock workers in the Sekondi-Takoradi area. As news of the strike spread, workers in Kumasi and the goldmining towns of Bekwai and Obuasi joined in. Within a few days the strike was beginning to affect municipal transport workers in Accra. As more and more workers were laid off the stoppage began to assume national proportions by the end of the week.

Nkrumah was at this time taking a holiday on the Black Sea coast. Despite Gbedemah's coolness over the budget issue, Nkrumah hoped that as the senior member of the presidential commission he would keep a wary eye on the activities of Adamafio and his followers. Ghana was at this time full of foreign journalists, recently arrived to cover the Commonwealth finance ministers' meeting and to gather local background material for the forthcoming visit of the Queen.

It was through these overseas journalists that news of the strike leaked to the outside world. For two days after the outbreak of the strike the domestic press and radio said nothing about it. In the absence of any official statement rumours about the trouble abounded. They were often exaggerated but contributed to a growing atmosphere of crisis. On the third day the party broke its silence. The *Ghanaian Times* opened with a barrage designed to hit all its enemies at once; a barrage which bore all the marks of Adamafio's authorship:

> For two days we have watched. For two days we have studied. Although the whole nation is aware of the immense benefits of the budget, the reaction of the workers has brought to light the utter fraudulence and ineffectiveness of the bogus British colonialist system which still pervades in various spheres of our national activity. Now the nation has come face to face with the realities of the continued application of the British parliamentary, yea, the cabinet and budgetary system.

Added to the general cause, the newspaper claimed that much of the trouble was due to 'enemies of the CPP and a few disgruntled elements within the CPP itself'.[37]

The strike was three days old and still spreading when the presidential commission decided to act. A cabinet delegation to which both Adamafio and Edusei were attached was sent to Takoradi to seek a meeting with the strike leaders. The latter were drawn principally from the executive of the railway and harbour workers' union and enjoyed the support of many local market women. Some of the strikers who had moved to Kumasi to organize there had been arrested by the local police. The Takoradi strike leaders took the hint and refused to reveal themselves. On 9 September the delegation returned to Accra empty-handed and a state of emergency was declared in Sekondi-Takoradi.

The course of the 1961 strike has been well recorded elsewhere.[38] There was no doubt that it was a crisis of the first magnitude. With Nkrumah and many of his senior ministers abroad, a potential revolutionary situation had emerged in which a struggle for power between Adamafio and Gbedemah and their respective supporters was on the cards. The key to the situation lay with the army under its joint Ghanaian and British command. Neither Gbedemah or Adamafio, however, could hope to swing the army behind them in an internal fight. But it was Adamafio who had seized the initiative. Shortly after the cabinet delegation arrived back in Accra, he called a meeting of the party's inner 'study group' at Flagstaff House. It was attended by the central committee and top party officials and under Adamafio's pressure, and without waiting for further information, it was decided to treat the strike as a political act engineered by oppositional elements to overthrow the government. Accustomed to posing as the champion of the masses, Adamafio was quick to denounce the strikers as 'agents of neo-colonialism', 'saboteurs' and 'traitors'. He promised to deal ruthlessly with the strikers, and in a broadcast made shortly after the study group meeting denounced them as 'despicable rats'.[39] He took this intransigeant line without consulting the presidential commission, claiming that he was 'acting in the best interest of the government'.

When news of the strike first reached Nkrumah in Russia he despatched John Tettegah, the secretary general of the TUC back to Ghana. After some hesitation, torn between loyalty to his former trade union colleagues and the prevailing political current in Accra, Tettegah decided to line up the TUC behind Adamafio's interpretation of the strike. The strikers were, he said, 'a mob bent on indulging in an illegal strike'. The members of the union executives linked with the TUC were themselves torn between sympathy for the strikers and fear of reprisals if they did not toe the line. On the day after the study group meeting the members of the railway and harbour union who had not struck called for a return to work, stating that they 'sympathized with the workers in seeking a redress for the hardships that the budget had caused'.[40] Their conciliatory statement also said that 'to the best of our knowledge any allegation of any sort of political influence is completely out of the question'. But their appeal fell on deaf ears. The strike leaders felt that they were too deeply involved to call off the strike without a promise from the government at least to listen to their grievances.

But Adamafio was in no mood for compromise. He was determined to get as much political mileage as possible from the crisis. 'We are sure', he wrote, 'with the lessons we have learned from our workers' reaction to this 1961 budget that our Party and Government will take steps to throw down the river of no return all remnants of the useless, age-old parliamentary system... and erect in its place a more progressive, better and effective system.'

The weakest of his opponents, the United Party opposition, played right into his hands. On 12 September the party's executive met in Dr Danquah's rambling old house in Accra and decided to issue a public statement 'as a responsible national party on the industrial and political unrest'. A copy of the statement was sent to the chief superintendent of police as well as to the foreign press men. Innocuous enough in its content, it called upon the government to adopt a more 'sensible' economic policy.

Yet this action, coupled with a clumsy attempt to break through the censorship of outgoing telegrams to get to the world's press, provided Adamafio with what he claimed was conclusive evidence that the United Party was behind the strike.

A few days later Nkrumah returned home and broadcast the following day. He called for a resumption of work the next week and, as a conciliatory gesture, lifted the curfew in Sekondi-Takoradi. The response was not promising and on the following Wednesday Nkrumah broadcast again. This time his message carried a note of warning. Those strikers who failed to return by Friday 'will have given a clear indication that they, and the instigators behind them, are determined to bring about the overthrow of the Constitution by illegal means'. Nkrumah thus endorsed the interpretation of the strike adopted by Adamafio and the inner party study group. He was not prepared to listen to the strikers' grievances, still less was he prepared to negotiate with their leaders. Badly shaken by the crisis, he had been reassured on his return to find his party and the union machinery holding firm. The army under its British Chief of Defence Staff, Major General Alexander, and the police were unaffected by sympathy for the strikers. There had been no suspicious movement from Gbedemah. Moreover, by the third week the strike showed signs of collapsing. Many of the strikers earned £12 a month or less and did not possess the resources to continue.

Late in September Napoleon Grant, the railway worker who had emerged in the closing stages of the strike, was arrested, taken to Accra and brought face to face with Nkrumah, Edusei, Adamafio and Tettegah. The government was to claim later that at this meeting Grant confessed that the strike was aimed at overthrowing the regime, and that the strike leaders had received large sums of money from disgruntled foreign businessmen. None of

Grant's alleged admissions, however, were supported by any evidence and he was never tried before a court of law. He disappeared, together with fifty other strike leaders, into Nsawam prison to languish in detention for several years.[41]

Soon afterwards the government moved against the United Party leaders. Detention orders were served on Danquah, Obetsebi Lamptey, and several others. At the same time the purge was carried into the ruling party. Nkrumah announced that, in accordance with the dawn broadcast, six members of his government, Gbedemah, Botsio, Emmanuel Ayeh Kumi, E.K. Dadson, W.A. Wiafe and S.W. Yeboah, were required to resign their posts on account of their 'varied business connections'. Six other ministers were obliged to surrender to the state properties and assets in excess of the limits laid down in the dawn broadcast. Furthermore, 'no minister should engage in private trade or business of any sort, nor should he use his position to obtain privileged terms.'[42]

On the same day as Nkrumah's announcement, Gbedemah issued his reply, claiming that the possession of business interests was merely a pretext for his dismissal.[43] His statement continued, 'it is most unfortunately that your new-found addiction to socialist principles mentioned in your letter should after thirteen years of close and almost brotherly comradeship cause a breach between us. In all these thirteen years not once have you impugned my integrity and ability as a loyal comrade... today we come to the parting of the ways.'

The September strike was the second major threat to Nkrumah's rule after ten years in office. The first threat had come in the mid-fifties from the National Liberation Movement. Then the CPP government could ultimately count upon the support of the British against any unconstitutional attempt to overthrow it. In 1961, however, the government stood alone. Yet the machinery had withstood the crisis, although at the cost of publicly flexing the ultimately despotic sinews of its power. But the international repercussions of the crisis embarrassed Nkrumah. His attempts to project himself as the leader of a strong, united country moving forward towards socialism and continental unity was henceforth less credible in the eyes of the other African leaders from the Commonwealth assembling in Accra for the finance ministers' conference. The United States government, providing the lion's share of the foreign money needed for the Volta project, found its fears for the future security of the government reinforced by the strike. On 22 September, the United States government informed Nkrumah that it would not be able to reach a final decision on the negotiations by early October, the date suggested by the export-import bank which was conducting the talks between the two governments. On 30 September, the British Commonwealth Secretary, Duncan Sandys, arrived in Ghana to assess the security arrangements in the light of the Queen's visit planned for November. Nkrumah urged strongly that the tour should take place, and instructed his High Commissioner in London, Kwesi Armah, to do everything possible to allay public anxiety in Britain.[44] Armah made a bland public statement to the effect that 'absolute harmony' prevailed in Ghana, and that the industrial troubles were a proof of the existence of democracy.

Nkrumah's endorsement of the policies of Adamafio towards the crisis marked the temporary rout of the conservative, loyalist wing of the party. If Gbedemah, Edusei and the other ministers could be pulled down, then nobody was safe. Further repressive measures were drawn up to strengthen the grip of the government and the party over the country. But the ultimate significance of the crisis

did not lie in the demonstrable fact that the party and
government had lost the confidence of a large and
important section of the working population. At the time,
few people realized the wider implications for the future of
the strike and its aftermath. In seeking greater freedom of
action in order to protect itself from future crisis,
Nkrumah's government had unwittingly kicked away one
of the major props upon which its existence depended. On
the advice of Geoffrey Bing and Tawia Adamafio,
Nkrumah terminated General Alexander's appointment as
Chief of Defence Staff and sought new arrangements to
replace the seconded British officers in the Ghana army
command.[45] Nkrumah ensured that the Ghana armed
forces, now entirely under Ghanaian control, would
henceforth be an interested party in the event of domestic
discontent.

The Criminal Procedure amendment bill was the
principal piece of legislation which the government
planned to introduce in the wake of the industrial
troubles. The bill provided for the setting up of special
courts to try political offences. The judges of the special
courts were to be appointed by the President, and there
was to be no appeal against their judgments. It was during
the second reading of the bill which took place in the
middle of October that Gbedemah fired his parting shot
against the movement he had done so much to create.
Aware of the strong sentiments against the bill within the
country at large, conscious of the doubts of many within
the CPP, and, of course, acutely aware of his own fall
from grace, Gbedemah considered that the time had come
for him to speak frankly. There had been a time, he said,
when both he and Nkrumah had been dedicated to the
freedom and liberty of the individual. After many trials
and tribulations, independence had been achieved, and in
1958, in order to safeguard the 'hard-won' freedom of

Ghana, he, Gbedemah, had supported the passage of the Preventive Detention act. But, he went on:

> What do we find in the application of the provisions of that Act? How many people are languishing in jail today? (Uproar) How many people are languishing in jail today detained under this Act? I do not wish to give the answer, but I think the Minister of the Interior knows, and I wish to say here and now that many of these, in fact, most of them, are alleged to have been in plots to overthrow the government. We passed that bill in all sincerity to prevent saboteurs and revolutionaries from overthrowing the government. It has today become an instrument of terrorism.[46]

Faced with this appalling defection, Kofi Baako came close to hysteria. He recounted to the Assembly how, when he had been sick earlier in the year, Gbedemah had paid him a visit, bringing with him a black powder which, he said, would cure him. That powder, claimed Baako, was nothing less than 'black *juju*'. Uproar drowned the rest of his remarks.[47]

At this point the Speaker intervened to complain of irrelevancy, but Baako persisted with his tale of the magical black powder brought to him late at night by Gbedemah. He asked whether Gbedemah was not a member of the Busia group who had tried to overthrow the government by force:

> ... the Honourable Member for Keta (Gbedemah) knows that every word I have said about his part in the black *juju* is true, and that he was given an opportunity at the Central Committee to deny or confirm this... This Bill is a very good Bill... for everybody, including the Honourable Member for Keta. It is very, very good indeed, for without it, who knows what Kofi Busia and his clique...[48]

Baako's remaining remarks were drowned in the general uproar. Gbedemah had been the principal member of the presidential commission which governed Ghana during Nkrumah's absence throughout August and September. Although he had forfeited the initiative to Adamafio when the strike broke out, he felt that not only had the crisis vindicated his doubts about the budget proposals, but that his own behaviour during that crisis should have proved his own loyalty beyond any doubt. He had had then an unparalleled opportunity to seize power, but had not done so. Nor had he at any time during the strike made contact either with the strike leaders or the United Party. Baako's wild accusations went beyond the government's official statements on the strike, and beyond anything in the government's white paper on the disturbances which Gbedemah had already seen in draft form.

Gbedemah felt that he had shot his final bolt. Any good he felt he could do for himself or his country could be done better outside Ghana, in exile, than within it. He had already made discreet arrangements to leave the country with his wife and children after the debate, anticipating arrest and imprisonment if he remained. A few days after the debate he flew from Accra, to remain outside Ghana for almost five years, waging a persistent campaign against Nkrumah and his government abroad.

Baako's accusations continued to annoy Gbedemah even after the latter's departure. In December, a few days after the government's white paper on the September disturbances appeared, Geoffrey Bing received a letter from him, post-marked from Keta, Gbedemah's home town close to the Togo frontier. Gbedemah complained that there had been no hint of an accusation against him in the draft version of the white paper; it had been inserted in the final version after he had left Ghana. He reproached Bing for his part in writing the white paper, which he called 'a gross insult to the intelligence of the people of Ghana'. Its allegations against himself were, in his view, the work of Tawia Adamafio:

> ...that pernicious, avid buffoon of a Minister, whose sycophancy merely for the dishonourable end of personal promotion works to the detriment of those who toiled for years to build up the Party and Government he has now so adroitly undermined.[49]

The conservative wing of the party, although it had lost a battle, had not yet lost the war. From his exile Gbedemah extended his campaign against Nkrumah and his policies by means of chain letters and leaflets smuggled into the country and discreetly circulated by his sympathizers. Leading spokesmen of the conservative wing had been relegated in disgrace to the backbenches, but they kept their seats in the assembly and in the following months crept back one by one into favour.[50] The radicals crowed in triumph, but their victories were largely insubstantial. The conservative position at the end of 1961 was by no means hopeless. The tissue of interests which held the party together was still intact and they were an important part of it. Despite his leftward lurch at the level of international politics, Nkrumah instinctively kept his sense of political balance in domestic affairs. He showed no disposition to stake all upon his radical wing and convert the party into an exclusive movement of ideological purity.

Yet a socialist party it had to become, and early in 1962 Nkrumah took steps to try once more to revive a spirit of unity and dedication within the CPP. A 'Work and Happiness' programme was drawn up to be rubber-stamped by the party's eleventh congress due to be held later that year at Kumasi. The party constitution of 1959 was amended, making explicit for the first time its aim of creating 'a socialist pattern of society adapted to African conditions according to the principles of Nkrumaism'. The new constitution made a gesture towards internal reconciliation, urging party members to 'accept criticism in good faith and spirit and make frequent self-examination for correction, remembering that criticism and correction should be made not to destroy but to build'.

But the in-fighting which now afflicted the party had too strong a grip to be much affected by these exhortations. Rumour-mongering, malicious gossip and character assassination had become weapons used by all sides which none was willing to give up. Superficially the radical wing from their entrenched positions in the information services and party machinery had the better of the propaganda battle. Only within the assembly could the conservatives counter-attack, although the effects of their criticisms were severely limited by the restricted reporting of parliamentary proceedings. However, developments later in the year were to bring down their arch-opponent and give them a temporary advantage over their rivals.

In August 1962, Nkrumah attended a meeting with President Maurice Yaméogo of the neighbouring state of Upper Volta at the Ghanaian border town of Paga. Relations between the two countries had not hitherto been cordial. Nkrumah viewed with suspicion Yaméogo's membership of the 'Brazzaville' group of moderate African states and his adherence to the agreements between Upper Volta and France concluded at independence. President Yaméogo, for his part, was suspicious of Nkrumah's ambitions. His own country, one of the poorest in Africa, was heavily dependent upon the Ivory Coast for access to world markets. The recent relaxation of tension between the moderate Brazzaville bloc and the more radical Casablanca bloc, however, enabled the two Presidents to meet with all the appearance of amicability. Yaméogo was anxious to reduce his dependence upon the

Ivory Coast by cultivating better relations with his powerful neighbour to the south. Both men took part in the ceremonial demolition of a customs post at Paga to symbolize their new-found accord.

Taking his leave of his fellow President, Nkrumah left Paga and started a tour of northern Ghana. At the small village of Kulungugu not far from the frontier, the President and his entourage, which included Adamafio fresh from the party congress in Kumasi, stopped to greet a crowd of cheering school-children. Shortly after he stepped out of his car a bomb was thrown at him. His ADC Captain Buckman, stepped between the president and the missile just before it exploded. Four people were killed outright and fifty-six others, including many school-children were injured. Captain Buckman, who was severely injured, had nevertheless succeeded in protecting Nkrumah from the full effect of the blast and the President was only slightly injured, although in a state of shock. In this condition he was taken to the nearest hospital at Bawku.

As news of the outrage reached Accra, ministers and officials made their way by road and air to the distant north to get a clearer picture of what had happened. At first the police and security service were in a state of confusion. There was little evidence upon which to base their enquiries. The Commissioner of the Ghana Police, Eric Madjitey, arrived to take charge of investigations. Large numbers of arrests were made in and around Kulungugu village and a temporary detention camp was set up in a Bawku warehouse to accommodate those detained.[51]

As the shaken President slowly recovered his grasp, Adamafio's enemies seized their opportunity. Now was the time to heap yet another unpleasant surprise upon the President. Every bit of circumstantial evidence was gathered to show that Adamafio and his lieutenants had engineered the assassination attempt. The extent of his 'empire' was pointed out to Nkrumah. His close association with Ga groups and his rumoured involvement with the illegal Ga Shifimo Kpee were adduced as evidence of his taste for conspiracy. Comments allegedly made by Adamafio during Nkrumah's Moscow visit in the previous year were retailed to show the extent of his ambition.[52] Adamafio's behaviour at the party congress lately held in Kumasi was commented on by Baako at the President's bedside. Adamafio, in contrast to his usual habit, had seated himself well away from the President on the platform and had taken only a listless interest in its proceedings. Against Baako's advice, he had refused to return to Accra when the congress closed and had insisted on joining Nkrumah's party for the northern tour. When the explosion occurred, Adamafio had been a safe distance away, but in the following half hour he had repeatedly tried to find out from the injured Buckman whether the President was alive or dead.

It was all hearsay, but it was enough. With that quick inversion of belief sometimes found in men who have been close to a sudden, violent death, Nkrumah was now convinced that his trusted companion, the strong man of his party, had been plotting to depose him. His conviction was strengthened on his return to Accra by a report from Anthony Deku, the head of the Special Branch, who had been in London when the bombing took place, that the Ghanaian students there were certain that Adamafio was behind the assassination attempt. What had been apparently clear to many Ghanaians had now become so to Nkrumah himself.

Adamafio himself became increasingly uneasy. He was still confident of his hold over the President, but he had been aware of the strong feelings against him since the industrial troubles the year before. After his 'despicable rats' speech during the strike, he had complained to Madjitey about the 'numerous threats and insults' he had received in anonymous letters. He also thought that certain members of the government were employing *juju* to make him mad. Not trusting entirely in the kind of protection provided by the police, he had visited the priestesses of the fetish shrines of Ada and Larteh to seek supernatural assistance against his enemies.[53] Towards the end of the month news leaked to him of a secret meeting in Flagstaff House to decide his fate. There was little else Adamafio could do, except to continue with his duties, one of which was to address the domestic staff of Flagstaff House warning them that women traders had been selling food in the neighbourhood wrapped in discarded draft cabinet papers.

After the arrest of Adamafio, Adjei, Crabbe, and others, and even before their trial took place, there followed a spate of denunciations of the 'Adamafio clique' from the conservative wing of the party. Their demands for retribution and a purging of the party were all the more strident because they claimed to have foreseen the ambitions of Adamafio and his colleagues long before Kulungugu. Francis Tachie Menson claimed that:

In February this year when we attended a seminar... at Winneba, those of us with X-ray eyes saw from afar what was being planned against the Party and the nation. I, therefore, said to Osagyefo, the President: 'Please, if you want to save the country, then ban the organization known as Emashie nonn'. Emashie Nonn is the offspring of the Ga Shifimo Kpee, and ninety-five per cent of the members of Emashie Nonn come from the defunct Ga Shifimo Kpee.

After the seminar at Winneba Tachie Menson went on

They continued to uproot the foundation members of of the Party. The old brigadiers have been removed not only from office, but also from the Party in order that these people could fit themselves in and use the state machinery according to their own wishes... They pursued this policy and drove many people, including myself, from office. A went, B followed, C followed, and so on and so forth. That is why Tachie Menson became the Minister of Fallen Affairs. (Uproar)[54]

A.S.A. Abban, the former Deputy Minister of Agriculture who had lost his ministerial post after being publicly attacked by Adamafio the previous year, recalled that Gbedemah, Wiafe, Botsio and himself, as early as the previous April were:

talking about the suspicious activities of this very Tawia Adamafio and his gang. After that, we were chased to our homes as being enemies of socialism and also enemies of the party. In fact, this action was supported by the press, radio and the Minister of Information.[55]

The blow fell on 29 August. Adamafio was arrested by Owusu Sechere, the head of the CID, driven in chains to Nsawam prison, and served with notification of the grounds for his arrest. Cofie Crabbe, the executive secretary of the party, and Ako Adjei, the Foreign Minister, were arrested on the same day. John Tettegah was also arrested, but that adroit trade unionist managed to convince his interrogators of his innocence and was soon released.[56] A fallen favourite has no friends; Adamafio's camp followers quietly folded their tents, struck camp, and stole away in the night to await a more propitious time to wage their battles. Adamafio's empire was in ruins and he himself, the overmighty subject, had been toppled.

Abban's outburst called for the purge of Adamafio's

appointees from the party and the press. He demanded a full investigation into Adamafio's activities, and also those of Kweku Boateng who had inclined to Adamafio's camp when he held the Ministry of Information in 1959. Boateng, now the Minister of the Interior, was held up to further execration by the now irrepressible conservatives in the House. He was thoroughly rattled by the accusation of his old enemies that he had acted as the willing tool of Adamafio and his associates. Caught at bay in parliament, he took refuge in proclamations of undying loyalty to Osagyefo. His account of his activities on the evening of the assassination attempt was bizarre, indicative of the stress he was under:

> Some of us had returned to Accra after the eleventh Party Congress, and when on the evening of 1 August, the Minister of Defence (Kofi Baako) and I heard of the outrage at Kulungugu, we immediately proceeded to the North that night to ascertain the condition of our Leader and do our duty by his side. It is said that the assassination of Julius Caesar is the greatest crime in history. But it is also true to say that the deliverance of the President from this cowardly crime is the greatest miracle the world has ever seen or witnessed. Members will recall that on that fateful day of 1 August there were two ominious (*sic*) portents, the first occurring at noon. The second was a heavy torrential storm after the bomb incident. These signs of the elements were the harbingers of the great tragedy into which, but for the intervention of Providence, the Kulungugu outrage would have flung this country, and indeed, the whole of Africa.[57]

The trial of Adamafio and his associates began in August 1963, before a special court convened under the act which, ironically, Adamafio had earlier supported against Gbedemah's misgivings. Nkrumah was by now utterly

convinced of Adamafio's treachery. Taking their lead
from their master, the writers and journalists who had,
until Adamafio's fall, been amongst the latter's greatest
eulogizers, presumed the certainty of Adamafio's guilt and
conviction long in advance of the trial itself. But a further
shock was in store for Nkrumah. The defendants had been
charged with, amongst other things, treason. Under the act
setting up the special courts verdicts were reached by a
majority decision of the judges, and the disclosure of the
minority opinion, if any, was prohibited. There was no
appeal from its verdict. The scales of justice seemed from
the beginning heavily stacked against the defendants. But
early in December the special court headed by Sir Arku
Korsah, the Chief Justice, returned a verdict of not guilty
against Adamafio, Adjei and Crabbe, and ordered them to
be discharged. Several minor defendants, however, were
found guilty. Nkrumah's reaction was angry and swift.
Two days later Sir Arku Korsah was dismissed as Chief
Justice,[58] and a bill was rushed through parliament
within a few days, amending the Criminal Procedure act to
enable the President to set aside a verdict of the special
court 'in the state's interest'. On Christmas Eve Nkrumah
declared all the proceedings of the treason trial to be void,
and arrangements were set in hand for a re-trial. The three
former ministers remained securely in preventive detention
where they were to languish until the coup.

Nkrumah's precipitate dismissal of his chief justice for
returning an unwelcome verdict attracted much unfavourable comment abroad. The President acted within his
constitutional rights, but the exercise of those rights
destroyed the last shreds of judicial independence in
Ghana. The conservative wing was delighted at the fall of
their arch-enemy, but it was a victory which served to
underline the unchallengeable powers of the President.
Adamafio's erstwhile supporters, quick to abandon him

without finding a comparable champion, used the Korsah affair for their own ends, calling for a purge of anti-party elements before 'another Arku Korsah treachery' occurred.[59]

Nkrumah never again permitted one of his lieutenants to build up a personal following within his party comparable to Adamafio's. He continued to tolerate private baronies of wealth and patronage, but only on the unspoken condition that the barons themselves eschewed any political ambitions. He allowed the radicals to continue to press their uncompromising view of revolution, but denied them the means of bringing it about. Sovereignty over nation and party remained firmly and exclusively in his own hands. The feuds within his party continued unabated, but after Adamafio's downfall they were sterile and defensive, devoid of any significant political content.

Nkrumah's sequence of unpleasant surprises, however, was not yet at an end. On New Year's Day, 1964, an armed police constable, Seth Ametewee, on guard duty in the grounds of Flagstaff House, fired several shots at Nkrumah, missed, and pursued the President, evidently intending to finish him off with his rifle butt. He failed and was eventually overpowered. Once again Nkrumah had come close to a violent death. Shortly afterwards he ordered the police service to be disarmed, sacked many of its officers, and detained the Commissioner and his deputy although no evidence was ever produced of their complicity in the incident. Indeed, no explanation of Ametewee's action was ever forthcoming.[60] But the police service as a whole felt publicly humiliated by Nkrumah's reaction. Increasingly the President turned for his protection to his personal security services, important sections of which were under the control of East European and Russian advisers. Henceforth the police service joined the silent but resentful mountain of opposition to the system and was later to play an important part in its overthrow.

In the months afterwards Nkrumah left Flagstaff House and retreated into the fortress confines of Christiansborg Castle, one of his official residences in Accra. His self-imposed isolation was more than merely physical. it reflected his moody, introverted isolation from his party. In these months — indeed, right up until the end of the Republic — ministers, faced with an increasingly desperate economic situation, found it difficult to get access to the President. More and more of the burdens of government and administration fell upon an already overworked civil service. The party was deprived of the close, personal contact with its leader, which was so indispensable to it, and was left to pursue its own internal squabbles. But with each successive crisis the party was becoming more and more unmanageable. It had weathered successfully the troubles of 1955-56 and gone forward to inherit full power. The 1961 crisis left deeper scars, but it had emerged largely intact. The 1962 crisis was to leave some wounds unhealed, and by the time it faced its final year the party was on the verge of open disintegration. Nkrumah's lack of interest in its affairs was matched by the failure of his name and authority to carry its old, healing magic into the divided ranks of his movement.

V The Political Deformation of Development

At the time of independence Ghana ranked amongst the richest tropical countries in the world. Income per capita stood at about £70 per year, well above that of most African territories and approached only by Gabon, the western region of Nigeria and the neighbouring Ivory Coast. In addition Ghana possessed large reserves of sterling — over £150 million for a country of seven million inhabitants — which had been built up during the cocoa boom of the fifties.[1] Cocoa, the principal source of the country's wealth, was grown exclusively by the peasant farmers of the southern, forested parts of the country, and the cash proceeds from its cultivation were widely diffused throughout the community.

Yet within a few short years after independence ordinary Ghanaians were faced with the disappointment of their hopes of an economic resurgence once the colonial shackles had been thrown off. Worse, their precarious standard of living was under threat. The large reserves evaporated relentlessly until by 1964 they had virtually disappeared. Over the same period the country's indebtedness to a variety of foreign creditors had reached unmanageable proportions, and repayments of capital and interest absorbed an ever-increasing share of the national revenue. In the towns the standard of living of the unskilled workers — the great majority of town dwellers — had actually fallen in real terms by 1963 to the levels of 1939.[2] In the countryside the cocoa farmers were forced to take successive cuts in the price they received from the marketing board for their labours. In the last years of the Republic, making visible the hard, statistical evidence furnished by the government's own agencies, inflation, shortages and rising unemployment were giving rise to widespread disenchantment. Rumours of corruption in high places and a general lack of confidence in the government's ability to cope with the crisis effectively undermined the popular support Nkrumah and his party had once enjoyed.

What had gone wrong? In the broadest terms the answer can be resolved into two large elements. Firstly, Ghana's was a one crop economy dependent upon the world price for her export of cocoa. Her prosperity was therefore subject to forces which were beyond her ability to control. With biblical similitude, seven years of high cocoa prices were followed after 1961 by seven lean years.[3] The catastrophic drop in world cocoa prices reduced the country's overseas earnings and forced the government to draw deeply on its reserves at the very time that it was heavily committed to expensive development plans. With some — although certainly not complete — justification Nkrumah could claim to have fallen a victim to under-development. But the thesis he advanced after his downfall — that the slump was deliberately engineered by hostile western interests to bring his regime to an end — has little to sustain it.[4]

The other element in Nkrumah's economic failure was equally serious but lay deeply embedded in his own attitudes and those of the ruling party. The prosperity which had prevailed during the early years of the party's rule — and which owed little directly to its activities — had been a vital ingredient of its political success. But with the onset of adversity the optimistic and cavalier attitudes which the party consistently revealed on economic questions were to work against any attempts to meet the crisis with realism.

Nkrumah's opinions on economic matters were secondary to his political beliefs. The solutions to the complex problems of development were for him to be found in the pursuit of the political kingdom. If Africa was poor, then it was because of colonialism. This was the gist of the simple message he had hammered home when seeking power. Once he had obtained the prize he saw no reason to change his argument. If Africa continued to be poor after colonial rule had ended then it was because of 'neo-colonialism'. The growing confusions and mounting difficulties he faced in the sixties were evidence, for him, not of the short-comings of his policies, but of the strength of the neo-colonialist conspiracy which had conceded the forms but not the substance of real power.

Nkrumah's grand economic strategy after independence was the transformation of his country into a modern, industrial state as quickly as possible. He was determined that Ghana should escape the fate of being 'a hewer of wood and a drawer of water' for the industrially advanced nations. The ultimate reward was political: success would demonstrate the validity of his policies to other African leaders and would provide Ghana with a strong domestic power base from which it could further the cause of continental unification.[5]

Nevertheless Nkrumah's approach to the central problem of development betrayed a mixture of casualness and ignorance. He seemed unaware of the enormous significance of the spontaneous peasant revolution in agriculture in the early part of the century which had created the cocoa trade. His ideological obsessions led him to hamstring indigenous private enterprise which was potentially a major force making for economic growth. And he largely ignored the vast body of research into tropical farming, forestry and medicine undertaken in the past by colonial agencies. Much as a householder might call in a plasterer to fill in cracks when the real trouble was to be found in the defective foundations of the entire structure, he invited a procession of experts from abroad to draw up development plans.

The obstacles to his grand strategy of development were enormous in their magnitude. Programmes of massive industrialization which seemed two decades ago to offer the best hope for a backward country of breaking out of poverty have not had very much success in the tropical world. They are unlikely to bring about even a modest, lasting improvement in general prosperity, and any material gains have to be balanced against the social dislocation which invariably accompanies them. It would be better for such a country to limit its immediate ambitions, aim modestly, and seek to build upon existing skills whilst seeking to preserve a degree of social cohesiveness. The results may not be spectacular, but the gains are more likely to be solid. But such an approach would demand of the government qualities of self-restraint and discipline no less than those required for massive industrialization. And it would require the exercise of a skill unpopular amongst contemporary governments — of knowing when to leave some things well alone. But the whole psychology of the CPP was against a gradual approach to the problem of development. It had achieved power by stoking up popular expectations. Once in power over-ambitious, meddling programmes maintained the illusion of progress and enabled the party to consolidate its hold over the country.

If Nkrumah was prepared to hand over economic questions to a succession of imported experts, equally there were many only too willing to supply him with the answers he sought. By giving the impression to the politicians who employ them that there are short, sure roads to material prosperity through the manipulation of the economy

according to their favourite ideas, economists have helped
to raise expectations far beyond their ability to satisfy
them.[6] The problem of making a poor country into a
richer one is, in fundamental respects, a human problem.
The economist deals in quantifiable things and regards
development primarily in terms of overcoming shortages
of capital, technical skills and managerial know-how. But
even if these shortages are overcome, there may be little
economic growth, unless a significant segment of the
population is disposed to improve its own material
standards by work and saving, coupled with a willingness
to alter its habits and values. But this disposition is rooted
in the psychology of men and therefore presents difficulties
for economists. Governments themselves produce nothing
but consume a lot. The only really free area of decision
available to them is whether to encourage or impede the
productive activities of their subjects. Inefficient or
malicious government can reduce a prosperous economy to
a desert, but even an enlightened government cannot in the
short run, at least, make its people prosper if they themselves lack the energy or the will to do so. It is Adam Smith
and Samuel Smiles, nor Karl Marx and the fifty-seven
varieties of socialism, who should be the inspiration of the
poor countries.

The successive development plans drawn up at
Nkrumah's request were not Ghana's first experience of
economic planning. During the governship of Sir Gordon
Guggisberg from 1919 to 1929 an investment plan was
drawn up to make use of the government's growing
revenue from the export duty on cocoa. Sir Gordon said
that:

We want this balance as a 'capital' by which to start our
great and extensive scheme for the provision of those
things which are directly essential to the progress of our

people; our system of colleges, technical schools and secondary education, water supplies, electric lighting, drainage, etc.

The largest and most economically necessary project undertaken was the construction of Ghana's first deep-water harbour at Takoradi which was opened in 1929. Other projects initiated by Guggisberg which were to have a lasting influence within Ghana were the Korle Bu hospital in Accra, and the establishment just outside the capital at Achimota, of what later became one of British West Africa's most famous secondary schools at which the young Nkrumah was for a time a pupil.

After the 1951 general election which brought Nkrumah and his party to power a five-year development plan was announced. This plan, drawn up largely on the initiative of the last Governor, Sir Charles Arden-Clarke, envisaged the spending of £117 million, concentrating on the creation of a sound infrastructure of roads and public services. But the plan proved to be still-born. Nkrumah invited the West Indian economist and Fabian socialist, Dr Arthur Lewis, then Professor of Economics at Manchester University, to come to Ghana and advise on the prospects for rapid industrialization.

Dr Lewis produced a report[7] which, although shrewd in its diagnosis of Ghana's condition, was not wholly welcome to Nkrumah. His report stressed that agricultural growth was the key to successful industrialization. He pointed out that the productivity of the food-producing sector was 'almost certainly stagnant'. Industrialization which took labour away from the land without increasing the productivity of those remaining would simply create a food shortage and a competition between industry and the domestic consumer for imports, leading rapidly to a balance of payments crisis. Lewis stressed that the government's sources of revenue were too dependent upon cocoa and therefore upon agricultural labour of low productivity to sustain a massive increase of public spending on new industries:

> ... very many years will have elapsed before it becomes economical for the Government to transfer any large part of its resources towards industrialization, and away from the more urgent priorities of agricultural productivity and public service.[8]

A further important obstacle to industrialization pointed out by Lewis lay in the lack of managerial experience. Too much attention had been paid to the lack of capital and the question of foreign aid, and not enough to the human problems of encouraging, acquiring and diffusing management skills and competence:

> An enterprise cannot be built up simply by lending Africans money. To lend money to entrepreneurs who lack managerial capacity is merely to throw it down the drain. What potential African industrialists lack is not primarily money; it is rather technical knowledge and experience of factory organization.

Lewis had pointed out two factors of great importance which Nkrumah in the following years failed to appreciate, much to his cost. The last years of the first Republic were indeed marked by a growing food shortage and a swollen import bill, caused in part by the government's neglect of the traditional farmers in preference for state intervention in agriculture. And the results of industrialization, largely undertaken by a variety of state corporations, were lamentably poor, run for the most part by inefficient and unskilled managers who frequently appeared to have little knowledge of their duties.

Despite Nkrumah's disappointment with the Lewis

Report, which seemed to him to err on the side of caution, promising no quick, spectacular results, there was no other blueprint available upon which planning could go ahead. In 1959 therefore a further development was drawn up on the basis of the Lewis report, to commence simultaneously with the new Republic in July 1960. The new plan envisaged the spending of £132 million in its first phase, to be spent largely upon improving Ghana's infrastructure of communications and transport services, followed by the spending of a larger amount to be raised from government revenue, private enterprise and foreign aid. But this plan was quickly overtaken by events and projects were started on an *ad hoc* basis. The country's second deep water harbour at Tema was its principal achievement.

During his long tour of the European communist states in 1961 Nkrumah had been impressed by the complex national planning machinery of those states. He was easily persuaded that Ghana's plan was merely a shopping list of public investment which depended for its success upon the emergence of an indigenous capitalist class. It would not fundamentally alter the structure of his country's existing economy and could not use the data yielded by the 1960 census. Before leaving on his tour Nkrumah proved receptive to the arguments of Dr Nicholas Kaldor who had advised the governments of other under-developed countries.[9] Kaldor considered the existing national plan antiquated in important respects. He urged Nkrumah to adopt a new plan incorporating sophisticated techniques, using the data provided by the 1960 Ghana Census. The appeal of Kaldor's proposals lay in its emphasis on centralized state control of the economy, which could provide the institutional framework of socialism.

Shortly after his abrupt return to Ghana, occasioned by the industrial unrest caused by the incorporation of some of Dr Kaldor's proposals in the budget for 1961, Nkrumah set up a commission to draw up a comprehensive development plan which would establish the primacy of the state over the country's economic life. The planning commission first met in October 1961, under Nkrumah's chairmanship, drawing its members from the civil service, the trade unions and local government. Its work was helped by the proceedings and conclusions of a conference of economists called to Accra in April 1963, which included Dr Kaldor, Dr Lewis, and professors from Hungary,[10] Poland, India and Egypt. Meanwhile the existing plan was allowed quietly to lapse. It had run into difficulties on account of insufficiently detailed statistical information about the economy, and its progress had been damaged by the alarming run-down of Ghana's foreign reserves which started in 1961.

Early in 1964 the blueprint of the new plan was published.[11] In Nkrumah's words, it embodies 'the proposals of the Party's "Work and Happiness" programme adopted by the eleventh Party Congress in July 1962, and accepted by the country'. The plan laid emphasis on the modernization of agriculture and the rapid expansion of the industry as the foundation of a socialist society. Although a place was reserved in the overall strategy for foreign and Ghanaian private enterprise, it was principally designed:

... to use the resources of the state to the maximum degree possible for productive investment in agriculture and industry.

The political motives behind this exercise were elaborated by Nkrumah early in 1964:

In every socialist country state enterprises provide the bulk of state revenues and we intend to follow the same pattern here. Our state enterprises will be set yearly financial and production targets so that they may work towards definite objectives and goals and thereby give every stimulus to operate efficiently and profitably. Hence, the managers of our state enterprises and those in charge of our state corporations should be men trained in management; honest, dedicated men; men with integrity; men who are incorruptible.[12]

But it was easier said than done. Nkrumah was attracted by the plan because it appeared to be the blueprint of a socialist society. The economists liked it because of its sophistication. But it required a more developed statistical service than Ghana possessed. It also required for its successful execution greater qualities of restraint and discipline on the part of the government than it had hitherto shown. And above all, it required honest, efficient managers at the executive level in numbers which Ghana simply did not possess.

Long before the seven year plan was drawn up, it was clear that Nkrumah intended state-owned enterprises to be the spearhead of his country's industrialization. A few large Ghanaian private businesses existed but on the whole they lacked the capital and experience to expand their scale of operations rapidly. The first state enterprises were set up shortly after Nkrumah came to power in 1951. These were under the control first of the Industrial and Agricultural Development Corporations which were also intended to promote local private enterprise. In 1961 the Industrial Development Corporation was dissolved and overall control of the state enterprises was vested in the Ministry of Industries. In the following year the Agricultural Development Corporation was wound up and its functions distributed amongst the Ministry of Agriculture, the Farmers Council, the State Farms Corporation and the Workers Brigade. By 1965 everything had come to rest with the State Enterprises Secretariat in Flagstaff House.

Such rapid and abrupt changes in the organization of the state sector were common during the Nkrumah period. They had a generally deleterious effect, producing administrative confusions, blurring the margins between spheres of responsibility, and having a bad effect upon the morale of those affected by them. The experience of Titus Petronius as governor of Bithynia in the first century had considerable relevance for Ghana in the twentieth. 'I was to learn early in life that we meet new situations by reorganizing, and a wonderful method it is of creating the illusion of progress, whilst promoting confusion, inefficiency and demoralization.'

The setting up of state corporations was speeded up after 1961. By 1962 the annual turnover of the state corporations and the joint state-private enterprises exceeded in value the annual revenue and expenditure of the central government. By the close of the following year there were over forty state enterprises with initial capitalizations ranging from a few thousand pounds sterling to several million.[13] They were intended to operate as independent and commercially viable enterprises, making a profit on their operations. This was to prove a vain hope. In practice the state corporations turned out to be bottomless pits into which the government felt obliged to shovel ceaselessly increasing amounts of public money. At the end of 1963 the total losses incurred by the state corporations on their operations alone amounted to well over £15 million, quite apart from the millions of pounds locked away unproductively in their assets.[14]

Their contribution to Ghana's economic development was negligible. These enterprises not only cost the government substantial sums to set up, but also increasingly heavy supplementary expenditure to make up for deficits incurred during their operation. Thus, for example, during the financial year 1962-63, four supplementary estimates had to be voted by the National Assembly, in March, June and September 1963, increasing the provision of public money for the corporations from an original £127.7 million to £155.8 million. Nor was there any improvement in the following years. In September 1965, the Finance Minister, F.D. Goka, presented the National Assembly with a 'little budget' once again to raise additional funds to meet government overspending and the deficits of the state corporations. He complained that:

> Year in, year out, it has transpired that the Finance Ministers in this country have, for one reason or another, found it necessary to appear before this House to ask for approval of supplementary estimates submitted by Departments and Ministers.

Hitherto these demands had been met largely by drawing upon reserves and government borrowings from the central bank. But by 1965 the reserves were virtually exhausted.[15] Government borrowing from the central and the commercial banks, in the form of treasury bills, served to increase the money supply and boost price inflation within Ghana in the absence of any statutory minimum liquidity ratios. These were not introduced until April 1964, but proved no more than a momentary check to deficit financing. Although the Ghana pound was officially at par with sterling, it exchanged on the black market at a considerable and increasing discount. Goka, faced with this situation, was obliged to raise new and existing taxes and once more announced a 'voluntary' reduction in the cocoa price received by the farmers.

Despite the massive transformation of the economy by the setting up of the state enterprises, and despite the large injections of scarce capital into the public sector, Ghana had reached the curious condition of 'investment without growth'[16] This condition was noticed and commented upon by the civil servants and statisticians most closely engaged in the execution of the government's policies. A white paper issued on the progress of the national plan reported that:

> In 1964, although the situation with regard to food supplies has been considerably easier, there has been no resumption of economic growth. Industrial production has been virtually stagnant, and commerce and other activities dull.[17]

But their warnings went unheeded by the President and the inner circles of the party. Indeed, as the economic situation steadily worsened and the hoped-for 'breakthrough' began to look more and more distant, their disastrous policies were pursued with even more assiduity. Trapped within an economic cul-de-sac, uncompromisingly bent upon a course dictated primarily by ideological considerations, Nkrumah proved incapable of turning back.

The poor performance of the state corporations can be attributed to many factors. One of these was the haste and lack of foresight which attended their establishment. The rapidity with which they were created after 1961 taxed Ghana's resources at one of its weakest points, noticed by Lewis — that of the supply of trained, efficient and enterprising managers. There were already too few of these available before the great growth of the state sector. With the spawning of new corporations and the expansion of existing ones, key posts became filled increasingly by people who lacked the qualities needed for them to make a success of their jobs. The chairmen and managing directors of state corporations were appointees of the party, and, with a few exceptions, their calibre was low. Few were concerned by — or even aware of — the activities of their subordinates. The state enterprises, in fact, began to suffer from much the same ills which beset the machinery of the government and the party as their numbers and offices multiplied. Morale at all levels within the corporations was damaged by the elevation to managerial level of party hacks and the incompetent cousins and nephews of prominent politicians. The results were entirely predictable. Mistakes and miscalculations which would have bankrupted private businesses occurred with monotonous regularity, and the deficits were made up by further raids on public funds. Given the generally poor quality of management, it was hardly surprising that productivity per man within the state corporations was in all cases lower than within the private businesses which were still permitted to compete with them.[18]

A further handicap of the state corporations arising out of the carelessness and haste with which they were set up, was the lack of any proper external means of control over their activities. Although their original instruments of incorporation made provision for the inspection of their accounts by the Auditor-General, and the submission for these accounts to the Parliamentary public accounts committee, there seemed to be no means of ensuring that this was actually done. In his report for 1963 the Auditor-General commented that:

... the existing provision of the management of some of the state corporations allow for considerable flexibility which could be abused by unscrupulous managers. In the absence of a Board of Directors of a Management Committee, the Manager or General Manager virtually becomes the sole administrator of the Corporation and, except in a few cases, no regulations are drawn up for the internal administration of the Corporation. The enforcement of an audit enquiry ... is therefore left to a General Manager who may decide to take no notice. In this situation audit reports cease to produce the results that are normally expected from them.[19]

The biggest losses amongst the state corporations were made by those which required large amounts of capital investment. Ghana Airways lost heavily because of a political decision to purchase aircraft from both Britain and Russia. Its prestige routes between Accra, Cairo and Moscow proved highly unprofitable. The majority of the small numbers of passengers were members of parliament, party officials and their friends whose expenses were paid out of public funds. Other large losses were sustained by the State Farms Corporation. Its accounts were in such a chaotic state by the time of the coup that the new regime was obliged to hire a private firm to sort them out. The State Steelworks Corporation at Tema operated a small plant which processed imported scrap. Its initial capitalization was almost £1.7 million, but in its first year it needed a subsidy of half a million pounds to keep it in operation. The State Gold Mining Corporation also made heavy losses. Its mines formerly belonged to a group of British companies which decided in 1961 to close them because they were no longer profitable to work. The government arranged to take them over and bought out the companies at a reasonable price. But the mines failed to show a return and by 1964 several millions had been spent simply to keep them in operation.

The Ghana National Construction Corporation, successor to the old colonial Public Works Department, secured the bulk of government contracts, including that for the erection of the vast palace intended to house a single conference of African rulers in 1965. But its losses were heavy and compounded by bad debts owed to it by other state corporations, and by 'former Ministers who apparently had no intention of settling their accounts'.[20]

Other corporations made more modest losses. The justification for giving managers such independence was that the government felt that boards of directors would be unable to make quick decisions. It was a defensible policy if only the managers could be relied on, but too often such posts were filled by men unequal to their job.

By the time the public accounts committee's first report was submitted to parliament in 1964, seventeen state corporations had failed to submit their accounts for audit as required by law.[21] The National Assembly was thus deprived of material with which to arrive at a reasoned judgment of the progress — or lack of it — of these state bodies. The committee remarked sadly that it was 'alarmed by such derelictions of duty on the part of a large number of corporations which had for several years failed to submit their audited accounts'. Such failures, it added darkly, 'might well give cause for suspicion'.[22]

Examining particular corporations, the committee published the evidence from which they drew their general conclusions. The Vegetable Oil Mills Corporation, for instance, was unable to provide figures of the cost of operation of its four plants. After inspecting them the committee concluded that 'there was not sufficient planning in establishing these industries which are beset with common problems.' These included the selection of unsuitable sites, obsolete machinery imported from abroad and poor transport facilities. The State Fibre Bag Corporation, plagued by frequent breakdown of its machinery, made a loss in 1964 of £141,000' In near despair its managing director spent £500 of the corporation's money 'allegedly for the purchase of a cow, sheep, drinks and other things for the performance of certain rites to clear the factory of evil spirits and dwarfs'.[23] The crust of modernity was wafer-thin and easily broken. Managers under stress were apt to seek traditional solutions of their frustrations.

With the extraordinary reign of Andrew Yaw Djin as Minister of Trade in control of the import licensing system[24] a further obstacle emerged to work against the efficient running of both public and private enterprise and against the smooth operation of the development plan. Breakdowns of plant were common within the state corporations and all spares and new plant had to be imported. Djin succeeded in making the quick, orderly import of spares and new plant impossible. The result taken in conjunction with manpower problems, managerial difficulties and the absence of a strong controlling framework — was that the state manufacturing enterprises achieved a level of production less than half of their proper capacity.[25]

Despite somewhat half-hearted attempts by the State Enterprises Secretariat to clean out the Augean stables of the state enterprises from 1964 onwards, the situation continued to deteriorate. In his sessional address to the National Assembly in January 1965, even the President felt obliged to point out that:

> ... our state enterprises — and that includes the state farms and the agricultural wing of the Workers Brigade — were not set up to lose money. The number of state corporations which have been established has been determined by our policy of socialist re-construction and the building of a socialist economy in Ghana. But the state enterprises like any other enterprise, have a duty to operate on a profitable basis and thereby earn sufficient returns on the initial capital invested by the Government. Those in charge of state enterprises must realize that the investments in the factories with which they are entrusted are financed from the hard-earned savings of the individual taxpayer.[26]

Nkrumah was made aware of the situation prevailing in

most of the state corporations by some of his top civil servants; an awareness no doubt sharpened by the worsening economic situation. His apparent rehabilitation of the profit motive and his new sympathy with the taxpayer, evident in his speech, were welcome signs of a possible new direction in the conduct of the economy, although the ills against which he was inveighing had been publicly known for some years.

Later in the year Kofi Badu, a new member of parliament and one of the few former district commissions to have had a university education, admitted that the experiments in public ownership and enterprise had not been successful. After watching the melancholy performance of the chairman of the State Farms Corporation, Atta Mensah, defending his record before the House, Badu was moved to remark that:

> ... one of the saddest spectacles of our national life is the low rates of labour productivity ... In general, in our state enterprises, labour productivity is at a low ebb. We have created a working class of clockwatchers rather than job-doers ... There are several reasons for this; amongst them the poor tools of work, absence of the manager-worker relationship, ... poor and inefficient management, I think we ought to concern ourselves a great deal with this problem. The State Enterprises Secretariat must itself look into the matter of its appointments and set a certain level of competence and experience...[27]

Badu called upon the government to draw upon the 'experienced and mature Ghanaian businessmen and see whether the state cannot draw fruitfully upon their knowledge'. Some of the President's more thoughtful followers, including Badu, were drawing close to two essential points; firstly, that Ghana was an under-developed country which lacked the resources to sustain a large, centrally directed state sector; and secondly that even if such resources existed, there was not much evidence that the state sector's activities would result in an upsurge of production. But time was running out and Nkrumah showed no sign of willingness to embark upon a 'new economic policy' and curb his headlong rush into state interference with economic processes.

The show-piece of Ghana's development ambitions was the Volta dam. It was not Nkrumah's brainchild, although it rightly remains as one of his monuments. The possibility of a dam on the Volta in the area of Akosombo gorge was thought of long before the war. But the capital was not forthcoming. The colonial government had doubts about the viability of such a scheme capable of generating huge amounts of electrical power for a small territory of four to five million people, most of them small farmers. After the war several feasibility studies reported favourably on the prospects of a dam to supply power, improve navigation on the middle Volta and provide water for the arid Accra plains. Other projects elsewhere, at Kariba and Aswan, demonstrated a growing international interest in Africa's water resources. Nkrumah was also encouraged by the interest shown by foreign companies in the possibility of using Ghana's large bauxite reserves for the smelting of aluminium at a site not far from the new deepwater port of Tema. This appeared to get over the hurdle of finding a large enough customer to consume the power profitably.

After Nkrumah's visit to the United States in 1958, negotiations were started in the following year with Kaiser Industries Corporation and Reynolds Metals for the construction of a Tema smelter. The total cost of the dam and associated works was estimated at £75 million. Ghana undertook to provide just over half of this amount from her own resources and the World Bank agreed to provide another £30 million. Kaiser and Reynolds agreed to form a consortium, the Volta Aluminium Company, to build and operate a Tema smelter costing £46 million. Despite the unhappiness of the Americans at the leftward swing of Nkrumah's policies in 1961, the Kennedy administration decided finally to give its approval in February 1962. With its usual bad manners, Nkrumah's own *Evening News* greeted the report of Kennedy's ratification of the agreement with the headline, 'Dollar Boss! Better Late than Never.'

The consortium which undertook to produce aluminium at Tema planned for a production of between 100,000 and 150,000 tons per year after completion in 1967. But its impact upon Ghana's unemployment problems was insignificant. In full operation it would employ just over a thousand workers. Although in its initial stages the smelter would import bauxite it was envisaged that Ghana's own resources would eventually be used. To date this has not proved the case. Compared with the magnitude of Ghana's investment in the project, the beneficial results to the country as a whole have been disappointingly small. The Volta project might at some future date prove a great asset to Ghana, but in many respects far more could have been done if the vast sum spent on it had been spread over many other less spectacular but more useful projects.

Apart from the Volta project, domestic private investment in Ghana's industry and commerce declined during the years of the first republic. In money terms, however, this was more than offset by the massive increase in public investment. Yet the national product showed a steadily falling rate of growth.[28] Hamstrung by tough exchange control, by capricious and unworkable import licensing arrangements, and subject to bullying by an unsympathetic regime, Ghanaian businessmen withdrew into their shells. Yet their activities, properly encouraged, might have laid the basis of the economic transformation which Nkrumah claimed to seek.

Nkrumah's attitude to private enterprise was a complicated one. Many local businessmen had supported the CPP since its foundation and their financial contributions had been of immense help to the early party. One Greek Cypriot businessman resident in the colony, A.G. Leventis, became an intimate friend and supporter of Nkrumah, advising him on ways and means of raising and investing money for the party. Some of Nkrumah's lieutenants possessed considerable business acumen as well as shrewd political skills. Nkrumah admired strong-minded, successful captains of industry and struck up personal friendships with a number of foreign capitalists whose interests naturally benefited from their association with the President. Nkrumah found Edgar Kaiser, the ageing president of the American corporation, a curiously congenial and sympathetic figure. Over the Volta project he said 'we certainly understood one another on the business side, but the sort of true and lasting friendship which is built on mutual understanding and trust develops naturally through that rare and indefinable personal bond of affinity.'

Once in power, however, Nkrumah's temperamental dislike of opposition and his desire to interfere with all activities within Ghana under the guise of building socialism impelled him towards an increasingly hostile attitude towards indigenous private enterprise. In the short run he could not do without it, and even advanced state assistance to some private companies. But it was clear that private capital would soon be forced into a subordinate role. Large foreign interests were welcomed so long as Nkrumah thought them useful. The Capital Investments act of 1962 — the 'businessmen's charter' — offered generous terms to foreign companies investing in Ghana. If such companies proved troublesome, Nkrumah considered that they could be expelled or brought to heel by political decree. Smaller expatriate concerns, mainly Syrian, Lebanese and Indian, were tolerated. Their owners could be — and in some cases were — summarily deported, and their general unpopularity within Ghana ensured that they would present no political danger.

But the prospect of a flourishing class of indigenous businessmen growing up outside the fold of the party was a different matter. All the ingredients existed for the growth of a local entrepreneurial class. Ghana's problem lay not so much in a lack of capital as in the absence of suitable local outlets for it, and perhaps more importantly in a lack of self-confidence amongst local businessmen to enlarge and diversify their activities. Their savings tended to find their way into British and overseas banks. What was needed to foster the emergence of a domestic self-generating business sector was an institutional framework to bring money, ideas and energy together. For doctrinal reasons, however, Nkrumah's government was unable to provide this condition, with the ironic result that it was driven to ever greater dependence upon foreign capital to sustain investment whilst local capital was driven into exile or sunk into unproductive outlets.[29]

When power is in the hands of those who may not themselves be good at creating new wealth, the position of those who are is often one of discouragement and jeopardy. When Ayeh Kumi, Nkrumah's financial adviser, was ordered by his chief to sort out the import licence muddle in 1964, he came across a memorandum prepared by Nkrumah's instructions by two of his ministers which suggested ways of stifling local enterprise. Ayeh Kumi explained that:

It had been the system to gradually stifle the big

businessmen and the small Ghanaian businessmen in this country to be replaced by state corporations, and there had been a move towards this by putting all sorts of inconveniences in the way of merchants and traders in the country... The policy was that good businessmen should be engaged as managers in the state corporations and the others gradually weeded out... the steps taken against them were by income tax, various types of taxation, licence restrictions. African businessmen must not be given licences and if they persisted, they would be given such licences as would make them incapable of doing business.[30]

One area in which private enterprise and a state corporation were in competition was that of sea-fishing. The Ghanaians eat a great deal of fish. Dried or smoked, it is an important source of protein for the inland population. An increasing proportion of the total fish catch was made by deep water trawlers imported from abroad. This valuable trade was one in which private Ghanaian companies operated on a large scale. Several such companies existed, but the largest was Mankoadze Fisheries, founded in 1953, which became a limited liability company in 1958. Between 1960 and 1961 Mankoadze Fisheries imported four medium-sized trawlers and equipment from the USSR on a long-term credit basis. By 1963 these trawlers enabled the company to increase its landings considerably. By the following year it was supplying a large part of the country's requirements of fish. In comparison, the Ghana Fishing Corporation, despite large sums invested in it, was persistently running at a loss. This situation led Nkrumah to offer Robert Ocran, the young managing director and part-owner of Mankoadze, the job of running the entire fishing industry of Ghana. Summoned to Flagstaff House in August 1963, he recounted what had happened at the interview.

> The President asked my age, and I told him, and he
> said 'you know the state is also doing fishing business',
> and I said yes. Then he said 'I want you to take it over;
> hand over your business to the state and I will make you
> boss of the whole fishing industry in Ghana.' So I
> scratched my head and said this was rather difficult
> because all my life I have worked taking decisions
> myself, so it will be difficult for me to work for anybody
> (else) ...[31]

Ocran was understandably reluctant to take up the
President's offer. In return for giving up his own highly
successful business, he would have to enter the labyrinthine
structure of a state corporation in which his independence
and freedom of initiative would either be lost, or would
make him political enemies. He was also aware, as were
others, of the rumours of corruption and malpractices
within the state owned Ghana Fishing Corporation. Rather
than accept Nkrumah's offer, Ocran declared himself
ready to sell Mankoadze's assets to the government and to
set up again on his own account in some other field.

Nkrumah persisted in his efforts to bring Ocran's
company under state control. The following month Ocran
received a letter from the secretary to the cabinet, Enoch
Okoh, urging him to hold discussions with a committee
recently set up by the President to take over Mankoadze
Fisheries, 'in view of the Government's general policy of
not encouraging the creation of large-scale Ghanaian
private enterprise which Mankoadze Fisheries would
shortly become ...'[32] Meanwhile Ocran carried on as
managing director. He applied for an import licence in
1964 to bring in machinery for the company's workshops
at Tema. But Andrew Djin, the Minister of Trade, refused
to grant the application. Mankoadze was given the

alternative of capitulating to public control or grinding to a halt for lack of spare parts. After representations by the company, a huge licence to the value of £3 million was granted, but only on the understanding that the merger between the company and the State Fishing Corporation went ahead. At this stage deadlock was reached, and the situation was only resolved by the coup early in 1966.

But these manoeuvres did nothing to restore the fortunes of the sagging morale of the Ghana Fishing Corporation. In February 1965, Djin, still Minister of Trade, made a statement of the Corporation's profits to the National Assembly. This was immediately challenged by Mary Korentang, the former deputy chairman of the Corporation,[33] who alleged that the Corporation owed substantial sums to the Ghana Commercial Bank, and that the announced 'profits' were merely window-dressing. Later in the year, in December, William Aduhene asked in the Assembly why it was that private fisheries caught more fish than the Corporation. The Minister of Fisheries, Benjamin Konu, denied that this was so, but refused to provide any figure of catches.

What lay behind Aduhene's question was an attempt to draw the minister on reports which had appeared in the *Evening News* of vessels of the Corporation selling part of the catch for hard currency in Freetown, in contravention of the exchange control regulations. The Minister admitted that this evasion was actually being practiced by the Corporation. Vessels had put to sea without sufficient victuals and had been obliged to sell part of their catch to make up the deficiencies. Relations between the Corporation's vessels and local supply agents in ports outside Ghana were poor because of the Corporation's slowness in paying bills for goods supplied on credit. The Ghana embassy in Freetown was unable to offer any help, so the crews sold part of the catch locally and used the proceeds to pay off the agents. But even this explanation did not totally allay suspicions that officials within the Corporation were engaging in illegal traffic in foreign currencies for their own profit.

Nkrumah's offer to Ocran was indicative of his stubborn opposition to indigenous private enterprise. Instead of seeking to understand and put right the persistent malaise which affected the Ghana Fishing Corporation as well as other state corporations, Nkrumah was driven to making the state sector parasitic upon the talents and enterprise of successful private ventures.

One of the principal reasons for the failures of the state enterprises was the absence of any effective central supervision over their internal affairs. The penalty of bankruptcy and liquidation suffered by private companies for mistakes and mismanagement was absent from the state corporations. Only strong supervision from the top could act as a substitute for the discipline of the market. But this too was lacking. Not only the state corporations but the entire financial machinery of government lacked rigorous control. The institutional framework was there; indeed, there were too many institutional changes between 1960 and 1965 which put an intolerable strain upon those expected to put up with them.[34] But once again, there were not men of sufficient experience or training to make them work. The few who were available too often saw their warnings and advice disregarded by their political bosses. Both the Auditor-General and the public accounts committee appealed to Flagstaff House for more trained staff to help with their work, but in vain. These two bodies, together with the Central Bureau of Statistics under its young, able director, E.N. Omaboe,[35] managed to function as watchdogs over the uses of public money, but it was uphill work.

The root cause of this demoralizing financial indiscipline

lay deeper than the defects of official machinery. It was embedded in attitudes found throughout Ghanaian society. Before the CPP came to power the Watson report had noted that:

> ...in discussion with many Africans we found a marked disinclination to face realities. A tendency existed to take refuge in ill-founded optimism — that things would come right in the end, or that someone would find the answers... The hard truth that every penny of Government expenditure comes out of the taxpayers' pockets has nowhere penetrated public understanding.[36]

The basic psychology of the CPP simply reflected this popular attitude. It had not come to power as a pinch-penny party. Its whole style was one of 'liberation' from what its leaders termed colonial stagnation and orthodoxy. Nkrumah was expected to cut a dashing figure on the domestic and world stage. And if this was to cost money, his followers were not going to begrudge the cost. So long as there was money in the national kitty, and so long as it was satisfactorily diffused at large by the party, then tomorrow would look after itself. The years of prosperity from the cocoa trade and the large reserves inherited by the government helped to sustain this attitude and concealed from the greater part of the population the true precariousness of the economy. The atmosphere of easy money rampant in the fifties was the undoing of public thrift. After 1960-61 when cocoa prices tumbled and the reserves began to shrink, the old habits stubbornly persisted. The government and the party began to cast around for other sources of money with which to maintain themselves in the manner to which they had become accustomed.

After 1951 Ghana had become a happy hunting ground for business entrepreneurs from many countries, attracted like flies to jam by the country's burgeoning reserves and the free spending proclivities of its new government. It was common knowledge amongst the business community trading with West Africa that 'dash' — bribes — paid over to the right people secured contracts or expedited business. The CPP, far from suppressing this practice, virtually made it into a national institution. Businessmen in the past have frequently proved more astute than academic theorists in discovering what politics is all about; they have had to be, for they prosper or perish by their judgments. They quickly discovered that Ghana's politicians spoke out against 'capitalism' with one side of their mouths whilst they sucked its sweets with the other. After independence an increasing part of the party's income, and the incomes of some of its prominent members, was derived from what was euphemistically known as the 'commission system'. Everybody, it seemed, benefited. By paying a commission, the businessmen secured their contracts; the ruling party received its cut from the capitalists; and a general air of bustle and activity impressed the population. But the cost of the 'commissions' was simply added by the overseas suppliers to the total cost of the contracts — to be borne eventually by the Ghanaian taxpayers. As the reserves declined and the economy remained stubbornly stagnant, increasing numbers of new projects were commissioned by the government from overseas companies on a suppliers' credit basis. It was a method of keeping up the level of expenditure which proved irresistibly attractive to the government, but it proved to be the broad, easy road to national penury.

The financing of development projects by overseas companies through the use of suppliers' credits is a common form of promoting trade and investment between rich and poor countries. The credits are not, strictly speaking, a form of foreign aid. Capital and interest have to be repaid by the recipient country. When the recipient country is able to establish and maintain a proper system of investment priorities, suppliers' credits can prove useful in promoting investment. But in Ghana's case this essential condition was absent. The government lacked both the machinery and the self-discipline to keep proper control of what was going on.

Ghana's total external debt in 1963 stood at £184 million. A year later it had risen to £349 million.[37] Over the same period her external reserves had dwindled to £32 million. The most rapidly growing component of the external debt were the suppliers' credits, which probably totalled £175 million in 1964. In most cases Ghana was committed to repaying the capital sums and the interest back within a period of four to six years — an obligation which entailed an increasing proportion of the budget for debt servicing.

Actual figures for the suppliers' credits were difficult to get. The Auditor General complained in his report for 1962-63 that:

> It has not yet been possible to obtain sight of all Foreign Credit Agreements, nor has a solution been found to the problem of verifying goods and services received by the Government under the agreements.[38]

Although nearly everyone in political life knew that the government was living on borrowed money, astonishingly, no-one — not even in the inner circles of government knew for certain just how much had been borrowed. The 1964 economic survey reported that an official committee set up to examine the debt position discovered a 'gross underestimate' of the amounts involved, because of 'the absence of a centralized control over the signing of suppliers' credits, and the maintenance of proper records of the national debt'.[39]

How had this chaotic situation arisen? The commission system encouraged those ministers who were in a position to do so to place as many contracts as possible with overseas suppliers. Their personal incomes and the income of the party increased with the government's debts. In theory, all overseas contracts were placed through the Ghana Supply Commission which was supposed to scrutinize the terms of such contracts and check the quality of the goods received. In practice however it proved easy for them to bypass the Supply Commission altogether and to pay scant attention to the Central Planning Commission which was responsible for overseeing the development plan.

The government appeared to have discovered a bottomless well of ready cash. It would cover the growing gap between its current income and its soaring expenditure by an ingenious device which was, in reality a mortgaging of its revenues for years ahead. For their part the foreign suppliers looked askance at Ghana's shrinking reserves and the viability of the projects they were invited to embark upon.[40] A few unscrupulous companies, both western and communist, entered the game with zest, taking advantage of the laxities of the system to palm off obsolescent equipment at new prices. Their money was safe, however, against whatever day of reckoning lay ahead — insured under the export credit guarantee arrangements of their own governments. For some mysterious reason, perhaps because of a sensitivity to the charge of interfering in Ghana's domestic affairs, the underwriting governments did little to discourage the practice. If Ghana defaulted, their own taxpayers, largely in ignorance of these commitments, would foot the bill.

What did Ghana get in return for shouldering this burden of debt? The illusion of progress was sustained. New roads, improved water supplies and public works did appear throughout the country. Work started on a host of new factories for the state corporations. But not all were completed and fewer still made any commercial contribution to offset the crippling cost of servicing the foreign credits. Nor could this kind of forced development be continued indefinitely. As one member of parliament graphically described it, 'it is like a car-owner who buys petrol on credit, and then when he is unable to pay at the end of the month, moves on to another petrol station.'[41]

This hectic rush towards bankruptcy could not be blamed entirely upon the unauthorized and capricious activities of Nkrumah's ministers. The President himself, acting with a characteristic mixture of impulsiveness and credulity, helped to swell his country's debts.

Dr Noel Drevici, a West German businessman, although a Rumanian by birth, struck up a friendship with Nkrumah during his first visit to Ghana. He returned with an offer to set up industrial projects at Tema and elsewhere; seventeen contracts with a total value of over £62 million. Nkrumah was interested, particularly as Drevici convinced him that suppliers' credits could maintain the pace of industrialization without making an immediate call on the country's fast shrinking reserves. Drevici was an astute salesman. With maps and models of the 'Tema industrial project' he readily engaged the President's interest, despite the doubts of some of his ministers and civil servants.

Drevici's plans provided for a cocoa silo complex, a chocolate factory, a margarine factory, a diamond mining project and a sugar products factory. As a testimonial to modernity, he also offered to build a tower with a revolving restaurant on the top in time for the Accra trade fair planned for 1965. Some of Nkrumah's ministers and advisers continued, however, to have grave misgivings. £62 million seemed to them an enormous sum for which to be indebted to a single company. Moreover, the total sum pledged in other directions in the form of suppliers' credits was mounting rapidly. Any surplus Ghana earned on her current accounts would be mortgaged ahead for several years. R.O. Amoaka Atta, who was then Minister of Finance, claimed later that he had opposed the project, but that contracts were signed by him 'under duress' at the President's insistence. Amoaka Atta, who was also chairman of the foreign credits committee set up under the seven-year development plan, claimed that:

> I was helpless under the circumstances, because Mr Ayeh Kumi, the general economic consultant, was always saying at the Committee meetings that Nkrumah wants this special contract signed.[42]

Amoaka Atta also maintained that the Drevici contracts had actually been signed before the Minister of Industries, Imora Egala, had seen copies. Egala was opposed to the Drevici project and understandably annoyed at the lack of consultation over a project falling within the concern of his ministry. He was opposed in particular to the planned silo complex which would cost £7 million. His technical advisers had told him that the silos were so large that, if fully filled with cocoa, there was a risk of spontaneous combustion starting at the base of the silo as the cocoa was compressed by its own weight. He decided to circulate a memorandum amongst his cabinet colleagues, but was warned off in a letter to him from the secretary to the cabinet. The letter read:

> In view of the categorical direction of Osagyefo himself ... that you should sign the contract with Mr Drevici, I suspect that your memorandum, if circulated in Cabinet, may embarrass you and your colleagues considerably. You will recall that many Ministers may try to advise caution in letters on many of the points

in your memorandum. But the President came down like a ton of bricks and virtually lost his temper...[43]

The contracts were signed soon after and the Drevici project went ahead. By the time of the coup it was estimated that he had already been paid about £9 million for work completed and in hand. The fears about the silos and the dangers of spontaneous combustion were shown to be only too well grounded. Nearly completed by the time of the coup, they could only be used for a small part of their total capacity. Other grounds for alarm were discovered. Officials at the Ministry of Industries were not satisfied that some of the machinery supplied was entirely new.[44] Breakdowns were frequent and spares hard to get. The enterprise proved so unsatisfactory that soon after the coup two thirds of it was abandoned.

But the foreign debts contracted so haphazardly by the government were not exclusively with overseas private interests. Of the total foreign credits contracted by September 1963, worth £93,640,000 — of which £72,600,000 were still outstanding — some sixteen and a half million were with Russian and East European state exporting corporations, of which only a fraction had been repaid by that date. On the whole, the interest payable on foreign suppliers' credits from the communist states was lower than that charged on credits from other sources, but economically the value of some of the projects financed by the communist states was equally as dubious as those financed by western companies. Over £5 million went on eight Ilyushin aircraft for Ghana Airways, £4 million from Yugoslavia for a naval base, and over £1 million for the disastrous state farms experiment.

The debts contracted by Nkrumah's government proved a fatal burden to Dr Busia's government during the short-lived second republic, and they are likely to be a heavy millstone around the necks of future administrations for many years. The few choices now facing Ghana as a result of the spendthrift years are difficult and bleak. The second military government of Colonel Achampong, now in power, regards the foreign debts as the principal obstacle to Ghana's prosperity and stability. But a unilateral repudiation of them could inflict upon the country a further degree of isolation from international trade and capital. Yet if the present government recoils from this consequence and undertakes to honour them, it will be forced to keep the general standard of living of the people at a low level, with all the risks that this entails.

The statistical evidence from Ghana's own sources leave no doubt that Nkrumah's development policy was a costly failure. It did not arise out of neglect or indifference towards economic matters. On the contrary, the economy of the first republic was distinguished by perpetual institutional innovation, detailed planning and heavy public investment, all designed to secure the maximum rate of growth. Notwithstanding all this energy, the failure came about because of Nkrumah's stubborn attachment to economic ideas and doctrines of questionable provenance which were fundamentally inappropriate to Ghana's circumstances. It was for him almost as easy to achieve an end as it was to conceive of it.

But his obsession with state control and centralization as the key to economic growth — as indeed to everything else — could not be matched by his ability to inspire discipline within the elaborate structures he had created. Arrogating all powers of decision to himself, he deprived those serving him of the opportunity to take new initiatives. Yet at the same time he allowed others to exploit the growing jungle of controls and protected more from the consequences of their incompetence. This strange combination of rigidity at the highest level of government and anarchy in the lower reaches vitiated any hopes of a realistic approach to development. Driven from one expedient to another, hoping like Mr Micawber that something would turn up, the declared arch-enemy of 'neo-colonialism' ended by leaving his country in pawn to foreign interests to a greater extent than any other contemporary African ruler. Admittedly the world economic tide had turned against Ghana in Nkrumah's last years. But her chances at independence of breaking out of the cycle of poverty were probably better than those of any other African country. By the time of his downfall this opportunity had been recklessly squandered.

VI The Fruits of Office

'It would be idle to ignore the existence of bribery and corruption in many walks of life admitted to us by every responsible African to whom we addressed the question. That it may spread as further responsibility devolves upon the African is a possibility that cannot be denied. No nation can rise to greatness on such foundations (although) its existence cannot be accepted as a barrier to self-rule', observed the Watson report in 1948.

Venality is such a common feature of political life that it is surprising that so little systematic attention has been paid to it as a proper subject of political science. Cynics might say that since all politics of their nature are corrupt, corruption in politics requires no special explanation. Politicians in office will either minimize its importance or deny that it exists at all. Academic students of politics are not close enough to the system to know what is transacted beneath the surface, or are puzzled by material which seems irrelevant to their critical frame of reference. Yet questions of who gets what out of the system, and how; the means by which private estates are built up and maintained by illicit transactions; the manner in which rival baronies of wealth within the system settle their differences, all surely affect the development and durability of a political order.

In many respects the scale of corruption in Nkrumah's Ghana was probably no greater than that which came to exist in some other African states, or indeed, than that in many wealthier countries of the world. Although Nkrumah spoke out frequently against corruption in his own party and even took half-hearted measures to curb it, his efforts were unsuccessful. Self-enrichment through the abuse of office was a great adhesive, a political glue, which bound his movement together despite the constant bickering within its ranks. Had he taken ruthless steps to enforce the virtues of austerity and rectitude which he so often extolled, he would have risked upsetting powerful interests and put the unity of his party at risk. Moreover his own position would have been in danger, for Nkrumah himself was not above reproach. Under the protection afforded by his own defalcations, his subordinates felt free to pursue their own private advantage with impunity. The CPP might have declaimed its ideology loudly to the world at large, but within its ranks money spoke more persuasively.

The wider background of corruption in Ghana is not our concern. It reaches back into the fabric of traditional societies under colonial rule. Sharing is one of the fundamental attributes of the extended family system common throughout Africa. The lucky individual who comes to enjoy prosperity is expected to use his advantage to help his kinsmen. For him not to do so would be widely regarded as selfish and unnatural. Colonial rule, however, superimposed over traditional societies a host of new functions, each regulated by an appropriate professional ethic. Doctors subscribed to the hippocratic oath, lawyers observed the code of their profession, and civil servants were bound by their standing orders. As more Africans entered these professions they worked within an establish-ment which favoured those who abided by their professional ethic and penalized those who allowed the exercise of their craft to be influenced by traditional moralities. The British sought not to destroy the existing fabric of native life, but to clear the way for a local élite which would eventually be capable of working to the standards of a modern administration. To a large extent they were successful in West Africa,[1] but with their departure and the removal of the constraints they had supplied, the strength of the older values revived. Family and tribal interests could no longer be so easily resisted, influencing every kind of transaction between the public and officials, from an application for a market stall licence to the award of major contracts. Laws against bribery and corruption remained on the statute book after the British had left — indeed, they were added to — but the unwritten conventions of traditional life proved to be stronger. And since all levels of society were so affected, even the enforcement of sanctions was subject to the same process of erosion.

In the small, gossipy world of Ghanaian political life little remained secret for long. Rumours of Nkrumah's own interests had long been put about, but it was only after his downfall that detailed evidence concerning them came to light. He seemed to have become more careless about money as he grew older.[2] The ease with which it proved possible for him to lay hands on public money made him indifferent to its value. After his fall the National Liberation Council set up a commission of enquiry into his personal estate.[3] Its method of investigation was simple, although the details revealed by witnesses were frequently confusing. The commission added up the earnings of the former President from his public offices and other known legitimate sources and compared these with the value of the assets owned or controlled by him at the time of his downfall.

Nkrumah himself had stated in his autobiography that he arrived in the Gold Coast 'penniless'. His passage money was provided by Danquah's Convention and his initial salary as secretary to the Convention was £300 a year. As 'leader of government business' from February 1951, he received an annual salary of £2,750 with allowances worth £600. From April 1952, when he became Prime Minister until July 1960, when he became President, he received a salary of £3,500 a year plus allowances. His presidential salary was £12,000 and he was paid in addition a pension of £2,500 as a retired Prime Minister. Up until his final month as President, Nkrumah had received a total of £118,863 as payment for his public duties. In addition he was awarded a Lenin Peace Prize worth £10,000 in 1962. His various publications brought in a further £5,310, making in all a grand total of £134,173. Of this total the commission estimated that roughly one third should represent his personal savings.

The commission's examination of Nkrumah's estate, as it stood in February 1966, led it to two conclusions; firstly, that he was a very wealthy man, secondly, that the bulk of his wealth came from sources other than his legitimate earnings. Nkrumah possessed disposable cash assets within Ghana of £402,294. In addition he controlled three limited liability companies, the National Development Company or NADECO, the Guinea Press and the Ghana Bottling Company whose combined assets were worth £1,061,851. Properties owned by him in Ghana were valued at £592,000 and properties owned by him or his family outside Ghana were estimated to be worth £265,862. In all, the commission considered that the total value of all assets which could with reasonable certainty be regarded as falling under his ownership or control at £2,332,008. This figure did not include other assets deposited abroad about which the commission had no reliable information.

Nkrumah did not seem interested in whether the money he acquired was from the party or the public. The commission remarked that

Although he is given to rather reckless spending... he seems to be frugal with his money. He hardly ever makes cash gifts, and it cannot be said on an examination of his bank accounts that he was anything like liberal. He certainly did not spend any of his large fortune on his Party. On the contrary, we find that sums ostensibly raised for the Party sometimes found their way into his personal account.[4]

Nkrumah's apparent generosity to loyal but hard-up party members was sometimes charged to public funds. The State Housing Corporation, for instance, was ordered to pay out of its own funds to provide new houses for the President's relatives in his native village of Nkroful, although Nkrumah took care to give the beneficiaries the impression that the houses were the product of his own generosity. Many other gifts were made out of money voted to the President's Contingency Fund. Madam Fathia, Nkrumah's Egyptian wife, received £10,000 from this source. Cars were bought out of the fund as presents for the daughter of the fair-skinned lady MP, Lucy Seidel, and for the fetish priestess of the Larteh shrine who claimed to have treated the President for what she described as 'head and chest, cough and sneeze'.[5] Houses were also provided for women loyalists of the party. The vice-chairman of the women's section of the party in Sekondi, who claimed to be an 'ex-lover' of Nkrumah's, received £2,000 on the direction of the President to enable her to complete her half-finished house. Ama Nkrumah — no relation of the President's[6] — was given £1,200 to enable her to purchase her rented home. Madam Susana Buadi petitioned Nkrumah in the same year. She described herself as a 'party activist' and asked for a house to be put up for her. The President agreed and instructed the regional commissioner of the Volta region to see to it. Under the impression that Nkrumah would underwrite the cost, the commissioner contracted for the house with a local builder. But Nkrumah repudiated the debt and the regional commissioner was obliged to raid funds earmarked for local development projects in his area.

In addition to his controlling interest in the three companies, Nkrumah also acquired ownership of considerable stretches of valuable land. Some of this land, principally around Accra, was acquired by purchase and evidenced by title deeds. Other lands, especially around Nkrumah's birthplace, possibly belonged under customary law to his family. Land owned by Nkrumah at Wenchi was given to him by the chief, the Wenchihene, and his council in appreciation of the CPP's support against the rival chiefly family, of which Dr Busia was the principal son. Land at Larteh was donated to Nkrumah in accordance with native custom by the chief linguist of the Akonede shrine to which Nkrumah was a occasional visitor. The chief of Jamestown, a poor district of Accra, also gave Nkrumah land in return for the support the party had given him and his elders in the past.

Nkrumah also owned land and buildings in Cairo and near Rabat in Morocco. The Cairo buildings were erected, according to Krobo Edusei, as part of the £200,000 'commission' received from a West German company in 1959. These buildings had been made over to Madam Fathia's relatives in Cairo. The land and buildings near Rabat appeared to have been a gift of King Mohammed V of Morocco in 1962 as an appreciation of Nkrumah's services to African unity. Morocco and Ghana were at that time members of the militant 'Casablanca group' of African states. The upkeep of these villas was, however, charged to Ghana's public funds.

In addition to his private fortune, continually augmented from public funds, Nkrumah also enjoyed the steadily increasing perquisites of his presidential office. His main residence was Flagstaff House in the northern suburbs of Accra. Formerly the headquarters of the Gold Coast commander in chief, it was progressively enlarged and improved during Nkrumah's tenancy. New buildings to house the proliferating official secretariats were built in the grounds. After the bomb attempts on Nkrumah, three concentric security walls were constructed around the grounds and a helicopter landing site was built just outside the main gates to facilitate a quick get-away in an emergency. Opposite Flagstaff House, new apartment blocks rose to house the growing security service with which the President increasingly surrounded himself. It was in the vicinity of these blocks that the rebel soldiers of February 1966, met the fiercest resistance. Within the grounds of Flagstaff House a large, well-equipped zoo was laid out in 1965 for the personal enjoyment of the President and his guests. Some of the animals for the zoo were donated by admirers overseas, and by Nkrumah's distant kinsman, Chief Biney, a wealthy Lagos business man.[7]

On the Aburi ridge, thirty miles to the north of Accra, lay a second presidential residence, the luxurious Aburi Lodge. The source of the money for this is still a mystery, although Gbedemah after the coup claimed that it 'was not from public funds' and that he was kept in the dark about it.[8] Rarely used by Nkrumah, the Lodge was sold by him shortly after its completion to the government, but was afterwards given back to him by his central committee on behalf of 'a grateful nation'. Nkrumah also used the old Danish castle of Christiansborg, formerly the Governor's residence, built on a rocky promontory along the coast near Accra. Finally the President also possessed a modern hillside retreat overlooking the Volta dam from which he could contemplate his masterpiece.

Part of Nkrumah's fortune came from the money-making activities of his party. Political parties have long financed themselves by contributions from interests that want something done and are willing to pay for it. The

CPP developed money-making into a fine art, becoming a self-financing machine bringing in several millions each year. The principal source of its cash came from 'commissions' paid over to it by local and foreign companies in return for the award of government contracts. The value of the 'commissions' varied between five and ten per cent of the value of the contracts. Throughout the first republic only an insignificant part of the party's income came from membership dues and public subscriptions. As government spending mounted and more and more contracts were placed, this source of the party's income grew *pro rata*, and in turn reinforced the pressures behind the uncontrolled rise of public expenditure.

The mechanisms by which the ruling party exploited its monopoly of political power to make money, although simple in outline, were complicated and varied in detail. One of the most important ways lay in the operations of the National Development Company. It became, in the words of the investigating commission, 'the clearing house for bribes paid over to the CPP or to Kwame Nkrumah personally'.[9] NADECO was founded as a limited company in October 1957, and was intended to replace the disbanded and discredited Cocoa Purchasing Company[10] as a means of acquiring funds for the CPP. It was a registered limited company and not, as widely believed, owned personally by Nkrumah. Nevertheless he 'exercised all the rights of a real owner in relation to the Company's business',[11] and was a principal beneficiary of its operations. According to Krobo Edusei, who was a part-time adviser to NADECO,[12] the decision to set up the company was taken in 1956 at a joint meeting of the cabinet and the central committee of the party at a time when public agitation for an enquiry into the affairs of the Cocoa Purchasing Company was building up. Kojo Botsio's explanation for the decision was that:

The Central Committee found that the Party was having plenty of surplus funds, and the idea was that the money could be profitably invested in a business for the upkeep of the Party.[13]

George Padmore had once explained to Nkrumah how the American political parties depended upon contributions from business interests and urged him to introduce a similar system in Ghana; foreign capitalists would pay for the introduction of socialism. Ghana had few large indigenous businesses, but expatriate firms could provide the party with a large income in return for favours which it was in a position to offer. It seemed an attractive, although spurious, way of bringing back into the country a part of the profits earned there by foreign capitalists.

The running of NADECO was entrusted to the general direction of Emmanuel Ayeh Kumi, a businessman who became largely responsible for the overall management of the financial affairs of the party and its leader. The first board of NADECO's directors was a close-knit group. This was Nkrumah's own private empire, and he guarded it jealously against the curiosity of his ministerial colleagues. All the directors were businessmen of a sort, although of varying pretensions. Most of them were Nzima and Fanti, with whom Nkrumah shared a common vernacular, and were amongst his oldest and trusted supporters, not prominent in public life but valued for their obscurity. Ayeh Kumi came from Axim, as did Isaac Amihere, and William Baidoe Ansah. The last two, together with Andrew Yaw Djin, had all served respective terms of office as treasurers of the CPP. Most of the directors had previously been active in the affairs of the Cocoa Purchasing Company. The odd man out in this Nzima-Fanti group was Obed Andoh, an Ashanti contractor, who had also served as treasurer of the party.[14] Apart from Ayeh

Kumi these people were relatively lowly figures, the 'collectors' of commissions. They lacked much formal education and were Nkrumah's countrymen — his creatures — owing their advancement solely to his patronage.

The top dressing of NADECO was provided by Emmanual Ayeh Kumi and W.M.Q. Halm, later to become Governor of the Bank of Ghana.[15] Born in 1913, Ayeh Kumi was roughly of the same age as Nkrumah. After a secondary education he started work as a produce clerk and served with the West African forces during the war. Afterwards he set up a variety of businesses, all with small turnovers, but his principal ambition was to create a business enterprise on a scale with the expatriate concerns. He was a Rotarian with a curious though harmless obsession with the collection of statistics and titles.[16] He joined the CPP at an early stage and was eventually appointed to the chairmanship of various public boards. Trusted by Nkrumah because he was totally lacking in political ambitions, he eventually became the President's personal financial adviser and consultant in 1962. The circumstances of his advancement to a position of intimacy and influence with Nkrumah were strange. In his own words:

... I was called by Ambrose Yankey, the deposed President's Chief Security officer, to go and see a Mohammedan who had been brought from Kankan to do certain things for the former President. When I went the Mohammedan told me to open my palm which I did and he fumbled through sand and a mirror which he had in hand and told me the deposed President liked me very much; I have a great future if I remain loyal to Kwame Nkrumah and do his wishes, and if I remain his right-hand man I should be great. He gave me some roots including what appears to be Arabic gum and incense to smoke myself once a week and also a bottle of a mixture which was basically Florida Water to rub myself and my face before I go to work.[17]

The magic was apparently efficacious. Ayeh Kumi kept his position to the end, virtually the keeper of his master's privy purse, representing his master in most of the transactions involving large sums of money paid over to Nkrumah and his party.

In the early years of NADECO's operations it concluded several highly profitable deals. In 1958 £300,000 was received from the Israeli shipping line, Zim, as commission on a contract worth £3 million to establish Ghana's own Black Star Line of eight merchant vessels. Another profitable deal which yielded £200,000 was concluded with a West German company of locomotive manufacturers on a contract worth £2 million for locomotives and rolling stock for the Ghana Railway. The public accounts committee of the National Assembly, which was not aware of the secret details of the transaction at the time, remarked that it was:

... particularly unhappy about the circumstances surrounding the purchase of locomotives and wagons to the value of £2 million. Our concern was based on the fact that these locomotives and wagons were purchased by negotiation with an individual firm instead of by competitive tender, and against all expert advice.[18]

The contracts had in fact been awarded against the advice both of the Crown Agents in London and of the general manager of the Railway. The latter pointed out that the tender submitted by an American company was cheaper and could be executed more quickly, and that in any case the West German price exceeded the budgetary provision for new rolling stock. It did not come to light until much later that the West German firm secured the contract through the good offices of Krobo Edusei who had cultivated friendly relations with the company. Within a short time, despite the high price of the equipment, the general manager of the Railway complained that the locomotives:

> ... have developed major faults in the form of advanced fractures in the bogie bolsters and the main bogie frames due to faults in design and construction.[19]

Naturally enough in the circumstances, no government action or enquiry followed. The locomotives were patched up at further public expense and the matter was quietly forgotten.

One of the biggest operations undertaken by NADECO was the purchase of the A.G. Leventis trading company on behalf of the Government. Nkrumah intended that the Leventis company should provide the nucleus of a state-owned retailing organization. He hoped that with a chain of 'people's shops' throughout the country, an increasing proportion of the retail trade would fall into state hands. Leventis, a Greek Cypriot, had cultivated a friendship with Nkrumah and Edusei, advising them on their financial affairs and donating money to the party. During the 1948 disturbances, Leventis's shops, unlike other expatriate-owned stores, had not been threatened by hostile mobs. Unlike many other Cypriot, Lebanese and Syrian traders in Accra, Leventis had refused to enlist in the special constabulary raised by the colonial government during the disorders. He perceived a future winner in Nkrumah and his party, and as early as 1948 began to prepare for the day when the British would depart from the Gold Coast and the CPP would take over the reins of power.[20]

Leventis's cordial relations with Nkrumah continued after the latter had become Leader of Government Business after the 1951 election. He was instrumental in bringing about the marriage of Nkrumah to the Egyptian Coptic Christian, Helen Ricz Fathia, in 1956 and became godfather to Nkrumah's son by that marriage. Sympathetic towards the independence movement, Leventis was also struck by the pliability of many of the leading figures of the CPP. He had himself been the subject of some icy comments in respect of his trading practices in an earlier official enquiry. By 1959 his company was running into difficulties. He asked Nkrumah for help and was given a government loan of £2 million. Two years later, early in 1961, the government revealed an interest in the possibility of taking over A.G. Leventis. A government valuation of the property and stock of the company reached a figure of £5.2 million. In February 1961, F.D. Goka, soon to be Gbedemah's successor as Minister of Finance and Trade, made a formal offer to Leventis of £4.5 million. Leventis refused on the ground that he would have to borrow half a million pounds to enable him to wind up his affairs properly.

Krobo Edusei said in evidence later that the purchase price was raised to £6 million. Under this arrangement Leventis received £4.5 million and agreed to remain as buying agent for the new state corporation. The remaining £1.5 million would be earmarked to establish a trust 'for the purpose of building schools, colleges and hospitals to perpetuate the name of Leventis in Ghana'.

Komla Gbedemah, then Minister of Finance, however was unhappy about the transaction. It seemed to him a highly irregular deal contracted for dubious reasons at the expense of the taxpayer who would have to find the £6 million purchase price. In a memorandum placed before the cabinet, he said that '... I feel that it is Ghana's money which is being placed at the disposal of the Ghana Government, and not the legitimate money of Mr A.G. Leventis.'[21] Gbedemah wanted the deal to go through only if a part of the money actually paid to Leventis was put into the proposed Leventis Trust.

As it turned out, Gbedemah's suspicions were justified. On 10 April 1961, — two days after the President's dawn broadcast — the cabinet approved the deal. Present at this meeting were Krobo Edusei, Dowuona Hammond, Kofi Baako, Tawia Adamafio, F. Goka and E.K. Bensah. All of them subsequently maintained that they were opposed to the deal, but that they were overruled by Nkrumah 'because he manifested personal interest in this particular transaction'. However, the commission of enquiry after the coup concluded that, although Edusei and Dowuona Hammond were vocal in their opposition, the claims of the others 'would impugn the accuracy of the officially authenticated record of the Cabinet decision'.[22] Commenting further on Leventis's view of the transaction, the commission remarked that:

> Mr Leventis himself does not appear to think a great deal of the personal integrity of the President. We are satisfied that he often told Krobo Edusei that Nkrumah was corrupt and would be exposed when his régime came to an end.[23]

When the transaction was completed, no Leventis Trust was set up for these worthy causes. The one and a half million pounds overpayment, added from taxation to the purchase price, disappeared in various directions; £750,000 went into Nkrumah's personal account,[24] a large sum went back to NADECO, and the rest remained unaccounted for.

The real purpose of NADECO as a clearing house for bribes was, naturally, discreetly hidden. But Ghana is a small country. Foreign businessmen talked, and rumours began to circulate. When Komla Gbedemah was Minister of Finance he was aware of the rumours but was careful not to get too deeply involved. He was worldly enough to a accept bribery and corruption as part of the Ghanaian way of business. He also knew that NADECO was part of the President's own empire, and that undue attention to its affairs would be resented. But he knew that the 'commissions' were simply added to the total price charged by the companies and therefore were not a kind of tax on foreigners' profits, but were borne ultimately by the Ghanaian taxpayer, and for this reason he was opposed to the practice. He was asked by the Apaloo Commission after the coup how much he knew about the collection of commissions:

J.W. Taylor (for the Commission):
You heard that this rumour about the ten per cent in effect meant that the members of the Government and the CPP were collecting these commissions from contractors, but you do not know who these mem- were?

Gbedemah: That is so.

Taylor: Having heard as a top CPP man and as a very responsible member of the Government, did you try to contact the ex-President to find out what could be done ... to save the good name of the Party?

Gbedemah: I did. I approached the ex-President and remonstrated with him that this matter had been raised at a Cabinet meeting and that I opposed it, but I heard that some people are collecting commission.[25]

In fact by 1960, Gbedemah's own days in the inner circle of the party and government were already numbered and there was probably little he could have done to suppress the traffic, even if he had earnestly wished to.

Wherever possible the party insisted that 'voluntary contributions' should be made over in cash rather than by cheque, and that official approval for the award of contracts solicited by commissions should be given only when proof of receipt of the commission was recorded in the party's accounts book. Ayeh Kumi maintained that in some cases Nkrumah himself had received cash contributions and handed them over to Ayeh Kumi to be deposited in one of the President's accounts. Under examination after the coup, Ayeh Kumi revealed further details of the way the system worked:

Chairman: Is is true that he (Nkrumah) sent people to collect from all the firms?

Ayeh Kumi: I would not say all the firms, because he handpicked where to go.

Chairman: Those who got the biggest contracts?

Ayeh Kumi: I should think so. I do not know how he did it, but if any of the people in this Court cared to say how many types of people go into his office to see him every day, then we might know. It so happened that these people went to his office and he spoke to them himself.[26]

In the last few years of its existence the CPP was drawing a large part of its income from NADECO's operations. Ayeh Kumi estimated that the party's annual expenditure during its final years was running at a level of between £10 and £11 million. [27] Some of the money which flowed into NADECO as commission payments was used by the company for its legitimate commercial activities. But the greater part went to subsidize the party and its financially ailing integral wings. An examination of NADECO's books after the coup revealed that a total sum of £588,404 had been transferred from the company to the party. Reliable figures are hard to get because regular accounting procedures were not always followed. Indeed, the illicit transactions of the CPP were marked by the same administrative confusion and lack of regard for proper accounting which were characteristic of government agencies and state corporations. Some of the party's 'collectors' were themselves suspected of taking their own cut out of the money paid over to them, particularly when cash payments were involved.

On being informed about the rumours circulating about the party's operations, Nkrumah gave a warning to his commission collectors during the course of an address to the National Assembly early in 1964 on the launching of the seven-year development plan. Admitting that such 'commissions' were in fact being collected, he said that official contracts would not be approved by himself or the economic committees in Flagstaff House unless the commissions were disclosed in detail and entered in the terms of the contract. 'These conditions are being made in the interests of the taxpayer who ultimately has to find the money to pay *for these gifts and bribes.*'[28]

The purposes to which the money collected by NADECO's operations were put were many and varied.[29] Some large amounts went directly into

Nkrumha's privy purse. In August 1965, for instance, £90,000 was paid into his personal account with Barclay's Bank in Accra. Other amounts went to reward the President's friends for services rendered. 'Kankan Nyame', the witch-doctor who endorsed Ayeh Kumi's appointment, received £2,000. A further £25,000 went to meet Nkrumah's personal expenses at the Commonwealth Prime Ministers' Conference in London during 1965.

Large amounts were paid over to financially ailing agencies of the party. One such pensionary was the Guinea Press which produced the *Evening News*, Nkrumah's own mouthpiece. Nkrumah was unwilling to abandon the Guinea Press but was continually irritated by its inability to make a profit. In February 1961, the President ordered NADECO to make a monthly subsidy of £15,000 to the Press, in which he had a controlling interest as majority shareholder, in the hope of making it financially viable. His hopes were disappointed, and the following year the cabinet decided to make a once-and-for-all payment of £360,000 to give it a last chance of becoming self-supporting 'in recognition of services which the Press has given the Party and Government'.[30] But even this measure failed. The *Evening News* rabid denunciations of the capitalists severely restricted its appeal to commercial advertisers and in October 1965, Nkrumah was obliged once more to come to its assistance.

NADECO was by no means the only source of funds available to the President. He enjoyed direct access to public money through the contingency fund. The first provision for this appeared in the estimates for 1959-60. it provided for the modest sum of £100,000 to be disbursed jointly by the Ministries of Foreign Affairs and Finance. Presidential drawings on the fund had to be countersigned by the permanent secretaries of both ministries. The official reason given for the creation of the fund at that time was 'the rapidly changing international situation and the expanding foreign service (which) necessitated expenditure to be met at short notice'. A more discreet purpose was to enable Nkrumah to finance the African political exiles in Ghana favoured by him.

But other items paid out of the funds were a little more bizarre. The deputy secretary to the cabinet said later that 'we think ... with a manifest regret, that the ex-President even caused to be charged on his Vote 'WATER' which he regularly imported from overseas for his consumption.'[31] Another item so purchased was a large, bullet-proof American Lincoln saloon car, complete with gramophone, tape recorder and cocktail cabinet which Nkrumah intended to add to his garage. The Apaloo commission felt obliged to place on record

> ... that the evidence we received generally about the Contingency Vote and the use to which it was put did not rest on what well may be the slippery memory of witnesses. These matters were fully documented. [32]

In the 1961-62 estimates, control of the contingency fund was transferred from the two ministries to the President's office, removing it from the regular audit of the civil service. The senior civil servant responsible for administering the fund testified before the Apaloo Commission that the President was empowered:

> ... to use this Vote as and when he pleased, and on the types of project and purposes he has specified.[33]

In succeeding years the sums paid into the contingency fund were very considerably increased. Although it was used partly to subsidize the President's admirers and supporters in other African states, it became in time virtually indistinguishable from Nkrumah's growing private estate, and was used by him, like the NADECO money, to reward his favourites and personal friends.

Nkrumah did not get his contingency fund without opposition. Komla Gbedemah was Minister of Finance when control over the fund was transferred to the President's office. Nkrumah's request for an enlarged vote of £2 million to be raised in the budget planned for 1961-62 came at a time of growing pressures on Ghana's reserves. Gbedemah was also alarmed at the freedom of manoeuvre which an enlarged contingency vote would give to Nkrumah. He therefore informed the President that he considered it 'inopportune' to give way to his request, at least for that financial year. Nkrumah's reply was to transfer responsibility for the budget from Gbedemah's Ministry of Finance to a new Budget Secretariat at Flagstaff House responsible to the President's office.

Gbedemah thought that being Finance Minister without responsibility for the budget was like playing Hamlet without the Prince of Denmark. He wrote to Nkrumah informing him that under the new and reduced responsibilities of the Ministry of Finance 'he was no longer interested in being appointed to that post'. Shortly afterwards Gbedemah was removed to a less important ministry. In September he was asked for his resignation from the government in company with several other ministers, and the breach between him and Nkrumah began to widen.[34]

Gbedemah's misgivings about the contingency vote under sole presidential control appear to have been justified. The initial sum of £100,000 voted to the fund in its first year jumped to £500,000 in 1961-62. In the following year it reached £1 million and in 1963-64 to £1.5 million. In 1965, when the food shortages were getting more acute, the reserves were at rock bottom, and the public was being exhorted to tighten its belt, the contingency vote totalled £2 million.

Under cover of the umbrella provided by Nkrumah's involvement in dubious financial dealings, other leading members of the government and party of this socialist state built up their own private empires and fortunes. The most notorious example of freebooting on an ambitious scale was that of Krobo Edusei — alias 'Moke' to his many admirers. Edusei had been a foundation member of the CPP, a member of its first central committee, and a 'prison graduate'. His record of loyalty to the party was therefore impeccable. After an elementary education in Kumasi, Edusei practised the varied arts of journalism, debt-collecting and trading in herbal medicines. During the disturbances between the NLM and the CPP in the Ashanti region, Edusei, then the propaganda secretary for the CPP, had held an important element of the Ashanti for his party. Nkrumah never forgot his obligation to Edusei for his loyalty at this critical time. Although irritated by Edusei's ostentation, which made his desultory attempts to give his party the appearance of austere rectitude look foolish, Nkrumah knew that Edusei was his man, one who harboured no ambitions for the succession.

Edusei was a successful man of the people and the most popular of Nkrumah's ministers. Of humble origin, he possessed a peasant shrewdness, coupled with a generosity and outspokenness which won him a large following. He was readily accessible to petitioners, pressing the complaints of his countrymen in the highest circles of the government and party — for a price. Socialism — indeed, any kind of ideology — left Edusei indifferent. His ambition was to make money and to spend it. In April 1961, at the height of the campaign waged by the radicals against parliamentarians with business interests, Edusei became very exasperated. Before the Assembly he recalled his earlier career:

I was myself formerly earning £7.10s a month on the *Ashanti Pioneer*. By the help of Almighty God and the help of my constituents I am now receiving £400 a month. When I get the money, am I expected to throw it into the sea? (Some Members 'No') They tell me that... I must not build a house or buy a car, nor enjoy the fruits of my labour and live as a politician. If that is so, then Osagyefo must explain again what he means by socialism...[35]

Edusei's talent for making money out of politics was revealed at an early age. During the boycott of expatriate stores in 1949 Edusei organized his own 'courts' to fine those who failed to comply. The proceeds were divided between himself and his henchmen. When he was first elected to parliament in 1951 he estimated his total business assets at £20,000. Three years later a report on allegations of corruption sourly noted Edusei's passion for expensive radiograms received as presents from foreign businessmen anxious for government contracts.[36]

Edusei received money from various sources between 1955 and 1966. He received a present of £6,000 from the CPP after the death of his sister during the political violence in Ashanti. A visiting delegation of West German businessmen gave him £4,700 in 1956 for unspecified services. The death of his uncle brought in a further £5,000, and in 1963 he received a donation of £2,000 from the Ashanti timber producers in return for his help in getting the Timber Marketing Board dissolved. Much of this capital he invested in various trading enterprises and properties. He told the Jiagge commission after the coup 'I have no farm. My brothers are farmers, I use my money in building.'[37]

Edusei told the Jiagge commission that he owned

fourteen houses, a luxurious beach hut, and had bought a long lease on a London flat, worth in all about £130,000. In addition he owned several expensive cars, imported furniture and other effects, valued at £66,000, and had six different bank accounts, some of them overseas. Asked about the furnishings of one of his Accra houses, he said 'when one stands in front of a big mirror one can see one's face twenty times.' He added, amidst laughter, 'I invite the Commission to visit my place.'[38]

Edusei made generous gifts to his relatives and friends. He had a house built for his son, Nana Osei Yaw, and for his daughter, who was in Europe. He was equally generous to his wife, Mary Jackson, his mother and his daughter. His business entertainment was similarly on a lavish scale, although he claimed to live frugally on a native diet of fufu, kenkey and fish. Shortly before the coup at a time of desperate shortage for most people in Ghana, he booked the entire nightclub of the luxurious Ambassador Hotel in Accra for a private party of one hundred guests. This alone cost him £1,200. He expected lavish treatment in return from his business friends. The expenses of his marriage to Mary Jackson in London in 1955 were borne by a Jamaican businessman living in Britain. The bridesmaid at the wedding became one of his mistresses and was lodged for five years at his expense in the expensive Star Hotel in Accra. Edusei told the Jiagge Commission that when he travelled abroad:

...his foreign friends who were his guests in Ghana usually met him at the airports of the country he visited and they usually presented him with envelopes containing money pulled from their breast pockets. He deposited such sums of money in his overseas accounts.[39]

But, although accessible to more humble petitioners, Edusei used his powers of patronage strictly for profit. In 1963 he was approached by a cocoa farmer, Appiah Kubi, from Juaso in Ashanti who wanted to become a chief. As Kubi later remarked, 'you have to pay before a Minister will help you', so he promised to pay Edusei £2,000 for securing his enstoolment. Edusei succeeded in getting Kubi officially gazetted as a chief, but Kubi only produced £300 of the £2,000 he had promised. He offered Edusei a house in addition to make the deficiency and Edusei agreed to accept it. Eleven months later, however, Kubi's enstoolment was withdrawn by the government and Kubi tried to get his house and money back. He sent his brother to Accra to plead with Edusei, but was threatened with detention if he persisted. Kubi told the Commission that he had not succeeded in getting his house returned. 'It is still with Krobo in the name of so-called Kwadwo Owusu'. Owusu was, in fact, Edusei's elder brother who admitted holding this and other properties on Edusei's behalf.

Between 1952 and 1966 Edusei made over forty trips to Europe. Some of these trips were in the course of his official duties, others were made to improve and cultivate his business contacts in Europe whose interests in Ghana he had helped to promote. The timber producers in Ghana were mainly Ashanti, and Edusei had done them a favour in 1962 by getting the Timber Marketing Board wound up.[40] In the course of his dealings with the foreign timber merchants Edusei had discovered a way of ignoring the increasingly tight foreign exchange regulations laid down by his own cabinet. He trusted neither his colleagues nor the value of Ghana's currency and accumulated £64,000 in foreign money in overseas banks. Edusei's countryman, Osei Bonsu, who was Ghana's ambassador in Rome, later described how Edusei granted loans in Ghana's currency to enable foreign importers to cover their local expenses, and had the money refunded in foreign currency to one of his several accounts overseas.[41]

On 18 April 1962 Edusei was dismissed as Minister of Industries. A scandal had blown up when news reached Accra that his wife had purchased a gold-plated bed for £3,000 in a London store. She had bought it in the hope of curing her infertility. Edusei was greatly embarrassed, for the news could not have come at a more unpropitious time. 'I am a number one Nkrumaist', he declared, 'I believe in socialism; a golden bed is not socialism.' His opponents played up the episode for all it was worth. Much to Nkrumah's annoyance it was widely reported in the overseas press. Edusei's house in Accra was singled out as unbecoming for a minister in a socialist government. It had, reported the *Ghanaian Times* 'fountains, mosaics, swimming pool, a hall of mirrors, gardens and a tennis court'. Edusei salved his conscience by renting the house to the government for the use of official visitors. After Adamafio's downfall in September, he was back in the government as Minister of Agriculture, thoroughly unchastened by his second demotion which was even briefer than his first.[42]

After the 'golden bed' episode the government hastily pushed through a Public Property and Currupt Practices bill which provided for a maximum sentence of fifteen years with hard labour for those convicted under it. The offences defined under the new act included grave damage to public property caused by any person who entered into an 'unprofitable' business transaction on behalf of the state or a state enterprise. Offenders could be tried by the special courts set up the year before, and as a final flourish commissions of enquiry could be set up to look into the affairs of any person against whom allegations of corruption had been proved.[43]

However, leading members of the party and government displayed extraordinary powers of survival, notwithstanding Nkrumah's attempts to give his regime the appearance of probity. The new act, for all its severe penalties and its invocation of the special courts, had little effect. It held no terrors for ministers who knew or suspected the extent of Nkrumah's own transactions. Late in 1962 Nkrumah sought once more to inject a spirit of revivalism within his movement, calling for a campaign '... to eliminate corruption, wipe out nepotism and expunge rumour-mongering and character assassination from our social fabric'.[44] But no action followed to disturb deeply entrenched interests or give effect to his words. On the contrary the eclipse of Adamafio later in the year temporarily silenced the shrill demands for a purge from the radicals and militants with whom he had consorted.

But early in 1963 the radicals had recovered sufficient confidence to resume their attacks upon corruption in high places. Nkrumah had no more intention of ditching the radicals and militants because of Adamafio's sins than he had of destroying the conservatives because of Edusei's. There were, of course, a few sea-green incorruptibles within his movement — expatriate advisers with dwindling hopes of putting the CPP on the road of socialist purity, and native-born radicals more interested in power than in wealth — but some of the radicals were themselves caught up in the web of corruption, although generally on a pettier scale than some of the ministers.

The chief target of the renewed attacks was the 'conspicuous consumption' of members of parliament, who lived 'apart from the people, practise social arrogance, resort to the issuing of threats and commands, and exploit the ignorance of the masses to enrich themselves'.[45] At no time did they dare to attack the most conspicuous consumer of all, the President himself, who was the keystone of the system of which they were a part. Nkrumah's calls for rectitude merely provided them with a puny weapon to beat vainly at the magnates of the party and, with a more stinging effect, upon weaker people.[46] They were obliged to fish for small fry under the shadow of their rapacious Leviathan. Ironically it was the parliamentarians, the subjects of indiscriminate attacks by the radicals, who exerted most pressure on the leadership over the corruption issue.

The act of 1962 against corrupt practices was followed by another early in 1964 which empowered the President to set up commissions of enquiry into allegations of corruption made against public officers. A further act that year widened the scope for commissions of enquiry initiated either by the President or by a two-thirds vote of the National Assembly. But it was not clear in the latter case whether the resolution to set up a commission should come from a government motion or a private member's motion. Baako was placed in a difficult position. He had to balance the risk of independent backbench activity giving rise to a commission which might seriously embarrass the leadership against the anger of the Assembly if he tried to restrict the scope of private members' motions. In the end he advised that resolutions could come from the floor of the house 'after advice' from the government.[47] It was a concession that the backbenchers were quick to exploit in the following months.

The laws against corrupt practices, were, however,

largely useless — except for the additional powers they gave to the leadership to deal with unwelcome outsiders who might intrude on their preserves. It was impossible to keep track of every fraud. The machinery and the will simply did not exist. Some culprits close to the President took steps to safeguard themselves. Krobo Edusei was reputed to have gathered information about the activities of Nkrumah and his colleagues when he was Minister of the Interior in 1957-58 and to have lodged it abroad with instructions for its publication should he fall too far from grace. Ayeh Kumi took out a similar insurance policy. He resisted Nkrumah's campaign to force party members and ministers to disclose and liquidate their overseas assets. 'All of us were in fear and advised others to do so, but I did not sell my property for two reasons, for if I were forced to liquidate my property in London I would also make known his property in Cairo and I felt determined to do so.'[48]

The proceedings of the National Assembly became preoccupied with allegations of corruption and malpractices, some of them no doubt arising out of malice and rumour. The debates on the anti-corruption bills of 1964 took place against the background of the Akainyah report on irregularities in the issue of import licences.[49] The Akainyah commission had been set up following persistent complaints in the Assembly and its report implicated the head of the CID in the traffic. It was widely believed, however, that some top politicians had been involved in the abuses. On publication the third chapter of the report had been completely excised, but through some oversight the chapters had not been renumbered. Far from assuaging suspicions, the report merely inflamed them. When the public accounts committee reported on £100,000 missing from the Cocoa Division of the Ministry of Agriculture the police started investigations. No prosecution followed and J.D. Wireko on the backbenches pointed out that:

When the matter came before the police... probably by design, all copies of the vouchers connected with the case were removed from the records, even up to the level of the Attorney General's office in Accra in order, no doubt, to make investigation into this case impossible.[50]

Only in one instance was a former minister charged, tried, found guilty of fraud and subjected to the full force of the law. Late in 1964 Francis Yao Asare, a former regional commissioner and minister of agriculture who had drifted into the fringes of political life, was arrested together with two Accra businessmen and charged with defrauding the government by selling to it imported cocoa-spraying machines at grossly inflated prices. In May the following year Asare was sentenced to twenty-one years hard labour and his companions to twenty-five. His sentence could safely stand as an exemplary warning to others without risking any great political disturbance.

The import licence racket reported by Akainyah was an important source of enrichment for certain ministers and their friends. Stringent licensing controls were introduced in 1961 to correct Ghana's worsening balance of trade and the drain on her reserves. A perfectly conventional response to the exigencies of Ghana's economic condition became, in the hands of those responsible for administering the regulations, an operation in which the country's vital interests were subordinated to the pursuit of personal profit.

Under the arrangements the government laid down allocations for various categories of imports at the beginning of each financial year. Notices were then sent out from the Ministry of Trade to importers calling for applications for import licences to be made within the limits of these allocations. When these applications were returned the chief commercial officer and the principal secretary of the ministry processed them and then issued the licences. The entire operation began each September, at the close of the financial year, and was completed by December, so that importers received their licences for the rest of the year and could make their plans accordingly. Simple in broad outline, the efficient execution of this system made exacting demands upon an over-strained civil service which lacked any previous experience of this kind of exercise.

In fact, as things turned out, in many cases import licences were issued to the highest bidder. Traders, especially small traders desperate for licences in order to survive, sought interviews with ministers or other important men in a position to influence the allocation and issue of licences. Licences were even obtained by individuals who had not hitherto engaged in the import trade in order to secure goods which could then be re-sold at a handsome profit to established importers unable to get licences for themselves. Different patterns of patronage and different avenues of approach emerged as relatives, kinsmen and friends of ministers greased the corridors of access to the issue of licences — in return for commissions paid over to them by the hard-pressed traders. There was little hope for the traders of redressing their grievances in the courts. The former deputy Attorney-General, Dr Ekow Daniels, commented on the plight of the legitimate trader between 1963 and 1966:

He could not go to the Courts and ask for an order of *Mandamus* compelling the Minister to issue an import licence to him. Even if he succeeded in an action in

Court, some more technical reasons would be found to drive him out of business if he was a Ghanaian, or he could be deported if he were a non-Ghanaian. Woe betide such an importer who would report to the Police an allegation of bribery or corruption in high places. The only course left to such an importer was to contact someone who knew someone who also knew a Minister, or simply to bribe his way through to get the import licence.[51]

The discovery of forged amendment slips attached to some import licences in December 1962 led senior officials of the Ministry of Trade to set up a departmental committee of investigation. Three junior officials were handed over to the police for questioning and their interrogation led to the arrest of three Indian traders resident in Accra. The forgeries allowed the holders to import goods from western countries rather than from the communist trade pact states. The profit in this was simple; goods from western countries sold well, those from the trade pact states did not.

These revelations, coupled with growing unease amongst the business community over the general administration of the import licence system, led Nkrumah to appoint a commission of enquiry with Mr Justice Akainyah as sole commissioner to look into the irregularities. He was given no power to initiate prosecutions on the basis of his findings, although all evidence given before him was on oath.

Akainyah unravelled a complicated traffic in forged import licences involving thirty-three trading firms in Accra, about half of them Indian-owned, and certain junior officials in the Ministry of Trade. In part this traffic stemmed from real frustrations amongst traders at the difficulties encountered in getting even simple requests answered by the Ministry. One Italian trader complained that he had to spend three days at the Ministry simply to have the port of unloading on his licence changed from 'Takoradi' to 'Tema'. Another source of irregularity arose because relatively junior staff were given the responsibility of amending licences and making out advice slips. The temptations for some of them to make a bit of spare cash on the side from desperate traders proved too much for them. One of the Indian traders complained that:

> The officials in the Ministry are corrupt and would not give licences to genuine importers. They gave licences to their friends and non-importers. They did not treat the genuine importers fairly at all.[52]

Several Indian traders complained that in 1961 and 1962 two clerical officers of the Ministry toured their shops in Accra demanding a 'commission' for effecting amendments on import licences. Several senior officials at the Ministry were aware of this practice and suggested to the principal Secretary that a prosecution of the offenders, in addition to dismissal, would be the best way of stopping the practice.

But the most startling revelation of the Akainyah Commission was the alleged involvement of the chief of the Criminal Investigation Department, Owusu Sechere, in private dealings with the Indian merchants. One of the Indian merchants arrested in September 1963 was a Mr Vashi. He had been discovered importing plastic sandals classified as raw materials, paying only 15% duty rather than the 33% required on manufactured goods. His release on bail was secured by another Indian merchant, Mr Patel, a friend of Owusu Sechere, and known amongst the Indian community as the 'Supreme Commander of the CID'. Patel then suggested to Vashi that he went to Owusu Sechere's house and offered him a few thousand pounds to drop the case, as Owusu Sechere was alleged to have done this before in other cases. Vashi followed Patel's advice, but Owusu Sechere asked for £15,000 to stop further proceedings. Vashi could not raise the money immediately, but Owusu Sechere agreed to accept £5,000 as a down-payment.

About the same time, Anthony Deku, the deputy head of the Special Branch, had been informed that Patel's name was one of those appearing on a forged amendment slip and he began to make enquiries. Shortly afterwards Patel and Vashi arranged for the £5,000 to be collected and delivered to Owusu Sechere's house. On 3 October, as the money was being handed over, Patel, Vashi and their other associates were arrested by Special Branch men. Owusu Sechere himself was sacked as head of CID, but he was not arrested, and a short time later, was given another responsible post.[53]

The trade in import licences became so prosperous that one former MP who had never previously engaged in the import trade, opened a new company called Sando Ltd in February 1962. He was favoured with import licences from a sympathetic source in the Ministry of Trade which he resold to hard-pressed Indian importers at a price fifteen to twenty per cent above the value of the goods inscribed in the licences. The trade in import licences was becoming more profitable than the import trade itself!

But the Akainyah inquiry failed to result in any effective action by the government to rectify the abuses.[54] A few junior officials of the Ministry of Trade were prosecuted on the evidence of its findings. But, as already mentioned, the excision of the report's third chapter merely reinforced suspicions amongst the trading community and the public that even more important figures than the head of the CID were implicated in the abuses. Ironically, it was later alleged that Akainyah's own wife was herself a principal party to improper transactions in the import trade, using her influence and connections with certain members of the government to secure licences for her clients and supplicants.

The advent of Andrew Yaw Djin as Minister of Trade in October 1963 threw the already unsatisfactory and confused licensing arrangements into chaos. The efficient issue of import licences in a proper order of priority was essential if the government's development plans were to progress smoothly. But such an important and obvious point escaped the new minister. Barely literate, his reputation already damaged by his previous careers with the Cocoa Purchasing Company and as Nkrumah's special representative in the Congo, Djin shared with his ministerial colleague, Kweku Boateng, a positive distaste for giving written instructions to his subordinates. The trade Ministry's Principal Secretary, H.P. Nelson, described Djin's methods of conducting affairs:

> he hardly put anything on paper. A lot of things he told me, and even if I minuted to him he would merely say, I do not like this or that, and when I asked him to put this on paper he would not do so. So these instructions came to us verbally.[55]

One of Djin's instructions required that each item of importation must carry a pro-forma invoice. As Nelson explained:

> It meant that if you imported, say, twenty different sizes of nuts and bolts, there should be an application for each item, indicating the size and also for each price ... considering that there are hundreds of thousands of customs items, I mentioned to the Minister that this was a colossal job ... there was no machinery in the Ministry to deal with this exercise.[56]

The new requirements produced long delays in the processing of licences before issue. They also meant that importers, faced with the time consuming job of itemizing all their requirements into detailed categories, were unable to take the usual commercial opportunities afforded by arbitrage. By the time they finally received their licences, the list prices of goods under order had changed, usually to their disadvantage. They then had to apply for more foreign exchange to complete the purchase of the goods they had ordered.

Despite frequent representations to the ministry from the Ghana Chamber of Commerce over these innovations, Djin remained obdurate. Then in February 1964 he decided to cancel all the licences already issued for 1964 because they were not supported by pro-forma invoices. This revocation played havoc with the import trade. Nkrumah, who was to launch the seven-year development plan the following month, seemed entirely oblivious to the effects of this decision. Goods which had already been ordered were in some cases already on the high seas, yet the licences admitting them to Ghana were revoked. The business community was at its wits' end. Nelson made further representations to his minister, but in vain:

> I naturally pleaded with the Minister that time had been far spent and the pipeline of importers was almost at a vacuum; there was nothing coming in; that pipeline which was once full of stocks was entirely depleted and I considered it was advisable that essential commodities should at least not be cancelled.[57]

Djin gave way only to the extent of permitting the licences issued for rice, flour, sugar and tinned milk to stand. After the strong pressures brought upon him by Nelson and his Chief Commercial Officer, Djin decided that he alone would in future issue licences through his kinsman, Mr

G.C. Odoi, as from March 1964. Shortly afterwards H.P. Nelson, to his relief, was transferred to another ministry. Odoi proved unable to clear up the increasing chaos caused by the revocation and his powers of issue were shortly shuffled on to another reluctant civil servant.

The revocation of the licences was a near disastrous setback to the economy of the country. Djin had been told by the President to 'get tough' over the problem of excessive imports, and not to brook any interference from the civil servants. Nevertheless Nkrumah hardly antici- pated the consequences of Djin's actions. The possibility of rational economic planning had been thrown overboard before the seven-year plan had a chance to move into gear. Ghana's ambitious industrial and commercial development projects, as well as her existing industries, depended upon a smooth and co-ordinated flow of vitally needed imports. By late 1964 and throughout 1965 many government and private enterprises were held up or were working at under capacity largely because of the difficulties of getting spare parts and raw materials from abroad.[58]

Complaints and representations were made to Nkrumah and to his adviser on economic affairs, Ayeh Kumi, from all sections of the business community and from the state corporations about the import crisis. Even the police and the armed forces were running short of much-needed equipment. Ayeh Kumi decided to interview Djin about his policy, but Djin claimed that he had suspended the 1964 licences on the orders of the President. When Ayeh Kumi raised this with Nkrumah, the President denied it, but as Ayeh Kumi later remarked dryly, 'we had known the ex-President to deny things which he said.'[59]

To deal with the deteriorating situation, Nkrumah asked Djin, Ayeh Kumi, W.M.Q. Halm, then Governor of the Bank of Ghana and Amoaka Atta, the Minister of Finance, to form an *ad hoc* committee late in 1964, to see what could be done about the licensing mess. But the mechanics of import licensing however did not arouse the same interest as other pursuits. Ayeh Kumi found his colleagues profoundly bored with the subject:

> At a certain stage during our deliberations I found most of the members of the committee either absent or late in coming to the meetings. I had to take it on myself to collect all such data as I could and work on it alone with the help of Mr Odoi of the Ministry of Trade.[60]

During his investigations Ayeh Kumi made several alarming discoveries. Firstly, the whole of the country's import allocation for 1964 of £80 million had been already exceeded; indeed, it had all been issued within the first quarter. Secondly, the procedures laid down for regulating the application and issue of licences had been over-ridden or ignored in many cases. Licences had been issued for certain classes of imports in spite of specific instructions to the contrary. Small, obscure companies had been given unaccountably large licences, while large, well-established companies with a good credit standing overseas were under-issued. It began to appear as if Djin had been using his control over import licences as a personal empire, a source of profit for himself, his friends and benefactors.

Djin had indeed established his own company, Ghana Trading Enterprises, in 1960. It consisted of two employees, one of whom was his son, Osei Yaw Djin, and its premises consisted of a single room measuring seventeen feet by twelve. In 1962, before Djin became Minister of Trade his company had applied for £100,000 worth of import licence and was granted £35,000. After becoming Minister of Trade Djin put the business under the nominal control of his son, but continued to direct its affairs. Thereafter the company was granted ever larger licence quotas. In 1964 it applied for £500,000 worth and received £722,261.[61]

Djin was well-known for his dislike of white faces and his particular detestation of Lebanese traders. If they failed to get their licences through the proper channels and complained to the police of extortion they were liable to summary deportation. One Lebanese company, that of Omar Captan, had been trading in Ghana since 1935. When the import licensing system was first introduced, Captan was granted a licence for £500,000 worth of imports. In October 1964 it applied for upgrading and was granted a licence worth £2.5 million. On this basis Captan travelled to Europe and Japan to arrange for the supply of imports on the long-term credit basis favoured by the government. On his return to Ghana, he discovered that his company has been downgraded and his licence cut to £65,000. Captan sought an interview with Djin and explained how damaging the cut was to the economy as well as to his company, but:

> Djin told him he did not care, and that he had the power to upgrade and downgrade just as he liked, and had downgraded him, and was not prepared to do anything about it.[62]

On the other hand Djin manipulated the issue of licences to suit the interest of his friends. A medical consultant on friendly terms with Nkrumah, had a grievance against the French trading company which had supplied a cold storage plant for his wife's fishery company. Because the wrong oil had been put into the machinery, the plant broke down. The consultant saw the manager and threatened to cut the company's licence unless it provided a new plant free of charge. It refused to do so, on the grounds that the maintenance of the plant was the responsibility of the owner. In October 1964 the company put in an application for licences for £1.3 million worth of imports. Its application was refused. The Ghanaian branch manager of the company remarked that:

> We were forced to lay off hands, but we feared we would be branded as saboteurs of this country because we had no alternative but to reduce the staff.[63]

However, Djin was at the end of his career at the Ministry of Trade. He had survived for so long, despite his incompetence, because he was one of Nkrumah's trusties drawn from the group of Nzimas and Fantis who knew too much of their master's financial affairs to be summarily disposed of. But Nkrumah could no longer ignore the popular unrest caused by the growing shortages of goods and pressures from his civil servants upon him to get rid of Djin. The radicals òf the party, eager for a scapegoat for the growing unpopularity of the party, were also after Djin. On 13 April the *Evening News* announced that:

> Comrade Djin, we are fed up... we wish to draw attention to the delay in the granting of import licences for certain capital goods and other vital commodities... We do not think that a Minister worth his salt should have to wait for the Head of State himself to push him on to the discharge of his vital responsibilities and not only show him every time the order of priorities, but also press him on to action on the interests of the people. Mr Djin, with all the best intentions, has definitely become a spoke in the wheels of the equitable provision and distribution of the goods to the people ... the time has come for him to come forward and tell the Nation's Fount of Honour, 'I have failed'.

The following day Nkrumah removed Djin from the Ministry of Trade. Even then, Nkrumah did not dispense with his services entirely. He made him Minister of Animal Husbandry where he hoped the grazing would be too thin to sustain Djin's appetites.[64]

The Ministry of Trade was then split up into two separate ministries dealing respectively with internal and external trade, and yet another committee of top civil servants consisting of Enoch Okoh, J.V.L. Phillips and H.P. Nelson was formed to undertake the almost impossible task of sorting out the import trade tangle and putting the licensing system on some kind of rational footing. Even this committee showed some of the defects of its predecessor and Nkrumah decided he needed a new man for the job. On 1 July he recalled Kwesi Armah from his post as High Commissioner in London and installed him as Minister of External Trade. Mr. Justice Akainyah, who had led the earlier enquiry into import licence malpractices, claimed a family relationship with the new minister. 'Auntie Victoria', as Akainyah's wife was known to her intimates, had also had considerable influence with Andrew Yaw Djin. The later Commission of Enquiry concluded that:

... the house of Mrs Akainyah was a clearing house for illegal transaction, bribery and corruption in connection with import licences.[65]

Another minister's wife, Mrs Inkumsah, the spouse of the Deputy Speaker and former Minister of the Interior,[66] also allegedly engaged in the trade of licences. She was also a businesswoman in her own right, owning dress and shoe shops in Accra. She was alleged to have secured licences for the African and Lebanese Trading Company and the Animo Trading Company. Of the latter company, the Ollennu Commission remarked that it was:

> ... a fictitious business ... promoted with the purpose of trafficking in import licences.[67]

Her husband had dealings with another reputable expatriate concern, a trading company and garment factory, which employed a large Ghanaian labour force. The manager of this company gave evidence of the assistance he received from Inkumsah. His company had been downgraded severely for import licensing purposes between 1963 and 1965. He had petitioned the minister, but received no reply. Inkumsah, however, offered to mediate with the minister. The manager applied for import licences to cover goods to the value of £100,000, but this was increased to £250,000. The manager thought that he was expected to pay over a "commission" proportionate to the increased value of the licences. He remarked that:

> ...if you can exist without indulging in these things you would like to refrain from it completely, but when it was apparent that our company ... had been downgraded, there was nothing to do but to go into it in order to exist, so we had to go into it.[68]

The cumulative effect of these artificial and capricious interferences with Ghana's external trade was to disrupt severely any possibility of rational economic development as envisaged by the government's own plans. Private enterprise — of a legitimate kind — and the state enterprises were equally hurt. The number of trading and industrial concerns registered in Ghana fell steadily each year between 1959 and 1966, while in the private sector the total labour force declined. The excesses of the import licensing racket, like the activities of the government in other spheres, weighed most heavily upon those least able to support them.

The story of corruption and mismanagement amongst those in charge of Ghana's destiny in these years is a long and monotonous one of which only a small part has been outlined.[69] The client-patron relationship had become a fundamental element in politics. Few sectors of the national life were free from the disease. Not all those busily engaged in the spoils system were politicians, although it was necessary for them to keep in good standing with the ruling party. Not all politicians were corrupt, or corrupt to the same degree. When the last finance minister, Kwasi Amoaka Atta, promised early in 1965 to issue minutes to the National Assembly explaining the action he was determined to take on the findings of the public accounts committee, Iddrissu's delighted exclamation, 'First in history: an honest minister!' indicated how low in esteem, even amongst their fellows, the politicians had fallen.[70]

Sometimes the thin line between the straightforward abuse of a political monopoly and the exploitation of administrative confusion became blurred. The number of laws and regulations promulgated increased far beyond the effective means of enforcing them. If you could afford it, bribery was a means of cutting through red tape. Official rules and statutory procedures were often ignored or overridden through ignorance or carelessness as much as through malice. The import licensing arrangements, for instance, would have taxed a more sophisticated administration than Ghana possessed. Honest and capable administration became increasingly difficult in the burgeoning paraphernalia of state control manned by political bosses singularly deficient in either quality. In the hidden interstices of the system a host of obscure placemen and parasites found a profitable living.

So long as Ghana's wealth could sustain the ruling party the CPP could always purchase the support of a considerable section of the community. In important respects the activities of Nkrumah and his lieutenants were aided and abetted by large numbers of their countrymen who actually favoured conspicuous consumption by their chiefs. Edusei's robust enjoyment of his wealth was vicariously enjoyed by his poor followers. It was after all a style they would have chosen for themselves had fortune so favoured them. In a poor country the temptation to join rather than oppose such an open-handed system was immensely strong. Critics of the waste and venality of the system certainly existed, but either as exponents of an alien, puritan socialism or as upholders of the old-fashioned colonial virtues, they were isolated from the majority.

In the long run it was not the improprieties of the system which led to the erosion of its popular support. If economic progress could have been achieved, the widespread corruption might have been tolerable — perhaps even regarded as a necessary price of that progress. But a disease merely vexatious in an increasingly prosperous community may become fatal in a poor and contracting one. By the early sixties Ghana had been brought to that condition. The money had run out. The profligacy of the political system could only be maintained at the people's expense, and this above all was to lead to their estrangement.

VII Workers and Farmers

Fifteen years of continuous rule by the CPP had failed to bring prosperity to Ghana's population. The party's 'Work and Happiness' programme of 1962 declared its intention of securing a cheap supply of food to enable workers to feed themselves and their families at a cost of two shillings a day, one third of the statutory minimum wage. This benevolent intention, far from being achieved, became less realizable as time went on.

The proportion of the working population engaged in trade, industry and services was small compared with the total employed in the countryside. The number of non-agricultural workers rose from 320,000 in 1959 to 392,000 in 1965,[1] an increase which hardly kept pace with the rise in population and the drift to the towns. As in other tropical countries young men were leaving the farms for the bright lights of the towns where the prospect of permanent employment were bleak.

Nevertheless, the settled urban workers in the early years of the independence movement possessed through their trade unions a political influence greater than their numbers. The relationship between the trade unions and the CPP before independence had sometimes been a difficult one, with the party seeking to extend its influence over the unions and the unions anxious to retain some degree of autonomy. By 1958, however, Nkrumah decided that the time had come to bring the trade unions fully under his party's control.

His instrument was the Industrial Relations act, largely drawn up according to the proposals of John Tettegah and

and given a final legal polish by the Attorney General, Bing. In effect the act made the legal existence of the trade unions dependent upon official recognition by the Minister of Labour who was empowered to grant or withdraw recognition at any time, without right of appeal. The right of a licensed union to call a strike was also made dependent upon the approval of the minister. In cases of dispute the act provided a conciliation procedure which the unions were obliged to follow. Only in the event of a total failure of the procedure to secure an agreement could the withdrawal of labour be envisaged, but this too rested on the final decision of the minister. In fact, during the entire history of the act, no strike was ever officially sanctioned. The right to strike had effectively been abolished.[2]

The act also made provisions designed to stop factional quarrelling within the trade union movement. The executive council of the TUC was given control over the internal affairs and finances of the unions, and the total number of unions was reduced by compulsory amalgamations. In 1957 there were about ninety-seven unions, many with a small membership and weak organization, with about 165,000 members. The Industrial Relations act cut down the number of certified — and therefore legal — unions to twenty-four and in 1960 to sixteen. Total membership, however, increased to 159,000 and in March 1960 the official TUC newspaper claimed over 350,000 workers in unions affiliated to the TUC.[3]

The majority of the trade union leaders and officials welcomed the provision of the new act. They were becoming part of the political establishments, which gave them personal security and enhancement of status after years of indiscipline and factional disputes. The recognized unions were given a permanent secretariat, paid for out of the £300,000 a year income yielded by the compulsory two shillings a month levy which the TUC was empowered to collect from all wage earners. The TUC itself was given a handsome modern building in Accra close to party headquarters and its newspaper received a subsidy from party funds.

In exchange for these perquisites, however, the trade unions and their Congress had become an 'integral wing' of the ruling party. Officials became increasingly the nominees of the party leadership. Branch meetings decayed into adulatory sessions in praise of Osagyefo and his policies, or ceased to take place at all. In the dawn broadcast in April 1961 the President announced that the party and unions were to be brought into an even closer relationship. Separate union cards were to be abolished and replaced by party cards, and in the regions the unions' local offices were to be housed in the same buildings as the regional offices of the party. Thus the trade union movement capitulated to the CPP without a struggle. Vestiges of opposition to the take-over survived in the industrial Sekondi-Takoradi area where an attempt was made early in 1959 to form a new union outside the TUC. But this was easily dealt with by an amendment to the principal act, compelling a union to join the TUC within twenty-four hours or be dissolved by order of the minister.

Whilst the settled town workers and their unions were brought easily under the control of the party, the large numbers of unemployed and casual workers presented another problem. Many of these were immigrants from neighbouring states attracted by the magnet of Ghana's prosperous years. The 1960 census showed that seventeen per cent of Ghana's male labour force came from outside the country.[4] During the Ashanti troubles of the mid-fifties the Ga Shifimo Kpee took advantage of the government's distraction to engage in sporadic violence against CPP supporters in Accra. With growing numbers of rootless young men in the capital and the major towns, rival quasi-political gangs of youths became a dangerous source of unrest and turbulence, especially when it became clear that independence was not going to bring about a golden age of prosperity overnight. Even those unemployed not attracted to violence were becoming a serious embarrassment and a nuisance to political leaders, seeking them out in their offices and outside their homes to petition for jobs and money.

It was to mop up this element that the idea of the Workers Brigade was conceived. It was partly inspired by Israeli advisers to the government who saw an opportunity of using the surplus town workers to help overcome rural underdevelopment, and partly by American policy towards the unemployed during the New Deal. Advice on the setting-up of the Brigade was freely given by the Israelis, notwithstanding Ghana's adherence to the anti-Israeli stance taken by the Arab-African countries at the heads of state conference in 1958.

The Workers Brigade was established under its original title of the 'Builders Brigade' by a bitterly contested act of parliament in December 1957. The objects of the Brigade, as defined in the white paper which outlined the bill, were 'to provide a useful occupation for the unemployed who are unable to secure either a formal apprenticeship or steady employment; to afford the youth of the country an opportunity to give patriotic service in the development of the country, and to assist in the execution of development projects, especially in rural areas'. Enlistment was voluntary, although the unemployed who refused work might be directed to join. Contracts from the Ministry of Local Government and other public agencies were intended to supply the Brigade with work. Base camps were set up in each of Ghana's administrative regions where inductees spent a few months in training before being sent out to work in the Brigade's field camps and farms. In theory the

Brigade was supposed to become financially self-supporting, with its own workshops to service its transport, garment factories to produce uniforms and an agricultural wing to grow food for the brigadiers.

Control and management of the Brigade — which was intended to be another 'integral wing' of the party — was exercised by a National Organizer and a board drawn from the TUC, ex-servicemen's associations and two members appointed by the Minister having overall responsibility for the Brigade. The Minister of Labour and Co-operatives, Nathaniel Welbeck, was given the job of supervising the Brigade in its initial stages. The first National Organizer was an Englishman, Brig. A.J.D. Turner, who had been an officer in the West African Frontier Force. He was assisted by American and Israeli advisers from March 1958 until his untimely death in October 1959.

The Brigade appeared to be the beginning of a promising experiment, dealing in an enlightened way with the very real problem of urban unemployment. Over 14,000 applications to join had been received, and the construction of twenty-eight camps commenced throughout the country, even before the act establishing the Brigade had been passed. But despite this auspicious start the Brigade quickly became infected by the usual diseases of the body politic. After the death of Brigadier Turner in 1959, John Tettegah was called in to be the new National Organizer. His interests, however, remained with the trade unions and he stayed only until April 1960, when a failed farmer, Jones K. Ababio, took over. Ababio remained National Organizer until his abrupt removal in August 1963. Responsibility for the Brigade was shunted from one Ministry to another during its first few years, until it finally came to rest, like so many other things, under the control of the President's office at Flagstaff House. At first under the Ministry of Labour and Co-operatives, the Brigade passed in quick succession to the Ministries of Agriculture, Transport, back to Labour and Social Welfare and then to Defence. These frequent changes from the charge of one ministry to another reflected the fact that the Brigade had become an encumbrance to whoever was supposed to be in charge of it.

In October 1959 the Ministry of Agriculture, then tenanted by Krobo Edusei, held sway over the Brigade. Edusei abolished the board of control which had been set up under the act to assist the National Organizer on the grounds that it would dilute the party's control over the Brigade. This action, which was not sanctioned either by the cabinet or the National Assembly, threw the Brigade's finances and administration into a state of chaos. It was soon apparent that the initial sum of £750,000 earmarked by the government to establish the Brigade was not enough. By 1961-62 the Brigade needed a supplementary vote of over £2 million merely to keep it afloat. After that record amount some attempt at economies were made, but spending on the Brigade never fell below £1.25 million in any subsequent financial year.[5] This state of affairs caused Kojo Botsio to refer to the Brigade as 'a public drain into which public money was poured without any visible results'. Far from becoming self-supporting, the Brigade made a heavy and increasing loss on its operations from the time of its inception until the coup of 1966. Although contracts worth £15 million were awarded to the Brigade by the government over this period, it made only a meagre and totally inadequate return from its operations.[6]

The formation of the Brigade aroused opposition from the beginning. Members of parliament, of the CPP as well as of other parties, feared at first that it might be turned into a para-military wing of the ruling party. Later criticisms fastened upon the evidence of maladministration within the Brigade, its costliness and its recruiting policy. Continuing pressures forced Welbeck to set up a departmental committee headed by a civil servant to look into the question of appointments and promotions within the Brigade. The results were never published, but excerpts were later made available by a commission of enquiry after the coup. The departmental committee commented adversely on the low level of morale within the Brigade and identified one major cause stemming from the practice whereby:

> ... individuals are sent to the National Organizer or other officials by highly placed persons, sometimes in no position of authority in respect of the Brigade, with a request that they be employed, often in specific posts, in the Brigade. Furthermore, the knowledge they have of their being employed by, and under the protection of a person in authority, often makes them insubordinate and difficult to work with. This has resulted in excessive numbers of staff and some staff insufficiently qualified for the posts that they hold, or even with criminal convictions, and has caused dissatisfaction among Brigade staff and lack of team spirit.[7]

In effect the Workers' Brigade had become a dumping ground for many of those who had provided the party in the past with mass support at its rallies and demonstrations, but whose continued importunities had become a source of embarrassment and a nuisance to ministers. The Brigade enlarged the empire of patronage available to ministers and politicians, conveniently enabling them to reward their supporters for past favours and to get rid of them at the same time. Not unnaturally, one consequence of this use of the Brigade was that many who enlisted and rose within its ranks regarded the official aims of the Brigade with cynicism and indifference. Some of them, as opponents of the Brigade were quick to point out, had past records of forgery, bribery and embezzlement.

The Kom Commission, in its majority report, found that:

> During the course of our enquiry it became clear that the whole organization was converted and used as an influential wing of the disbanded Convention Peoples Party and politicians and their friends recruited all and sundry into the organization without any regard at all to what the inductees could do or be trained to do ... the number of officers in the Brigade who before their induction had been convicted for offences involving fraud and dishonesty and who hold important positions in the Brigade is far more than one would expect, particularly when it is considered that those concerned are in a position to influence large numbers of Brigadiers.[8]

Deep resentment was generated in country areas by the manner in which the Brigade acquired farmland for its agricultural activities. Like the State Farms Corporation, the Brigade used a mixture of threats and bribery to make local chiefs grant stool lands for the Brigade's use, without regard for the interests of the farmers already in possession. One such case concerned the paramount chief of New Juaben, Nana Kwaku Boateng II, who granted a few hundred acres of stool land near Koforidua for the establishment of a Brigade camp. The families already on this land were moved out and their crops destroyed without compensation. Traditional law in Ghana relating to the ownership and use of stool land is extremely complex, and the legality or otherwise of the chief's action could not easily be established. The families, however, brought an action in the High Court against their chief. Their case was dismissed on the grounds that the Administration of Lands act of 1962 gave the President power to settle by direct intervention any dispute involving stool land. The Court's view was that the plaintiffs would be wasting their time, and the Court's, by pressing their case.[9]

Many other instances occurred in which the Brigade and local chiefs came to satisfactory mutual arrangements over the heads of farmers and in defiance of customary usage. The New Juaben affair, however, revealed other interesting and by no means untypical aspects of the Brigade's activities. In return for his co-operation Nana Kwaku Boateng was made a 'welfare officer' to the Brigade at an annual salary of £300 per year. There is no evidence that he attended personally to his duties. This was left to his three wives whom he insisted should also be placed on the Brigade's payroll. They were required 'not to work, but to stay in the Omanhene's palace and render service to the Brigade officials who visit the palace.'[10]

The agricultural activities of the Brigade, apart from exciting local resentments, did not add anything worthwhile to the country's overall agricultural effort. Returns on the capital invested in their farms were very low, and the quality of their management was poor. Rumours flourished and multiplied about over-manning, clock-watching and misuse of expensive imported equipment. In September 1965, hard on the heels of the dramatic debate on the dawn broadcast, a northern back-bencher tabled a motion calling for every encouragement to be given to the Brigade to achieve maximum production. P.C. Atuahene, the member for Bandu, spoke during the debate which followed as a former Brigadier from the Somanya farm. He complained of over-manning:

In the 1960's there was a slogan by which members of the Brigade worked at Somanya, and that slogan was 'one man, one acre' .... But what do we find now in the Brigade? That slogan can be described as 'one hundred men, one acre.[11]

There was not much hope for an improvement in the Brigade's affairs from those placed in charge of it. Atuahene spoke of the scorn and derision aroused in the countryside by the airs the leaders of the Brigade were accustomed to give themselves on their occasional excursions outside headquarters to inspect their farms:

> Is it not astonishing? We have one leader in Ghana, and that is Osagyefo. When Osagyefo goes to a place, he can be carried in a palanquin accompanied by a retinue carrying a state sword and an umbrella. That is understandable. But how can a National Organizer go to Tafo and be carried in a palanquin accompanied by people carrying state swords and umbrellas? Is he a chief? (Uproar).[12]

Jones Ababio, during his term as National Organizer, managed to tighten up discipline within the Brigade to a limited extent by dismissing several officers and many brigadiers, but he made enemies by doing so and rumours began to circulate about certain activities of the National Organizer himself early in 1963. Kofi Baako, then Minister of Defence and at that time responsible for the Brigade, appointed another departmental committee to enquire into these rumours. The committee, chaired by Colonel Ewah of the Ghana army, set out to discover whether Ababio had given his sister, a trader, the monopoly of supplying cassava to the Brigade's kitchens; a trade with an annual turnover worth £17,000. As with the earlier committee, the results of the Ewah committee were not made public, but Ababio was relieved of his duties in August 1963.[13]

Apart from the complaints of corruption, tribal favouritism and mismanagement within the Workers' Brigade, deep suspicions about its ultimate purposes continued to exist. The government's original white paper presented it as an instrument to alleviate urban unemployment and rural under-development. This aim made sense to many, but the quasi-military organization and titles of the Brigade did not. When the establishment of the State Farms Corporation was announced in 1962, it appeared to be in direct competition with the agricultural activities of the Brigade. A back-bencher CPP member, M.O. Kwatia, the member for Koforidua, asked:

> Why is the government establishing state farms? This is an indication that the Workers Brigade has failed to produce food for the people of this country.... Is the Brigade a military organization? An organization for constitutional purposes? A police organization? Or simply an organization? What purpose is it for? We must be very serious about this matter for the country's money is going ... down the drain.[14]

The government had, in fact, drawn up plans for turning the Brigade into a 'people's militia' on Chinese lines — a para-military wing of the party. These plans, however, remained in abeyance for some years. After the fall of Adamafio Nkrumah began to share the doubts of some of his followers about the risks of creating an armed wing which might fall under the control of a faction within the party. The idea met with fierce resistance from regular officers of the armed forces who disliked the prospect of a political army outside their control. Senior civil servants also warned against pouring yet more money into an organization already under fire for its inefficiency and mismanagement.

But the arming of the Brigade remained an option which Nkrumah wished to keep open. Bringing the Brigade under the control of the Minister of Defence was a preliminary step to taking this option.

In May 1964 the ministerial secretary to the Ministry of Defence, K.O. Thompson, announced that within the Brigade:

It was proposed to introduce a para-military training for all personnel below the age of forty. This will involve weapons training, elementary tactics and battle-craft. Eventually a volunteer unit of the Ghana armed forces will be established within the Brigade.[15]

Thompson also revealed that the first steps towards military training had actually been taken the previous November. But Nkrumah's security advisers, including the East Europeans whose influence was in the ascendant within Flagstaff House, were not impressed with the overall quality of the brigadiers. Unskilled and illiterate 'verandah boys' were not good soldiering material, hardly worth the expense of arming and training. Much more effective for internal security duties, from the advisers' point of view, was the investment in the growing Presidential Guard unit recruited from amongst the regular armed forces.

From 1962 onwards, while the affairs of the Brigade were administered jointly by Flagstaff House and the Ministry of Defence, real power over the Brigade fell increasingly into the hands of Ambrose Yankey senior, the President's personal security officer. Yankey used the Brigade to provide men for security duties and as cheer-leaders to embellish official celebrations. One such event took place less than a fortnight before the coup, early in 1966. When Nkrumah requested a parade to mark the fifteenth anniversary of his release from prison, the Brigade was ordered to assemble 'not less than 5,000 Brigadiers' from all parts of the country in Black Star Square. This undertaking — code named 'Operation Rainbow' — cost the Brigade over £30,000 for transport, food, accommodation and new khaki uniforms out of its already precarious financial resources. What had started out eight years earlier as a promising experiment to deal with the pressing problems of unemployment and under-development in a poor country was, by the end of the first Republic, reduced to an inefficient, chaotic, and, ultimately, purposeless part of the political kingdom.[16]

The negative achievements of Nkrumah's rule on behalf of the town workers produced seething discontent by 1965. But the persistent failure of his policies in the countryside was perhaps more fatal in the long run to his administration. The small farmer is the backbone of Ghana's economy. He and his dependants form by far the largest segment of Ghana's population.[17] In broad outline, there are two major, distinct zones of agricultural activity. North of a line running east-west about fifty miles north of Kumasi is the zone of open tropical woodland, of shifting agriculture and stock-raising. The rainfall of this northern zone is between fifteen and forty inches a year, and its amount and reliability is the principal factor influencing the distribution and nature of agricultural activity. South of this savana area lies the forest zone, ranging from open woodland on its northern margins to dense, tropical rain forest around the coastal town of Axim, in the south western corner of the country. It is in this forested region that the country's cocoa and hardwood timbers are produced, together with the bulk of its domestic foodcrops. In both zones traditional rules and customs relating to the possession, tenure and usage of land are extremely complicated and local in character.[18] Ultimate ownership of farming land, notwithstanding the impact of colonial rule, tends to be vested not in individual farmers but in the 'stool' or 'skin', the sacramental objects which symbolize and embody the identity of local communities.

About forty per cent of the three million acres farmed in Ghana is based upon shifting cultivation.[19] Unused or fallow land is cleared by burning and the cutlass and crops are grown on it until its fertility begins to decline. Cultivation then shifts to a new patch and the old one is allowed to revert to weeds and grasses to recover its fertility. This system obviously requires a large supply of land relative to population and is more commonly found in the savana lands of the north than in the forested south. A typical farm in the forested area consists of scattered plots or strips around a nucleated village. The average size of a farmer's holding of such strips or plots is about six acres, although in the Ashanti region it rises to about eight.[20] By western standards traditional agriculture appears wasteful. Yields per acre are low, as is output per man. The possibility of permanent improvement of the land, by drainage or enclosure, is limited and the small size of the plots precludes the extensive use of machinery. The size of the farmer's crop depends primarily upon his own, his wives' and his children's labour, although some are able to employ migrant labour.[21] Yet the traditional systems represent a fine adjustment between the labour of men and the survival of their societies on the one hand, and on the other, the difficulties and opportunities of nature. The tropical environment is a harsh one and the traditional ways of coping with it are backed by the powerful argument of survival.

In most West African societies land is much more than the factor of production which it has become in the western world. Land possesses a mystical significance which is indissolubly linked with the identity of the local community. It is the repository of the community's ancestors and gods and the guarantee of its continued existence. But the strongly conservative attitude of farmers and local people to land has never proved an obstacle to the exploitation of land for profit. The history of cocoa farming in Ghana reveals how a conservative peasantry may rise to the opportunity of making money with the alacrity of any capitalist, modifying their traditional institutions and customs whenever necessary, but without sacrificing their basic communal identity.

Cocoa was first introduced into the Gold Coast towards the end of the last century, but it was only after the first world war that the territory's export trade really got under way. Although the colonial government provided an infrastructure of roads and works necessary for the development of the trade and set up a cocoa research institute to seek ways of fighting crop disease, it left the actual cultivation of cocoa in the hands of the farmers and migrant labourers. Commercial banks arrived to supply the farmers with credit and agencies of the importing companies were established to deal with the purchase, grading and shipment of the crop.[22]

But the principal achievement was that of the farmers themselves. As the authors of the seven-year development plan acknowledged, 'the small scale farmer with his hoe and cutlass has virtually created Ghana as she is today.'[23]

The country's total income from cocoa sales abroad between 1951 and 1961 was £700 million of which the farmers received £420 million for their labours. The difference lay in the hands of the cocoa marketing board set up shortly after the second world war. Independence did not alter this arrangement. It gave the CPP government easy access to the already socialized savings of the country's producer class. As one writer pointed out before independence, the funds:

... present a great opportunity to politicians to entrench their position, extend their control and increase their power. It is not unlikely that African political parties gaining power will use the machinery and funds ... to further the general political aims of the parties, and that they will neither abolish the system nor greatly moderate the boards' policies.[24]

The crucial question was whether the cocoa funds would be used for their intended purpose of cushioning the farmers against hard times, or whether the CPP would annex them for its own purposes. In the event the latter happened. The marketing board's funds were raided by government and party to subsidize development plans and ailing public boards. By 1965 even the pretence of using the funds exclusively for 'development' was dropped when the board's managing director was ordered to pay £100,000 every quarter directly into the coffers of the party.

After independence the CPP was determined, as with the trade unions, to bring the farmers and their co-operatives under the control of the party as an 'integral wing'. The United Ghana Farmers' Council was its chosen instrument — the rural counterpart of the Trade Union Congress. Like the Congress, the Council was provided with a new, modern building in Accra and given a subsidy of £100,000 a year from the marketing board funds. Moreover the Council was to take over from the licensed purchasing agents of the overseas companies the loan arrangements for cocoa farmers. The companies were not opposed to these changes which could have no effect upon the world price of cocoa. Indeed, they would be freed from the expense of maintaining buying agents in the countryside. In theory, the companies admitted, the Council's monopoly might lead to desirable economies of scale in the handling of the crop. As a representative of Cadburys observed:

When a monopoly buying organization is fully efficient there is no reason why it should not be the correct medium for this particular purpose. The question arises as to whether a monopoly organization can be maintained as a fully efficient organization.[25]

Whatever the companies thought, however, the farmers were dismayed. Memories of the party's earlier and unsuccessful attempt to politicize the farmers through the Cocoa Purchasing Company were still green and they were sceptical of the ability of a party-run Council to do honest business.[26]

In November 1960 the Ghana Co-operative Bank which had hitherto been central to the cocoa farmers' loan arrangements was suddenly forced into liquidation and its assets and share capital taken over by the state-owned Ghana Commercial Bank. 'Overnight the thrift and credit habits which had been inculcated in farmers over the years were given their rudest shock imaginable.'[27] The government's proposal that the Farmers Council should take over the existing farmers' co-operatives, some of which had existed since the nineteen twenties and now numbered several hundred, came as an additional blow. It was followed by an announcement that the Farmers Council would also supervise the distribution of cutlasses and gammalin, two essential tools of the cocoa farmers. The farmers' apprehensions were shared by a former minister of co-operatives, Robert Amoaka Atta, shortly to become regional commissioner for Ashanti.[28] Amoaka Atta pointed out that some of the independent co-operatives had existed for thirty-three years without any complaints from the farmers. The Council, on the other hand, was frequently a target for criticism. It had received a loan of £500,000 in October 1959 from the Cocoa Marketing Board, but by 1961 there had been no sign of any repayments. Amoaka Atta revealed that he had earlier arranged a meeting between himself, the Minister of Agriculture, the banks and the Council, to discuss ways of improving the running of the Farmers Council; but the Council executive refused to attend, so nothing had been done. He observed that many local branches of the Council were 'one-man shows', with a single person acting as agent, president and treasurer, drawing all three salaries. The representatives of the independent co-operatives should be allowed to meet the President and put their point of view 'even though' he said 'Osagyefo may refuse their proposals in the interests of politics'.[29]

But it was too late. Nkrumah had already announced in his dawn broadcast in April that the new arrangements would come into operation during the following month. The Council — retitled the United Ghana Farmers Council of Co-operatives — would undertake the work of purchasing, grading, storage and transport of the cocoa crop from the point of sale from the farmers to the dockside. Under arrangements which were speciously hailed as an advance over those already existing in the cocoa industry, the farmers were finally delivered over to the party.

Whatever theoretical or economic justifications the government's new arrangements possessed, the real test of their efficacy would be found at the human level. If the Council officials had been honest, competent and incorruptible, if the organization had allowed the farmers' voices to be heard at all levels, then the arrangements might have worked to everyone's advantage. But it was not to be. The fears that the Council would simply be the discredited CPC up to its old tricks but armed with greater powers, turned out to be only too well-founded.

In February 1961 Charles Donkoh, the member for the cocoa growing constituency of Wenchi, expressed these fears. Donkoh, who was a cousin of Dr Busia, the exiled opposition leader, was nevertheless a CPP member. But he consistently displayed a tough horse-sense when commenting on the government's policies in the country-side. He remarked that:

> The one thing which is worrying the farmers now in this country is the tendency towards monopoly. That sort of monopoly is not good for a socialist country like ours. Many young men in the co-operatives have been going round telling the farmers that they will take the whole business into their hands.

Donkoh claimed that the UGFCC officials were unlikely to gain the trust of the farmers as the commercial purchasing agents had done. Already Council officials had:

> ... begun to spit at those people who have been buying cocoa for so long a period in conjunction with the commercial houses. These people have not done badly; on the contrary, they have done something for this country.... They have helped the farmers ... and they should be encouraged to continue. The farmers are grumbling and crying. When I went home last they were saying 'We sent you at long last to parliament. We have voted for the CPP but we are being exploited by those who call themselves supporters of the CPP.'[30]

Donkoh was by no means the only CPP member of parliament made unhappy by the proposed changes. Daniel Asafo-Agyei, the member for a Kumasi constituency, pleaded in vain for the government to pay careful attention to the representations made by the farmers' co-operatives associations. Christopher Takyi, the CPP member for Techiman, complained of the treatment farmers had received at the hands of the Farmers Council:

> Farmers sell cocoa to them and wait weeks or even months before being paid for it. We do not want to be

embarrassed by the statement that the Ghana Farmers Council will be the sole buying agency in the country. [31]

Another CPP back-bencher, Yeboah Afari, who had been Minister of Agriculture in 1956 the year when the Jibowu Report appeared, was sceptical about the proposed change:

We are too fond of destroying old institutions and setting up new ones. We did that with the Cocoa Purchasing Company and brought untold hardship upon the innocent as well as those who committed the offences leading to the destruction of that establishment. [32]

The farmers' co-operatives, however, did not submit to the take-over without a struggle. The previous year in 1960, the co-operatives within the Ashanti and Brong Ahafo regions had broken away from the state-sponsored Ghana Co-operative Marketing Association, in protest against the government's proposals, and had formed the Ashanti, Brong-Ahafo and Sefwi Co-operative Association. This short-lived coalition petitioned the government in June 1961 against giving the Farmers Council a buying monopoly. The government's only reply to its representations was to direct the Council to take over all the assets and liabilities of all the five hundred or so marketing associations and co-operatives in the country. These were estimated at the time of the take-over to be about £2 million and the value of their annual turnover about £10 million. The assets of the independent co-operatives were never paid for; nor were their liabilities properly assumed by the Council.[33] Thus with one stroke the government ended a tradition of independent self-help within the countryside which stretched back over forty years.

Henceforth the dictum that 'the party is supreme' was to be upheld by its puppet, the UGFCC, throughout the farming community.

The possible advantages which might have accrued to the farmers from the concentration of purchasing, storage and transport of cocoa in the hands of the Council were more than offset by the malpractices which began quickly to emerge in its dealings with the farmers. On a broad scale the Council was fairly successful with handling the bulk operations of an increasing volume of cocoa, getting it from the farms to the ports expeditiously. It even managed to make a modest profit, although this was dissipated amongst other chronically ailing state enterprises also engaged in agricultural activities. But this achievement was bought at the cost of a further enormous loss of confidence amongst the farmers in the government's policies towards them.

There was no means of redress for their numerous grievances, and complaints at their treatment at the hands of the Council's officials went unheeded. A few back-bench members of parliament continued to vent publicly the feelings of their rural constituents. But the days had long passed when the government might have felt obliged to listen seriously to the representations of its own back-benchers. In theory all offices of the Farmers Council were elective; in practice it was dominated by Martin Appiah Danquah and his lieutenants, who decided policy and filled the posts of the Council with their nominees.

Although the manager of the cocoa marketing board remarked, quite rightly, that one did not have to have university degrees to market cocoa, it was widely rumoured that recruitment to the Council depended more upon the applicants' political and tribal affiliations than upon their qualifications or their competence and honesty. By 1964 the UGFCC had swallowed up 1130 co-operative associations embracing almost 400,000 farmers.[34] It disposed of nearly fifteen thousand jobs amongst party supporters. The revised constitution of the UGFCC published in 1965 required its employees to 'accept the political leadership of the Convention Peoples Party, and to support the Party and its Government materially, financially and morally'. Vacancies within the organization were rarely advertised publicly. The highest posts were filled by the central committee of the party. The middle and lower ranks of the Council were recruited from 'persons who had never completed their middle school education, ex-taxi-drivers, and (party) action troopers'. [35] Like the Workers Brigade and so many of the party's other 'integral wings' the Council became a source of jobs for illiterate and semi-literate supporters of the party. In June 1963 Suleman Iddrissu openly accused the chairman, Martin Appiah Danquah, of recruiting his staff almost exclusively from amongst his fellow Ashanti. This charge was denied by Kofi Baako, who reproached Iddrissu by pointing out that there were many 'efficient Ashantis'. Iddrissu countered with the observation that:

Ashanti farmers cannot feed the whole of Ghana. (Laughter.) Almost all the high officers from the deputy General Secretary down to personnel officers are Ashantis. This sort of practice must stop. Osagyefo, the President of this country, is a Nzima, yet he has not filled this House with Nzimas. (Laughter and shouts of 'Good Case'.)[36]

Complaints about the poor quality of management at all levels in the Council were common. The Council was required to submit its accounts for annual inspection by the Auditor General, but the accounts rarely arrived on time or in a satisfactory state. Even the Ministry of Agriculture, nominally responsible to the Assembly for the affairs of the Council, found it difficult to extract any sensible information about its transactions. In May 1963 M.O. Kwatia, a persistent back-bench champion of the small farmer, attempted to get a commission of enquiry set up, during the second reading of the government's Commissions of Enquiry bill, to investigate the activities of the Council. He had been alarmed by reports reaching him that farmers were having difficulty in obtaining money due to them from their crop, but his attempt to repeat Mr Justice Jibowu's success failed. Baako fobbed him off with a technical objection and the Council continued on its cavalier way.

After the coup a clearer picture became available of the Council's transactions with the farmers. The farmers' grievances concerning under-payment, delays in payment, inaccurate weighing and grading of their crop, and political intimidation at the hands of agents of the Council were investigated in detail. 'Everywhere we went', commented the commission, 'farmers expressed strong feelings against Secretary-Receivers.'[37] No adequate safeguards existed against malpractices by the local buying agents at the point at which cocoa was brought in by the farmers for weighing, grading and sale. The commission commented that:

> ... Secretary-Receivers were not inclined to weigh the cocoa themselves and often entrusted this task to illiterate labourers who had never been tutored to register weights ... it was common practice for farmers to be forbidden to read the scales and if a farmer made an attempt to contravene this injunction his cocoa was promptly put aside and he was often left waiting until the next day before receiving attention.[38]

Farmers often suspected that the weighing machines at the collecting stations had been tampered with. Cocoa was sometimes 'accidentally' spilled during weighing and the farmers forbidden to retrieve it. The spilt beans found their way into the Secretary-Receivers' hands and were sold for their own profit. Delays in handling and weighing the cocoa were often contrived by the Secretary-Receivers in the hope that farmers forced to wait several days, sleeping at night on the office verandahs, would be willing to part with their crop at a lower price than that officially recorded, the difference once again finding its way into the agents' pockets. Collusion between the receivers and the quality grading officers of the marketing board was also widely suspected, so that farmers received a lower price than the quality of their crop entitled them to.

Farmers had frequently complained of delays in getting the money due to them from the sale of their crop. This could lead to serious trouble between the hapless farmers and their labourers impatient for their wages. In one instance a luckless farmer was burned to death by his labourers 'who could no longer accommodate the farmer's plea that he had not been paid for his cocoa'.[39] On the allegations of political discrimination, the Commission found that:

Secretary-Receivers sometimes deliberately delayed attending to farmers who were not members of the Convention Peoples Party, or who were known to be lukewarm towards the Party. It was further alleged that in the distribution of cutlasses, gammalin, etc., UGFCC officials were given an opportunity to accord preferential treatment to their favourites and Party members.[40]

The Council had been empowered to make deductions from payments made to farmers for specific development projects, such as new feeder roads, culverts and water supply. This practice had the sanction of the government and party but no machinery existed to counter possible abuses.

By 1965 more than a quarter of a million pounds stood in the Council's books as 'contributions' to development, but the farmers were sceptical about the uses to which this money was put. Some of it found its way directly into the pockets of the local party and Council officials. Some was loaned to needy farmers at usurious rates of interest. Some was used by officials to enable their wives to make down payments on commercial vehicles for their own business ventures or to provide them with trading capital.

The cocoa farmers found themselves ground helplessly between the millstones of falling world cocoa prices and the depredations of the ruling party. When cocoa prices fell alarmingly in 1960-61, the government resolutely refused to curtail its own expenditure with the inevitable result that the cocoa farmers, the principal producers of the country's wealth, were squeezed even more severely. In 1959 the Farmers Council announced that the cocoa farmers had 'agreed' to a reduction in their producer price of twelve shillings, leaving them with sixty shillings a load. This new exaction brought the government an extra £32.8 million. The July budget of 1961 introduced compulsory savings in the form of development bonds which were in theory redeemable. The farmers provided a contribution levied at ten per cent of their producer price. In October 1963 the development bonds were abolished and replaced by income tax. Although most wage and salary earners got back their contributions, the Farmers Council announced that the farmers had 'voluntarily' agreed to hand over their accumulated contributions to the government — an amount totalling over ten million pounds.[41] at the same time the Council announced that the farmers had further 'agreed' to another deduction from their producer price equal in amount to the abolished bond contributions.[42] In September 1965 a further deduction was made, leaving the farmers with a price of forty shillings per load for their cocoa. In ten years the farmers' producer price had been almost halved in money value. In real terms they had lost much more since the value of Ghana's currency had been deeply eroded by inflation over the same period.

The cocoa farmers had few weapons with which to fight back. Unlike the town workers who had given the government a bad scare in 1961, they could present no direct threat to the regime. Although far greater in numbers and economic importance than the workers, they were too far from the centres of political power, too widely dispersed and too tied to their farms to take concerted action. Their discontent had to be matched, moreover, against the existing local rivalries in the countryside which the party was able to exploit to keep the peace. The powerful combination of disgruntled farmers and tribal nationalism which had made up the National Liberation Movement of the mid-fifties was no longer possible under the coercive acts passed since independence.

But great damage was done to the farmers' confidence in the rule of their own countrymen. The economic pillars of the regime, they had become its abject pensioners. Many began to look back with nostalgia to a past golden age when obligations were honoured, when redress could be sought in the courts, when corrupt and dishonest officials were punished, and when the threat of arbitrary arrest did not exist. After travelling the countryside taking evidence from hundreds of farmers, the De Graft Johnson committee observed sadly that the farmers 'saw the re-introduction of white faces in the cocoa business as the surest hope for honesty and prosperity'.[43]

Cocoa farmers also supplied a large proportion of the country's domestic foodstuffs. Intimidated by the party, subjected to the arbitrary exactions of government, they retreated into a defensive shell. So long as they farmed their land, they and their families at least would not starve.

Despite official attempts to prod them into greater production of foodstuffs, the government's policies were working inexorably in the opposite direction.

Between March 1963 and September 1965 the prices of locally produced foodstuffs increased throughout the country by 82.3 per cent.[44] In certain of the larger towns the increase was even steeper. Over the same period the prices of imported foods rose by 30 per cent. The worsening shortages drained away any remaining popular enthusiasm for the regime and brought about a crisis of confidence within the party in the policies of the leadership. The stage was set for the forcible overthrow of the first Republic.

The fundamental cause of the shortages lay in the chronically low and stagnant level of agricultural productivity noted earlier by the Lewis report. The prosperous years of the fifties had masked the problem by enabling Ghana to make good its shortages by imports of foodstuffs, such as rice, sugar, maize, which it was possible to grow from its own resources. The increasing haemorrhage of young men away from village life into the towns, however, left the farms to be worked by an ageing labour force. Moreover, the ability to import foodstuffs in the early sixties was severely curtailed by the shortage of foreign exchange and the government's own rising expenditure.

Ideally, the solution to Ghana's agricultural problem lay in finding ways and means of increasing the efficiency of the peasant farmers, encouraging them to take advantage of the demand and persuading them to improve their traditional methods, capitalizing upon the countryside's long tradition of self-help which had been demonstrated historically to be a major factor for progress. But although the CPP was able to make its presence felt in the countryside it was unable to think of means of improving peasant agriculture within the existing social fabric. Nkrumah was more attracted by the notion of outflanking the problem of the peasant farmer by creating a 'new order' in the countryside. The way ahead lay in the direction of state farms and collectives, in large-scale mechanization and centralization of agricultural effort. Like all his other policies, Nkrumah's agricultural policy was based upon political rather than economic and social considerations. The industrialization of Ghana was his aim and farming was to be made subservient to it. The peasantry were to be turned into a rural proletariat and their farms into an extension of the factory.

Ironically, just as Nkrumah's state farms project was getting under way in Ghana, Krushchev's 'virgin lands' campaign was reaching a disastrous climax in Russia — a campaign which was itself a confession that thirty-five years of collectivization had failed to resolve the problems of some of the richest, settled agricultural land in the world. Yet this bleak episode escaped the notice of Nkrumah and his advisers altogether. The sheer size of the Russian experiment seemed to make it weaknesses invisible to them. But although his adoption of a formula which had failed in Russia was risky enough, Nkrumah was about to compound it by applying it in a tropical environment in which the peculiar and only partly understood ecological factors presented an additional hazard.

Cautionary examples lay within Africa itself, warning of the dangers along the road Nkrumah was about to take. In 1945 the Labour government in Britain launched an ambitious scheme to grow ground-nuts in an empty area of Tanganyika to provide vegetable fats and edible oils to help relieve the dollar shortage in Britain. It was an expensive failure. In 1951, after an investment of £30 million and much acrimony, it was abandoned. The British government, backed by immeasurably greater resources than any African state was later to possess, had:

> ...entered on the ground-nuts scheme in much the same
> spirit as had dictated the financing of war operations.
> But it is not possible to find any justification for many
> of the measures actually taken in the execution of the
> project, and in particular for the hasty assumption that
> mechanization would overcome the climatic and other
> defects of the notoriously unsuitable area selected for
> the operation of the major part of the scheme.[45]

Nearer home, in 1950 the Gold Coast Agricultural
Development Corporation set up the Gonja Development
Corporation to grow food crops in an area of the savana
near Damongo. After seven years of struggle the attempt
was abandoned. The Development Corporation pointed
out at the end of the project that:

> the fundamental lesson is, without doubt, that the new
> ways cannot at present compete with traditional
> methods of agriculture...[46]

The chairman of the Agricultural Development at that time
was Emmanuel Ayeh Kumi. He did not pass on this lesson
to his master in later years — or if he did, it was ignored.

Large-scale, mechanized agricultural projects have
sometimes proved to be a temptation to administrators and
politicians in tropical Africa impatient for modernity and
quick returns. One French agronomist has remarked that
'the problem of mechanization is crucial, because African
élites are seduced by the idea of modern machines. It is
difficult to convince them that agricultural progress does
not depend upon immediate and complete mechanization.'
[47] It was, however, an enthusiasm which Nkrumah
shared, despite the fact that the rain-fed agricultural
characteristic of his country is, of all economic activities,
the least suited to central direction and mechanization.

The State Farms Corporation was formally set up in January 1963, although it had been effectively in operation during the previous year when it inherited the assets of the dissolved Division of Agriculture and the Agricultural Development Corporation. Twenty-seven farms had been set up during 1962, but by the following year the corporation was running over a hundred farms and employing fifteen thousand labourers, most of whom it had inherited from the dissolved agencies. Although Nkrumah assured the peasant farmers that their interests 'will not be made subservient to those of the state farms and co-operatives'. It was clear that it was to the latter he looked, not only to produce plantation crops for export, but also to take over from the traditional farmers the task of providing the bulk of the country's domestic foodtuffs.

Meanwhile the task of bringing the peasant farmers under the control of the Farmers Council would go on. Immediate collectivization *en masse* was out of the question. His party lacked the coercive machinery to enforce it, and if it were attempted, it would certainly be resisted, placing Ghana's major source of income and food in jeopardy. Until full collectivization became feasible, however, the state farms would demonstrate 'the advantages of large-scale, mechanized socialist agriculture over small-scale peasant farming'.[48]

The seven-year development plan sought to bring about the end of shifting cultivation in the savana by introducing large farms cultivated by mechanical means as part of the total expenditure of £67.5 million it envisaged for agriculture. Half this amount would be spent on providing services for traditional farmers, £10 million would go towards setting up state farms, £5 million to the farms of the Workers Brigade, and £3 millions to the Farmers Council. The plan anticipated that the state farms would be under the control of trained managers provided with initial working capital but expected soon afterwards to run their farms on a commercial footing. It was the planners' belief that:

> Because these farms will be state-controlled and will be managed by people trained in modern agricultural techniques, they are the easiest way of getting early results in agriculture such as are now needed for nutritional and balance of payments reasons.[49]

By 1964 the State Farms Corporation had acquired control over 250,000 acres of land, although only about 40,000 acres were actually cultivated. A year later its holdings had increased to over 345,000 acres. In addition the Workers Brigade held 280,000 acres of which less than one tenth was actually farmed. As the total area of cultivated land in Ghana was about three million acres, the state agencies had acquired within a few years holdings amounting to about one-fifth of the entire cultivated area of the country.

It was hardly surprising that the small farmers viewed this rapid expansion with apprehension. The Wenchi MP, Charles Donkoh, reported some of their misgivings voiced to him during a tour of his constituency during the 1964 referendum on the one-party state:

> I went from village to village and was asked many questions such as these: 'Are you sure that when we vote "Yes" we are not going to be given uniforms?' 'Are you sure that when we vote "Yes" we shall not form long queues for food?' They thought that the government were going to nationalize their lives and property.[50]

The fears of the peasant farmers of their eventual destruction by the state farms were reinforced by the arbitrary methods of the state agencies used to acquire lands far in excess of their ability to cultivate them.[51]

The ultimate political purpose behind the behaviour of

the state agencies was seen by one agriculturist working in Ghana at the time:

> ... to be a means of breaking down the customs and traditions of the villages and their social cohesion, which were felt to threaten the rule of the President and his party. The peasants were shown 'where power lies' by the seizure of village lands without compensation, and by a calculated and ostentatious waste of resources — of land, labour and capital. This intimidation was remarkably effective, and to this day the peasants remain voiceless, politically impotent and cowed in the face of an all-powerful bureaucracy.[52]

It is, however, unlikely that the sole object of the state farms was to bully the farmers — if only on the grounds that Nkrumah's domestic policies were rarely so clearly defined. Certainly he wished to strengthen his party's presence in the countryside, but he was also concerned with finding a quick solution through socialized agriculture for the ever-growing shortage of food.

Whatever his motives the failure of his agricultural policies could not be concealed. By 1965 only 0.5% of the country's food supply came from the state farms and Workers Brigade farms, despite the heavy investment in them. As far as available statistics show,[53] by practically every criteria the performance of the state farms was inferior to that of the traditional farmers. The yield of produce in long tons per acre in 1965 was 0.21 compared with 1.17 on the peasant farms. In terms of output per worker the state farms produced 0.59 tons per year compared with the traditional farmer's 2.18 tons.[54] Official sources acknowledged that the state farms fell short of every one of the modest production targets set for the crops they were engaged in cultivating. Throughout their existence they never came close to making a profit.[55]

As the food shortages worsened the Corporation and the agricultural wing of the Workers Brigade were ordered to turn their efforts away from growing cash crops — the one area where they might have had a modest success — to growing foodstuffs. But they were handicapped by high overheads and running costs from which the traditional farmers were largely free. One important component of their costs derived from the prodigious use of tractors and machinery, easy to obtain through suppliers' credits extended by some overseas companies. These mechanical aids had little impact upon productivity, and the deep ploughing and extensive clearing they made possible was soon observed to have a damaging effect upon the soils of many farms. Consequently, although the import of tractors did not slacken they were from an economic point of view under-utilized. The other uses to which they were put, however, were many and varied:

> Tractors were frequently used for short journeys or shopping trips to the nearest village instead of a bicycle. At one state farm taxis used to call regularly to fill up with petrol. On the land a good deal of reckless use is evident ... Front-end damage is very common when inexperienced drivers drive straight into the bush. The number of spare parts is poor and is made more difficult by the number of different makes — Russian, Yugoslav, Czech, British, German and American wheeled and tracked tractors ... perhaps nowhere else in the tropics can so many tractors be seen lying in yards or abandoned in the bush. Management seems to have preferred to buy new tractors rather than attempt to repair unserviceable machines.[56]

The poor performance and great expense of the Corporation's tractors became a subject of constant complaint in the Assembly whenever the agricultural situation was discussed. But the tractor had become almost a sacramental object, an outward and visible sign of progress, and as such was seemingly immune from vulgar considerations of cost and efficiency.

The State Farms Corporation suffered both from excessive centralization and inadequate control over its local operations. Its top-heavy headquarters staff preferred life in the capital to service in the countryside. Few knew what was going on down on the farms. The system of 'district accounting stations' for local groups of farms made it almost impossible to make proper comparisons of costs and yields for individual farms, so no-one knew whether money was being spent wisely or not. Individual farm managers sometimes sent back to headquarters falsified or over-optimistic reports of their progress. Each farm was supposed to supply its labourers with building materials to enable them to construct their own cottages and to provide its labour force with a medical dispensary, but no machinery existed to ensure that these facilities were actually provided. Local farms were open to the interference of party officials who sometimes availed themselves of the produce for their own purposes. Remote from Accra and the Corporation's headquarters, farm managers had little choice except to submit to these demands.[57]

In 1965 few believed that the state farms were an answer to the food crisis. In the National Assembly complaints against the Corporation and its officials grew bolder and more specific. But there was little hope of the government revising the basic direction of its policies on the evidence abundantly supplied by experience. It was one thing to point out the state farms' shortcomings and quite another to correct them. The Corporation and the Workers Brigade had become part of the official establishment, secured against their failures and their critics by the will of the President.

The economic cost of the state farms can be measured by the large sums invested in them. By the end of 1965 the government's total investment in the Corporation's farms — excluding those of the Brigade — stood at fifteen million pounds. At the same time the cumulative loss made by the Corporation amounted to three millions.[58] All this was scarce capital which might have been put to better use. The contrast between the millions poured into state agriculture and the inability of many peasant farmers to acquire even the basic tools of their livelihood — their cutlasses and hoes — could not be concealed. No way has been found to measure the decline in morale of the peasant farmers faced with an experiment which they were powerless to control and which seemed to threaten them with extinction. As two investigators reported, 'If the government had used the same amount of money and talent that were expended on the state farms programme to develop techniques and to provide incentives for the small farmers, there would probably have been a far greater increase in domestic food production'.[59]

VIII The End of the Political Kingdom

Nkrumah's final year of office began with a bad omen. In the early hours of 4 February 1965 Dr Danquah died in Nsawam prison. Nkrumah felt considerable remorse at the death of his former mentor in one of his own jails. He retired for two weeks to his birthplace at Nkroful to reflect upon his own career since his return to Ghana in 1947. His meditation, although certainly in the wilderness, was not exactly solitary. A posse of photographers followed him on the instructions of the Publicity Secretariat to ensure a daily supply of pictures for the press, showing Osagyefo in a variety of brooding postures. Four days after Danquah's death, sentence was passed by Chief Justice Sarkodee Addo upon Adamafio and his associates who had been found guilty after their second trial. The five men were condemned to death, but in the following month Nkrumah commuted their sentence to twenty years imprisonment and promised a review of the cases of all other detainees.

But the worsening economic situation had to be faced. For the first time since the war food queues had become a common sight in the major towns. In Accra the hungry crowds stood against the background of the towering structure of 'Job 600', the palace which Nkrumah ordered to be built to house a single conference of the OAU heads of state scheduled for later in the year. Costing several million pounds, it symbolized Nkrumah's preoccupation with grand, futile, international gestures at the expense of his countrymen's welfare.

Within the party there was no unanimity either about the causes of the crisis, or about the measures needed to counter it. The radicals, strengthened in numbers in the new Assembly which opened later in the year by the entry of members drawn from the party machine and its integral wings, attributed the shortages to profiteering and black market activities by businessmen — some alleged to be within the bosom of the party itself — who were intent on sabotaging the socialist policies of the leadership. From this stance they stepped up their demands for even tighter control over the economy. The conservatives within the party saw things differently. For them, the shortages arose predictably out of the restrictive economic policies followed by the government since 1961. Import and exchange controls, costly experiments in state farming, massive and unfruitful spending on the state corporations and other 'white elephants' were sufficient explanations of the shortages of which high prices, corruption and the black market were the inevitable consequences. The President's own opinion of what had gone wrong differed from these interpretations. In his sessional address to parliament at the beginning of the year he admitted that 'the Government is seriously concerned about the shortages of some essential commodities that developed during the latter part of 1964.'[1] But the programme of development and industrialization demanded some control over imports which had to be accepted by the 'self-denial and thrift' of the people.

In his national day broadcast to the nation on 6 March Nkrumah asserted that:

> ... there is nothing like a crisis in our economic position. There are no grave shortages of anything essential to the personal or industrial needs of the people of Ghana.

The talk of a crisis was due to 'malicious criminals, who take advantage of temporary shortages and balance of payments difficulties to spread alarming rumours'. They were only listened to, he went on, because many even within the party were not armed with the 'correct ideology'. He promised in future to intensify ideological education in the party. Only if all party members actively espoused and practised Nkrumaism, he claimed, would the party purge itself of dissension and recover its former vigour. Individual aberrations would no longer be tolerated, and the party would 'wage relentless war against ideas ... that are contrary to our chosen ideology'.

In the middle of March a backbench member of parliament, M.O. Kwatia, gave notice of his intention to bring before the Assembly a private member's motion asking the government to ensure that the Ghana National Trading Corporation 'reviews its system of distributing essential commodities'. The debate on Kwatia's motion turned out to be one of the most important in the first parliament of the Republic. Meanwhile the radicals of the *Evening News*, not to be out-manoeuvered by their old enemies, the backbenchers, started collecting information about passbooks held by wives or friends of MPs and ministers. When the debate opened on 23 March Kwatia began by warning the government that the grave shortage of food and other commodities was likely to grow worse. 'The imperialists and their agents', he warned, 'were no longer to be found amongst the capitalist companies in Ghana but within the party itself.' He outlined the practices found amongst the managers of the state-owned trading corporation. 'When the goods come, these unscrupulous persons distribute about one-third of them to stores, and give the remaining two-thirds to women traders with whom they have certain arrangements. It is high time that the government set up a commission or some sort of machinery to re-organize the whole thing and make the people more patriotic.'

Kwatia was supported by other backbenchers, including

Iddrissu who claimed that the food situation was worse than in colonial days. 'The situation is pathetic', he said, 'and it pains me to say it, that today in the market a cigarette tin of rice is one shilling and twopence.' Some other members shouted, 'You will not even get it!' 'Perhaps', he went on, 'this has not come to the notice of the Minister of Trade? We should not beg the minister but rather force him to give us our needs.'

The passbook system which Kwatia claimed was being abused by the managers of the trading corporation originated in colonial days. The holder of a passbook — usually a market woman or itinerant trader — was entitled to purchase goods on credit from the warehouses of European and Lebanese trading firms for sale in the town markets and countryside. The system had advantages for both sides but had declined over the years as more trading firms opened up their own retail centres. But the import restrictions of 1961 and subsequent years had given it a new lease of life, and the Ghana National Trading Corporation was one of the principal users of the arrangement. At a time of import scarcity a passbook holder was able, in return for a cut paid over to the managers and stockkeepers of warehouses, to enjoy privileged access to recently landed goods.

Complaints about the favouritism of GNTC managers towards certain passbook holders began to be made in 1962. In 1964 a steering committee of the CPP which met in Kumasi resolved to warn the GNTC and other state corporations against employing managers who had criminal records. The GNTC was a vulnerable target, since the appointment of an expatriate managing director, Sir Patrick Fitzgerald, had proved unpopular with the radical wing of the party.[2] The passbook affair raised by Kwatia gave the *Evening News* an opportunity to hit several targets at once.

At the end of the debate on Kwatia's motion the *Evening News* published the results of its enquiry into passbook holders. It named the wives of Joseph Wireko, K.A. Ofori Atta, Nathaniel Welbeck, and of four ministers, Owusu Afriyie, Amoah Awuah, B.A. Konu and Kofi Baako, as possessors of passbooks. In addition the maidservant of Kojo Botsio, and the sister of R.O. Amoaka Atta were also alleged to possess them. In fact, the *Evening News* probably pulled its punches as other MPs and party officials almost certainly had access to passbooks through their wives and relations.

The revelations, coupled with the temper of Kwatia's motion, embarrassed the government considerably. Both Baako and Amoaka Atta admitted the truth of the newspaper's allegations. Baako said that it was 'a small thing' and promised to get rid of his wife's book. When the vote was taken on the motion, it was passed by the Assembly and the government promised to adopt it. As a direct consequence of the motion a committee chaired by Professor Abraham of the University of Ghana was set up to look into allegations of trading malpractices, and a tough amendment to the Price Control act was promised. Meanwhile, in the third week of April, the egregious Djin was moved from the trade ministry to a less important portfolio. Thus a temporary but powerful alliance between the parliamentary wing of the party and the radicals had succeeded in forcing the government to take steps to deal with a situation which threatened to bring about open revolt within the party.

After Djin's departure, John Ghann, a former native treasury clerk from Ashanti, took over as Minister of Internal Trade with Nkrumah's instruction to take vigorous steps to improve the situation. By now the food situation was so bad that the Accra sports stadium was being used as an emergency distribution centre for basic foodstuffs. Ghann ordered the surrender of all passbooks held directly or indirectly by party officials and politicians. He endeavoured to give a public display of energy by visiting the Accra markets in person and ordering the seizure of all goods being sold above the prescribed price. He also speeded up the drafting of the promised amendment to the price control bill.

But Ghann was not the first minister in history to experience the frustrations of controlling prices by decree. The market women simply withdrew their stocks once word got about that the minister was on his way. Nor could he ensure that the army of price inspectors enrolled when the new amendment became law was not itself open to bribery from the traders. Benjamin Kusi who had known Ghann years before when the latter was himself a petty trader thought that the real object of the new law was 'to suppress individual traders. The Minister is creating a false impression that there are many goods in the country and it is the traders who do not want to sell them.' Rebuked by Krobo Edusei, Kusi turned on him and said, 'Do not link this bill with Osagyefo's name, because it is work and suffering, and not work and happiness.'[3]

The party radicals had blamed the 'sabotage' of the private traders for the food shortage, but as the government's attempts to curb prices by decree were seen to be failing, they began to shift their attack towards the state agencies engaged in food production. In a mood of near-despair the *Evening News* rounded upon the management of these organizations:

What the masses would like to know from the State Farms and the Workers Brigade is the actual tonnage of foodstuffs produced in each of their farms, where and to whom it was sold, and the operational costs involved … We are surprised to hear from the Director of the

> State Farms Corporation that the organization was 'not
> set up to produce food'.[4]

In their new line of attack the radicals were again moving
closer to a tactical alliance with the conservatives who had
been sceptical from the start about state activity in
farming.

After the general election — or non-election — of July
which brought both the chairman of the State Farms
Corporation and the head of the Farmers Council into the
National Assembly for the first time, their critics at last
had the opportunity of taxing them face to face with the
dismal performance of their organizations. In August
Joseph Braimah said that:

> The shortages and high prices of local foodstuffs at
> present have proved that mechanized farming has failed.
> We warned in this House that Osagyefo was not being
> given factual reports about our mechanized farms, and
> time has proved us right. Our policy was to see that the
> worker in the near future spent only 24 pesewas (two
> shillings) on food a day. That hope is now a dream.[5]

Braimah argued that collective farming was alien to the
strongest beliefs of the peasant farmer. As for the state
farms, 'in the end they belonged to no-one, and therefore
no-one paid any particular interest in them'. As long as the
President showed 'sympathetic interest' in the sycophants
and incompetents in the state organizations, Braimah
continued, there could be no hope of improvement. Attah
Mensah accepted unhappily that there were drawbacks in
his State Farms Corporation. Trying to look on the bright
side by drawing the attention of members to the increased
acreage under his management, he was howled down by
cries of 'More eggs! More food!' from the sceptical
backbenchers.

Attah Mensah cast no light upon the purpose of having several state agencies engaged in agriculture, each with its own administration. It had, he said, been urged upon him to combine the State Farms Corporation with the agricultural wing of the Workers Brigade, but he had opposed this because he thought competition was healthy. Yet almost in the same breath he claimed to have arranged frequent meetings between the two managements 'so that production can be co-ordinated'. His critics were mystified by this confusing exposition of high policy and the publication of the Abraham report a few days later did little to reassure them.[6]

The report certainly uncovered evidence of trading malpractices, principally amongst market women holding passbooks. But these were small fry, and in view of the furore created by Kwatia's motion and the *Evening News* revelations earlier in the year it was not surprising that the report found that these abuses had 'since abated considerably', although the commission was sure 'that we have not been able to discover all the wives of public officials involved in the trade, or indeed, all the public officials who themselves engaged in the trade'. The report also criticized the monopoly given to the GNTC over the import of essential domestic commodities, since the commission did not believe the corporation possessed the resources to move large quantities of goods quickly over a large area. In addition, the government's statistical resources for planning distribution were almost non-existent, so that it 'knows very little about what happens'.

After reviewing other contributory causes of the shortages, the report touched upon the fringes of the central problem — the malaise which afflicted the peasant farmers:

There is some sign that our traditional farmers look

upon the state farms with anxiety. They feel that if unceasingly backed by the tax-payers money, state farms may well be spelling the doom of traditional farmers. We believe that if the traditional farmers should, out of a premature feeling that their days are numbered, cut down on the scale of their farming, there could be a very serious shortage of foodstuffs in the country.[7]

The report urged that the state agencies' further expansion into agriculture and distribution should 'in our opinion be limited':

It has not produced foodstuffs in quantities which would seem to justify their capital ... Some of the working habits of employees have been unsuitable. There is a definite hour to begin work and a definite time for closing. These hours, unfortunately, are not necessarily related to the demands of farming.

Although the report, given the limited time available for its completion, was workmanlike, there was no indication that the government would act quickly upon its recommendations. Other such reports had been produced in the past — with no result. The economic crisis had grown worse. Nkrumah showed no disposition either to modify his policies or to reconsider his chosen strategy.

Yet he alone was the source of all effective action within his political kingdom. If he could not be moved towards other directions, then nothing could change. Hitherto the mounting tide of discontent had not touched him. He had been above reproach; the anger of his party had fallen upon his lieutenants. But suddenly, in the opening weeks of the new parliament, there was a dramatic change. In their desperation a few backbenchers rounded on the central committee of their party, the supreme collective authority of their movement, handpicked by Nkrumah himself. The magic of Osagyefo's name was beginning to desert him amongst the ranks of his own movement as it had already deserted him amongst a growing section of the nation.

The attack on the Holy of Holies — the central committee — shook the party to its foundations. It was not the production of a deep-laid plan or conspiracy. It was led, unsurprisingly, by Suleman Iddrissu who allowed his temper once more to get the better of him. His first outburst took place on the same day as the publication of the Abraham report:

> More than a dozen times has the President ... given advice to the nation. We are all witnesses to the fact that in most cases the get-rich-quick have always been removed from their posts by the Central Committee, but later on are put into higher posts. What punishment has been meted out to them? Does it mean, sir, that the Central Committee is trying to be irresponsible, to tell all of us to get rich quick, so that ... we shall use the riches to get promotion?[8]

Baako, the leader of the house who had often had to deal with rebellious backbenchers, was caught off guard by this unexpected attack. Was Iddrissu, he wondered, suggesting 'that the Central Committee of the CPP is, or even can be irresponsible?' Iddrissu countered by saying that the central committee should not be afraid 'to give punishment to the people who get rich quick'. Baako was incredulous at this *lèse majesté*. He did not know 'what power had entered the Member to enable him to say things like that'. Iddrissu, not to be put down, replied that Baako himself was not being attacked — 'he is not amongst those people who get rich quick — otherwise I know what I would say.'

Iddrissu then referred to the case of Ambrose Yankey's son, the head of a 'special intelligence unit' at Flagstaff

House, who had recently been arrested for accepting bribes from some traders. 'What did we see?' asked Iddrissu, 'the action stopped in the courts.' Baako warned him that the case was 'delicate' and that Iddrissu had better drop the issue. Iddrissu did so, but only to take up another. The head of the CID in Accra had been censured in the Akainyah report for private dealings from Indian traders. He had been dismissed, but, continued Iddrissu:

> not long after this incident, this man was re-engaged and even today is head of the security branch. Does it mean that he will use that office to do the same thing again? I am saying that the whole fault lies on the Central Committee, because they are the greatest eye of the nation.[9]

At this point one of the new members angrily interjected to remind Iddrissu of his oath of loyalty to the CPP, but Iddrissu now had the bit between his teeth:

> Now, sir, you might be a witness that the *Evening News* which is the political mouth-organ (*sic*) of the party acted after the Member for Koforidua (Kwatia) brought a motion before this House, and as a result the Abraham commission was set up to enquire into the malpractices. What should have been the duty of the Central Committee? To suspend all those people who are now involved or suspected. What do we see now? People who were involved or suspected ... have been transferred ...

Iddrissu went on to complain that the people around the President were making it difficult for himself and other members 'to tell him what is happening in the country'. It was, he continued, the central committee's job to act against nepotism and corruption, and it was failing in its responsibilities.

The attack on the central committee worried the

leadership. It made a determined attempt to get the private member's motion calling for an implementation of the President's dawn broadcast which Iddrissu insisted on submitting, removed from the parliamentary timetable. A few days after his outburst Iddrissu was summoned before the 'parliamentary disciplinary committee' of the party, but he refused to appear before it.[10]

On 6 September Iddrissu was given a second chance to appear before the disciplinary committee by its chairman, Kweku Akwei. Otherwise he would be reported to the chairman of the central committee, who was Nkrumah himself. Iddrissu was not put off. 'I will not appear before you', he told Akwei, 'you can do your worst.' Akwei then appealed to the Speaker to defer the motion. Iddrissu, by now completely out of control of the leader of the house, broke in with the accusation that:

> When people steal you return them to high posts ... I know my one foot is in parliament and the other in Nsawam, but I have no fears: I will speak; we are in parliament.

The other members sat in awed silence at Iddrissu's recklessness, only broken when the Speaker announced that the motion would be deferred 'in view of the statement made by the chairman of the disciplinary committee'. At this the backbenches erupted in anger. J.K. Twum got up to demand a ruling from the Speaker on whether a parliamentary committee's work took precedence over the work of parliament itself. Shortly afterwards the house adjourned in uproar, but its battle was almost won. It was not prepared to be gagged without a struggle.

Iddrissu's motion, 'that this House requests the Government and the Central Committee to see to the thorough implementation of the aims and objectives of the President's dawn broadcast', was debated on the following day. Akwei tried another dodge to suppress it, trying to get the Speaker to declare it *ultra vires*. 'The Central Committee' he said, 'cannot be requested to do anything because it is not part of this House: it deals with party organization.' Boateng joined him, claiming that 'the unconstitutional nature of the motion cannot be questioned'. But he was opposed by I.K. Chinebuah, who held Boateng's old post as Minister of Information but had little regard for his predecessor. He wanted to know how the alleged 'unconstitutional' nature of the motion had escaped the scrutiny of the Assembly's business committee. [11]

In spite of these last minute delaying tactics, which thoroughly aroused the anger of the backbenches and divided the frontbench, Iddrissu opened the debate on his motion — which was seconded by Kwatia — by referring to the Kulungugu incident, the Akainyah report and the Djaba case:

> The President thought that the expatriate firms were exploiting the people, and for that reason he set up the GNTC. But the offenders, the people who went against the dawn broadcast, were some of us here assembled in this House; some of them were in the Cabinet, and this time, I say again, some of them are in the Central Committee ...

> Today we have swarming into the Party men who have arrived from Damascus like Saul and have changed their name to St Paul. They are more marxist than the man Marx himself. They have become more Nkrumah than the man Nkrumah himself. They are more 'Consciencists' than Consciencism itself ... Our generation is witnessing an era where a new aristocracy, a new class, absorb an enormous part of the nation's income ... If a poor man steals, conviction follows rapidly. If a rich

man steals, he is usually bound over on a plea of nervous breakdown. (Laughter)

We have at present in our midst certain dogmatists, the Adamafio's who in the long run will be proved to be more dangerous than Adamafio himself. They can only babble phrases. They call themselves true marxists and want to be revered with all the impudence they can muster. What they are after is leadership, and so they often use the eulogy 'Oh, Nkrumah, we hail you'. In fact they are preparing the ground so to forcibly take over the leadership ... Without being chosen, they climbed into positions of authority by undermining others, they issued orders and abused everything in the Party. They wilfully attacked and punished our Party members and pushed them around. Who here had forgotten the demands that one of our true leaders, a stalwart of the Party, be shot at Black Star Square?[12]

Now that Iddrissu had gone off like an explosion of rockets, fizzing in all directions, one after another of the backbenchers stood up to make their feelings known. The pent-up frustrations and disappointments of the last years suddenly welled up to the surface in an extraordinary burst of self-criticism. Kwasi Ghapson, a lecturer at Winneba, called for a change of heart within the party as a whole. There had been too much hatred and hypocrisy in the past. 'When Osagyefo is speaking, everyone says "Yea, Yea". Are they sincere?' he asked. 'I, Kwesi Ghapson, the member for Kibi, am not sincere. All of us are not sincere because we say yes, even when we mean no.'

A recurrent theme in all this heart-searching was the isolation of the leader from the mass of his party. One member complained that 'the dual carriageway from the masses to the President is not operating as it should.' He was contradicted by a new member of parliament who said that if members had grievances, there existed the party machinery by which their complaints could reach the highest levels. His only evidence for this assertion was the party constitution, but it failed to carry conviction:

> Mr. Speaker: 'Order! Members have been saying "people who are close to Osagyefo". All of us are very, very close to Osagyefo.'
>
> Members: 'No! We are far from him!'
>
> Mr. Speaker: 'There is not a single one of you who when he wants to see Osagyefo will not be allowed to see him.'
>
> Balagumyetime: 'Mr Speaker, even you cannot see him so easily.'[13]

Baako summed up as best he could a debate which had proved as dramatic as anticipated.[14] The motion which he had earlier failed to quash was, he said, 'completely acceptable' to the government. It was unfortunate, he went on, that the spirit of brotherhood found in the early party was indeed lacking; much more would have to be done to restore the unity and comradeship of former days. But he did not comment upon the fact that the Assembly had won a signal victory. It was not going to be the docile tool of the party leadership. Grievances had been brought into the open and aired with more frankness than at any other time, and in the few remaining months left to it the Assembly showed itself determined to keep up its pressures on the government.

The principal consequence of the debate on Iddrissu's motion was the latter's expulsion from parliament a few months later. Nkrumah had been made uncomfortably aware of the seething discontent within his party. Shortly after the debate he summoned the party's parliamentarians to Peduase Lodge to thrash out their differences. It was an extremely acrimonious meeting with each faction accusing the other of disloyalty towards the President.[15] Nkrumah could offer no palliative, except a promise once again to improve the organisation of the party. But similar measures had been taken before with little effect. The party needed surgery, not melioratives, and Nkrumah could not bring himself to use the knife.

Iddrissu had not been overawed by the formidable pressures against him and until his expulsion continued to raise motions potentially dangerous to the government. Fortunately for him, his expulsion was followed nine days later by the military take-over of the 24th February. The turmoil within the party which he had done so much to precipitate had not gone unnoticed by some officers of the armed forces.

The previous few months had seen a rash of military take-overs in independent Africa.[16] A few days after the *coup* in Nigeria in January, Nkrumah had delivered his valedictory judgement upon the murdered Prime Minister, Sir Abubakar Tafewa Balewa, as the victim of forces he had failed to understand.

Addressing the National Assembly on 1 February Nkrumah had referred to the 'unfortunate military incursions into the political life of several independent African states'. He warned that 'it is not the duty of the army to rule or govern because it has no political mandate'. Where the military had usurped power, 'the root cause can be found not in the life and traditions of the African people, but in the manoeuvres of neo-colonialism.'[17] The best defence against such a take-over, he went on, lay in the one party system which he had introduced in Ghana and which he hoped the rest of the continent would adopt.

It is difficult to see how Nkrumah could be so wrong. His political sense of survival seemed to have deserted him entirely in these last months. He was aware, of course, of the dangers of a military rebellion in Ghana. The East African army mutinies of 1964, which had been put down only when the new governments had called for British help, had come as a rude shock to him. As a matter of prudence he had taken steps to safeguard himself by building up his security services, calling in foreign intelligence advisers and strengthening his own praetorian guard. But, ironically, all these measures helped to precipitate the very event they were designed to frustrate. In exile his assertion that the coup which deposed him was the work of the western powers was never supported by any evidence, because, indeed, there was none.[18]

The first Ghana coup sprang exclusively from internal forces reacting to indigenous pressures. There is no need to blunt the edge of Ockham's Razor by explaining it in terms of army officers acting as British 'neo-colonialist' or any other kind of puppets, at the prompting of external interests. The dangers of his situation were staring Nkrumah in the face, but he could not, or would not, see them. Yet in the debate following his last address before the National Assembly, Joseph Braimah spelled out the risks inherent in Ghana's condition of widespread corruption and the government's indifference to public unrest. 'It is in such circumstances', he warned, 'that the armed forces step in to defend the masses against a corrupt government and in the process seize power.'[19] Braimah's prescience went unheeded. Nkrumah, the world statesman and African messiah, was wrapped up in the affairs of Vietnam and Rhodesia. At such a level he was oblivious to dangers perfectly obvious to everyone else who was not blinded by the brilliance of his vision.

The relationship between Nkrumah and the army which overthrew him had always been a delicate one. The Ghana army — like the armies of other newly independent tropical states — was not a national revolutionary force like the armies of Russia and China. Force had played little or no part in the liquidation of the French and British African empires. Independence had been little more than a ceremonial incident for the Gold Coast armed forces. The

Ghana army stood in direct line of descent from the local forces raised by the British before the first world war. It was as much a colonial creation as the civil service or the judiciary, but had drawn upon a wider social and geographical cross section of the Gold Coast peoples than either. Gold Coast units had fought with the Royal West African Frontier Force in both world wars, ranging as far afield as Burma and the Middle East in the second. Many of the Ghanaian officers at the time of independence had served in the second world war and a number had risen to senior posts from the ranks. There existed no other national institution at independence which possessed a comparable antiquity and tradition. From the start, the army, with a strong sense of identity which owed nothing to the nationalist movement, was likely to interpret the world in different ways from the politicians.

The army was also the last Ghanaian institution to be freed from British influence. Nkrumah's pan-African stance meant that Ghana must be seen to have a credible defence force if his country's voice was to carry any weight in the rest of Africa. He was anxious to maintain the army's combat standards and the presence of seconded British officers until 1961, like their Ghanaian counterparts, under the British chief of defence staff, Major General H.T. Alexander, acted both as a guarantee of efficiency and of the stability of the government. Spending on the defence forces rose steadily until it stood at a total of £15 million out of a budget of £203 million in 1964-65. At the same time the total strength of the armed forces stood at about 17,000 men of whom 15,000 were in the army. The latter consisted for six infantry battalions, an armoured car reconnaisance unit, transport formations and a unit of engineers.[20] The steady expansion, coupled with a rapid indigenization of officers complete by 1961, improved the career prospects of all experienced officers.

In June 1960 Nkrumah assumed supreme control over

the armed forces as head of state under the republican constitution. On 5 July the Congo crisis broke out with the mutiny of the Force Publique. By October Nkrumah had agreed to Lumumba's appeal to send out a contingent of Ghana's army and police force, but as part of the international force under United Nations command. The experience of the Ghana contingent in the Congo was not entirely a happy one. Although it acquitted itself well — despite a mutiny at Luluabourg — it suffered from confusion at the highest levels of command. Officially part of the United Nations force it became evident that Nkrumah thought it should serve his own and Lumumba's purposes. Nkrumah's political emissaries in the Congo, Welbeck and Djin, succeeded in making themselves as unpopular with the Ghanaian officers in the field as they later became to the Congolese government which expelled them.

A further consequence of the change to the republican constitution related to the oath which members of the armed forces swore at enlistment and on receiving their commissions to Nkrumah personally as head of state and supreme commander. This oath replaced the former one to the Queen. Paradoxically the new oath worked to weaken the soldiers' commitment to Nkrumah. No matter how much he presented himself as a substitute for the crown, as a living symbol of the nation's enduring existence, he could not conceal the fact that he was a mortal and political figure and as such, subject like other men to the winds and tides of political fortune. His soldiers had become the servants of a paramount chief and as every Ghanaian knew, chiefs who proved intolerably despotic might be deposed in the larger interests of their community.

Despite growing doubts amongst serving officers about the kind of men running their country after independence and despite their experience of political meddling during the Congo episode, one of the strongest conventions inherited from the British was that of non-interference in the affairs of the civil power. So long as the politicians respected the army's corporate traditions, the army was prepared to remain aloof from political issues in the service of its civil masters. But the ruling party proved unable to observe its side of the bargain. The coup, when it came, was not so much a simple matter of the army intruding into politics, but of politicians thrusting themselves increasingly upon the army.

Tawia Adamafio had long been irritated by the strong British component in the Ghana army and whilst still a law student in London had submitted a plan to the central committee for the 'cipipification' of the army.[21] Nkrumah had laid it aside at the time, fearing that it would cause unrest and impair morale and efficiency. But it was an option he kept open for the future. At that time, in 1958, an enquiry was being held in the 'Awhaitey affair' in which a senior officer, a camp commander in Accra, was alleged to have been involved with certain opposition MPs in a conspiracy to overthrow the government.[22] But the army officers as a whole were uninvolved in the affair. If anything it confirmed them in their desire to stand aloof from politics. Three years later the possibility arose during the September strike that the army might have to be called in to support the civil power. This faced the government with the unpleasant prospect of having to use British-officered troops against sections of its own civilian population. On the urging of Adamafio and Geoffrey Bing, Nkrumah dismissed Major General Alexander and ended the secondment arrangements with the other British officers.

Both Adamafio and Bing, however, were less concerned with rescuing their master from a potentially embarrassing situation than they were with substituting Russian influence within the armed services in place of the British. During his tour of the communist states in 1961 Nkrumah was offered facilities by the Russians for training about four hundred army cadets in the Soviet Union. General Alexander was against the proposal.[23] So were most of the Ghanaian officers under his command. Their views, however, were not consulted by the President. When Nkrumah returned home to deal with the strike he dismissed Alexander, who had flown in from the Congo hoping to dissuade him, and announced his acceptance of the Russian offer. Apart from the practical difficulties likely to arise from having two groups of officers trained in two different command systems within the same service, it seemed to some serving officers to be only a matter of time before the CPP annexed the army and converted it into an 'integral wing', as it had done with the trade unions and the farmers.

Their fears were further increased by the steady expansion of the President's Own Guard Regiment into something very like a second army under the exclusive control of the President. Nkrumah first requested General Alexander to set up a presidential guard company as part of the regular army late in 1960. Alexander thought that the training of a section of the army for ceremonial and security duties entailed a disproportionate amount of effort at the expense of the main force, but he went ahead, thinking that it might be useful for Congo reliefs and provide 'a home for old soldiers unfit for active service'. In January 1961 the guard company became the President's Own Guard Company, a formation increasingly set apart by its training and weaponry from the rest of the army.

After General Alexander's abrupt departure, the way was open for Nkrumah to expand his own guard company, with the help of Russian advisers, into something quite different to the home for old soldiers envisaged by the former chief of defence staff. Late in 1962 the regiment was brought under 'a Presidential Detail Department' at Flagstaff House, which included civilian as well as military personnel, and it became clear that regular officers from the main army were to be excluded from its activities.[24] Officers began to feel that the presidential regiment took an unfair share of the money available for the armed forces as a whole. The regular army's equipment and supplies, on the other hand, were beginning to deteriorate. The National Defence Council, set up in 1957 to govern conditions within the armed forces, met only once between 1960 and 1966 and found itself powerless to bring about improvements. Brigadier Ocran observed that there was a widespread feeling that 'when the British were here our interests were better protected'.[25]

The activities of increasing numbers of Russian, Chinese and East German 'advisers' within presidential circles and in the Bureau of African Affairs were also causing concern. Officers were not encouraged to enquire into the activities of the secret training camps where exiled Africans from neighbouring countries were being given guerrilla training under Russian and Chinese advisers. Under the control of the Bureau of African Affairs, Nkrumah regarded this enterprise as a potential arm of his African policy, designed to exploit upheavals within nominally friendly states in the hope that opposition movements which he favoured on ideological grounds would eventually seize power.[26]

However, a few army officers were selected to help with these clandestine activities. Nkrumah took care to pick those officers who were by birth and background outsiders to some degree amongst their fellow officers. Inevitably, those he chose were regarded by their brother officers as 'political soldiers' and regarded with considerable suspicion. A northerner, Brigadier Charles Barwah, was the most important regular officer selected for work in this shadowy area. He was quickly promoted to Major General and chief of staff. Barwah remained faithful to the President who had favoured him, and in the end paid with his life, the only senior officer to die in the 1966 coup.

In 1963 the question of political indoctrination for the army again cropped up. Barwah, however, thought that its introduction would be premature and nothing further was done. However, the CPP strengthened its hold in other ways. A party branch was opened in the military academy and cadets were obliged to apply for party membership, sending their applications to party headquarters through Kofi Baako, who was at this time Minister of Defence. In their own messrooms, officers were forced to be circumspect in their conversations by the presence of party spies acting as stewards and cleaners. The next step feared by the officers was the attachment of party commissars to each unit to ensure its political reliability.

Under all these threats to the tradition and independence of their service, conscious that for some reason the President seemed to have turned against them in favour of his private army, the army officers watched the steadily worsening economic situation and the inability of the party to put its own house in order. The idea of deposing Nkrumah had occurred to a few of them after the stormy debate in 1961 which led to Gbedemah's abrupt departure. But his absence deprived the opposition of their strongest political candidate for the succession. If it had been possible to remove Nkrumah and replace him with Gbedemah in one short, sharp operation the CPP might have survived the loss of its founder. But after 1961 the party had become so much the creature of Nkrumah that the removal of one could come about only with the removal of the other.

The first men to entertain thoughts of removing

Nkrumah after 1961, however, were not soldiers but policemen — Anthony Deku, later Deputy Commissioner of Police, and John Willie Harlley, the head of Special Branch. Both were Ewes and had known each other over many years. From their work with the Criminal Investigation Department and Special Branch both men acquired a detailed knowledge of the financial transactions of leading politicians, including those of the President himself. Early in 1963 they discussed the possibility of arresting Nkrumah under the Public Property and Corrupt Practices act of the previous year, but a successful arrest hardly seemed practical. From this point onwards they began to think in terms of the forcible overthrow of Nkrumah, his party and his government.

But neither of them had much pull with the army. Without the army's active assistance any move by the police must fail against the firepower of the presidential guard units. Deku, however, had a friend, Major Kwashie, the secretary of the military hospital, who promised to make discreet soundings amongst his brother officers about their opinions of the party and government. Nevertheless the police service possessed considerable resources invaluable to the army in the event of a take-over. It had nine thousand men throughout the country and a good system of internal communications. The police headquarters in Accra housed both the Special Branch and the CID and lay close to the main army camps in the city. There was also a police armoured car section equipped with twelve Ferret vehicles.[27] In the event of a coup the police would prove extremely useful for arresting members of the party and keeping disorder at a minimum whilst the army delivered the main blow.

Before coming to power Nkrumah had repeatedly attacked the police in his newspaper and had been successfully sued for libel by the expatriate Commissioner shortly before becoming leader of government business in 1951. He had marked antipathy towards Special Branch in particular which he maintained 'was a typically British creation which really has no place in our society',[28] although once he was in power he made use of its skills and experience against his political. enemies. Nor were the senior police officers entirely happy with their position after independence. The Commissioner of Police, Eric Madjitey, a genial, bluff Ga, had to endure constant sniping from the party radicals. Moreover, his men were in the uncomfortable position of having to execute the detention orders made by the politicians. As John Harlley later testified:

> Things became very difficult indeed to manage, as politicians went about ordering the detention of people by the police. This made me issue instructions that no police officer should detain any person without my authority, and as a result of this many police officers who were unco-operative were expelled from the service.[29]

Late in 1963 Commissioner Madjitey was ordered to withdraw the police from security duties at Flagstaff House to make way for a unit drawn from the Presidential Detail Unit. It seemed to Harlley and Deku that the opportunities their men had for remaining close to the President and of effecting his removal were running out. Whether the attempted assassination of Nkrumah by an armed constable in January 1964 was inspired by Harlley or not, Nkrumah's reaction unwittingly made Harlley the chief beneficiary of the incident. The police service was disarmed, several senior officers were detained and Madjitey was sacked. Harlley was made acting Commissioner in his place.

Meanwhile Harlley, Deku and Kwashie continued to meet from time to time to review the situation, but they had no stronghold in the army until Emmanuel Kwasi Kotoka joined them.[30] At that time Kotoka was an administrative officer with no troops under his command. It was not until 1965 that he was promoted full colonel and regained command of the second infantry brigade group quartered in Kumasi.

Kotoka was a major catch for the conspirators. Popular with him men of the second battalion and of proven ability in the field, he shared the grievances of many officers at the treatment Nkrumah was meting out to the regular army, and like them was unhappy about the burgeoning security services working from Flagstaff House. Kotoka possessed drive and talent and enjoyed a greater degree of working contact with his fellow officers than did Kwashie who was tied to his hospital.

By 1965 time was running out if a conspiracy was to be successful. Before long it seemed certain that military intelligence would fall totally under the control of the President and his communist advisers.[31] The department of military intelligence was already part of the Presidential Detail Unit. Its director was another political soldier, Brigadier Hassan, like Barwah a northerner. He had served at one stage in the Sudan army and was married to a Sudanese woman. Despite his difficulties with English, he had been promoted personally by Nkrumah and his appointment as director of military intelligence was unpopular with many officers. So long as the department operated out of Burma Camp, the regular officers would enjoy at least partial access to its operations, but if it were removed to Flagstaff House, it would be totally out of their reach. A successful conspiracy would be almost impossible if the army lost all control over its intelligence arm.

Early in May Harlley showed a private paper which he had prepared to the chief of defence staff, Major General

Stephen Otu. The paper dealt with the country's acute economic plight and the drift of its argument was that many of the problems could only be resolved by a change of regime. Otu took the point and was gently inducted into the circle of conspirators. Shortly afterwards Major General Ankrah, the deputy chief of defence staff, was brought in by Harlley. With the addition of these two soldiers, the two most senior officers in the army and both generally popular with the troops, the tribal composition of the conspiracy was broadened. Neither was an Ewe, and it was sensed by the ringleaders that the conspiracy should not seem to be dominated by Ewe elements alone. If Otu and Ankrah could succeed in sinking their personal differences their seniority and popularity would be invaluable for stabilizing the situation after the seizure of power.

The outlines of a plan emerged very shortly afterwards. In the following month Nkrumah was due to attend the Commonwealth prime ministers' meeting in London. The National Assembly was to be dissolved and the first parliament of the Republic ended at the end of May. The second parliament could be available by the end of June to endorse Nkrumah's overthrow and proclaim a successor. So far no hint of what was afoot had reached the President's security services. Nkrumah left for London as scheduled, accompanied by his entourage, which included Deku. But during the conference news arrived of Ben Bella's overthrow in Algeria.

In the consternation caused by this in Nkrumah's camp, Hassan suddenly arrived in London. Somehow he had received an intimation of what was being planned. Nkrumah was inclined to be sceptical — he thought Hassan sometimes over-zealous — but he gave him instructions to deliver to Otu and the security services. On Hassan's arrival in Accra, Harlley and the others called off the attempt whilst they were still unidentified as the principal agents of the conspiracy. Hassan had picked up only a patchy idea, and had moved before he could pinpoint the conspirators. But on 28 July Otu and Ankrah were retired and their places taken by Brigadiers Aferi and Barwah, both promoted at the same time to Major Generals. Ironically, in this reshuffle Kotoka was promoted full colonel and given command of the second infantry brigade. Otu and Ankrah, although not arrested, were henceforth under constant surveillance by the security services and therefore useless to the conspiracy.[32]

The collapse of the July move, however, did not lead to the break-up of the conspirators' circle. The security services could gather only the most meagre information. Harlley, Deku and Kotoka continued to meet discreetly to discuss likely opportunities. They brought into their circle the only politician belonging to the ruling party, B.A. Bentum, recently made Minister of Forests. Bentum had been a party member since 1949 and had risen in the trade union movement until, in 1964, he had been undermined by his rivals in the TUC and dismissed. Unemployed for several months afterwards, Bentum felt that his eclipse was due to his reporting of bribery amongst TUC officials to the police. Harlley befriended him and on his restoration to favour, Bentum passed over information to which he had access as a junior minister.[33]

Towards the end of the year several factors were beginning to work once again in the conspirators's favour. The September debate revealed the degree of demoralization within the ruling party. The retirement of Otu and Ankrah had not been welcomed by the majority of soldiers. 'The arbitrary dismissal of our two generals', wrote Colonel Afrifa later, 'pained us most.' When the reshuffle had taken place Nkrumah had also announced that he was taking direct command of the armed forces.

Baako's Ministry of Defence was reduced to dealing with civil defence and ex-servicemens' affairs whilst preparations were made for the armed forces to be placed under a new 'defence secretariat' in Flagstaff House. The long-feared take-over of the armed forces seemed finally about to take place.

The cover for this take-over was provided by the rebellion in distant Rhodesia. On 12 November Nkrumah called upon Britain to end the rebellion by force. If Britain failed to act, he promised to place Ghana's forces at the disposal of the Organization of African Unity. Two weeks later the National Assembly was recalled to an emergency session to pass an Africa Defence bill, conferring on the President wide powers to send the country's forces to 'wherever the peace and security of Africa is threatened'. All military leave was cancelled and enlistment centres were opened to enrol volunteers for service in a Rhodesian invasion. To most of the officers, as well as to the conspirators, it seemed as if the President had finally taken leave of his senses.

Early in the New Year Nkrumah, putting aside for the moment the Rhodesia question, announced what was to be his last performance as an international statesman. At Ho Chi Minh's invitation he was to fly to Hanoi via Peking with new proposals for ending the war in Vietnam. His new chief of defence staff, General Aferi, would be absent at the OAU in Addis Ababa. The conspiracy once more became active. Nkrumah's absence might well prove to be the final opportunity. New men with troops under their command were urgently needed. Early in February Kotoka drove north to see Major Akwasi Afrifa, the commander of the Tamale garrison. Taking a gamble on the young officer's reaction, he told of his plans and was gratified to find Afrifa fully in sympathy with them.[34]

Meanwhile, within the National Assembly, the ruling

party was once again squabbling fruitlessly over the same allegations of corruption, mismanagement and inefficiency which had been its staple diet for the last six years. Nothing had changed — except for the worse. As a melancholy testament to the fifteen years of CPP rule, Iddrissu described the total failure of the policies to alleviate the condition of the masses in whose name it had claimed the mandate to rule:

The poor worker outside this House is always after the moneylender. He takes a lorry or a bus from Accra to Tema to work and back, and that costs him a shilling a day, and he is expected, if we had raised our production to a certain standard, to live on two shillings a day. And so three shillings out of the six shillings and sixpence a day he is paid is gone. Out of the remainder he is expected to buy clothing for his wife. If he pays rent of thirty shillings a month, then a further shilling is gone. Five shillings gone. Now, funeral expenses, outdooring ceremonies and so on and so forth, let us say a shilling a day. Now six shillings are gone, leaving sixpence. Because the worker is a polygamist and has two or three wives, about three of his children may be attending school and he has to give them twopence a day to buy food, and so the remaining sixpence is gone. Now what is he to save? How can he save? Who are the people to encourage saving? They are the lieutenants around the President himself who have their money inside and outside Ghana who should do the saving.[35]

But as the Assembly frittered away its last days in recrimination, a *deus ex machina* was preparing to intrude into a paralysed situation where political argument had ceased to be of any significance.

Kotoka, having outlined the operation to Afrifa,

returned to Harlley in Accra. There was an additional reason for haste on his part. He feared that his command might be taken from him at any moment and given to another officer, the son-in-law of Margaret Martei, the powerful head of the CPPs women's organization. In Accra Kotoka contacted Col. Ocran, the commander of the Accra garrison, and told him for the first time of the planned take-over. Ocran's support was essential. He had been at Eaton Hall with Kotoka and was recently promoted in the August reshuffle. In Accra he commanded four infantry battalions and several other units. He was at the centre of military communications and in daily contact with the company commanders. Ocran was also believed to have some influence with the commanders of the presidential units stationed close to Accra and might be able to ensure that they remained in their barracks for the operation. Ocran had doubts when he heard of Kotoka's plans, but they were about the timing not the principle, and he agreed to join.[36]

At four in the morning of 23 February the troops of the Tamale garrison began their long journey south. The regional commissioner's office in the town remained in deep, unsuspicious slumber. Ironically, the government's mobilization exercise to test the army's readiness for the Rhodesian adventure had accustomed the townspeople to unusual troop movements before dawn.[37] Later in the morning the Tamale units under Afrifa encountered Kotoka and his men on the main road between Tamale and Kumasi. In a different time zone on the same day, Nkrumah was in Rangoon visiting the mausoleum which housed the remains of the twelve Burmese cabinet ministers assassinated in 1947, unaware that the end of his own career was only a few hours away.

By the end of the following day, 24 February, the army's operation was virtually over, entirely successful and relatively bloodless.[38] The Presidential Guard units in Flagstaff House and at their depot outside Accra at first resisted, but all other vital power centres in the capital fell quickly to the rebel troops. By six in the morning of the 24th, Kotoka was able to broadcast over the national radio announcing Nkrumah's deposition, the dissolution of the party, and the formation of a 'National Liberation Council' of army and police officers. He called upon,'all citizens' to 'assist in the arrest of all party heads, party chairmen and party secretaries' of the dissolved CPP. There was no doubt about the popularity of the coup. Even whilst sporadic firing was still going on in the vicinity of Flagstaff House, crowds gathered in the streets of Accra to welcome the soldiers and tear down the signs and banners of the party.

The most astonishing aspect of the February coup was not that it took place at all, but that the ruling party and its integral wings collapsed so completely within the course of a few hours, offering no resistance to the take-over. Those who were making money out of Nkrumah's regime and those who were most deeply committed to the ideals of its leader were bewildered by their sudden turn of fortune. The rest of the population easily and quickly detached themselves from a movement which had forfeited their trust. Nkrumah's calls from exile for resistance over the next weeks fell on deaf ears. No elements of the party went underground and carried the struggle into the hills and forests. The armed guerrillas in the secret camps submitted meekly to the new masters. It was as if the party had lost the will to survive in the face of its own inner dissensions and the country's intractable problems. Once its leader was deposed there seemed to be no point in carrying on. One by one, district and regional commissioners, members of parliament, headquarters officials reported as ordered by the radio to their local police stations for arrest.

In his absence Nkrumah had entrusted his country to a presidential commission comprising Nathaniel Welbeck, the Minister of State for Party Propaganda, and two obscure chiefs. The first leading politician to hear of the army's operation was Kofi Baako. He contacted the deputy secretary to the cabinet, I.K. Impraim, who was in charge of security matters in the absence of his chief, Enoch Okoh, who was with the President. But Impraim could not — or would not — make contact with Welbeck who might have emerged with Baako as one of the strong men of the party in its most desperate moment. At four thirty on the morning of the 24th, only Baako, Impraim and A.E. Inkumsah, accompanied by the two bewildered chiefs,[39] succeeded in meeting at the Ambassador Hotel as the army dealt the death blow to the regime a mile up the road at Flagstaff House. There was no contingency plan for mobilizing the party; no safe means of contacting the President's Guard Regiment. The once mighty CPP ceased to function on the terrace of Accra's biggest hotel. At six o'clock Baako left the hotel to give himself up to Harlley. Unable to find him, he went to the Roman Catholic cathedral to await arrest.

IX Nkrumah in Retrospect 1966-1974

As the crowds enthusiastically smashed the images of their fallen Caesar in 1966, it seemed to them that they had been given a second start, freed at last from a regime which had become more oppressive than the one it had replaced in the name of freedom and justice. But second chances rarely occur in history; the slate cannot so easily be wiped clean. Nkrumah's rule had commenced with many advantages which were exhausted or beyond recall. In particular it had started with hard cash in the bank. All that the National Liberation Council possessed to set against the debts and the run-down economy was an asset of the most fragile and evanescent kind — a state of popular euphoria.

The new government, although directed by army and police officers, was careful not to impose an oppressive military presence. The work of devising new policies was handed over to senior civil servants who were given a more or less free hand to do many of the things that the hostility and inefficiency of the previous regime had prevented them from attempting. Ghana's international and pan-African ambitions were cut down to a scale more commensurate with her depleted resources. The new government turned sharply away from the communist bloc which had wooed Nkrumah so assiduously and towards the western powers and to Britain in particular. In economic matters the first steps were taken to cut down the high government spending of the previous years. At first this trend was hopefully accompanied by a slight recovery of the world cocoa price. The outlook for the immediate future, although still daunting, began to give grounds for modest optimism.

On the political front the NLC initiated discussions for an early resumption of 'normal' political life. It regarded itself as a provisional government with no desire to hold on to power permanently. Its members sought to revive political life faithful to the British traditions which they regarded Nkrumah as having betrayed, but which, in fact, he had probably destroyed. No group was to be driven into intransigent opposition towards whatever form of polity might eventually emerge. Only those totally unrepentant of their former careers were to be excluded from public life. Former politicians were to be subjected to trial before the regular courts only if the evidence produced during the enquiries into their affairs was deemed sufficient to justify their prosecution. But there was to be no witch-hunt of Nkrumah's men over and above this kind of process. The arbitrary, capricious arrests and political bullying, so hated during the first Republic, were, it was hoped, a thing of the past.

Within Ghana there was a mood of critical self-examination. What had gone wrong under Nkrumah? And how could similar disasters be averted in the future?

If Nkrumah's early success had been due in part to his successful courtship of the young men, the NLC represented in some respects a revival of the authority of the elders. Dr Busia, who returned to Ghana shortly after the coup, initiated a 'civic education programme' designed to revive a spirit of moral sensibility inspired by Christian and traditional values. For the conservative elements of the population this offered one way of resolving their perplexities. For many of the younger Ghanaians, especially in the universities, Dr Busia's revivalism was unattractive and irrelevant. Amongst these there was a desire to make politics once more a serious business concerned above all with the central problem of development.

When the constitutional proposals finally emerged in January 1968 it was clear that the second Republic was to embody the fruits of the lessons painfully learned after independence. The central lesson was that power should not be concentrated in the hands of a single man. To secure this end the constitutional commissioners[1] drew heavily upon the anglo-saxon political tradition. Provision was made for a president and head of state distinct from the prime minister, the leader of the majority party. The president was to be elected for a term of eight years and thereafter would be ineligible for re-election. He would exercise his executive power only on the advice of the cabinet and would be assisted by a council of state. Other safeguards against arbitrary rule were provided, including an ombudsman to provide a point of appeal against the actions of officials. The constitution of the second Republic was certainly on paper a model of western political liberalism, although of a conservative flavour. But would good intentions alone ensure its survival?

The results of the first general elections under the new constitution reflected the continuing distaste for further experiments in political radicalism.[2] Dr Busia's party was returned with a good majority and in October 1969 he became the first and only prime minister of the second Republic after years in exile. But the legacy of debt bequeathed to his government by Nkrumah's regime presented him with problems which he was unable to solve. Caesar's ghost relentlessly stalked his successors in sharp contrast to the insubstantial influence wielded by the living Caesar exiled in Conakry. Population and unemployment continued to increase whilst the economy remained largely stagnant. The repayment of the massive debts dominated the country's economic policies. Busia was forced to steer a course between Scylla and Charybdis. Every policy designed to put Ghana on the course of financial prudence, to stabilize the currency and to repay its debts, increased urban unemployment and the cost of living. By the end of 1971 the economic situation was worse even than it had been at the time of Nkrumah's downfall. After a massive devaluation late in 1971 the second Republic itself was unceremoniously bundled into history by the second military coup of January 1972.

It was perhaps natural that the fallen Nkrumah should become a scapegoat for all the failures and shortcomings of his rule. But he was not merely a greedy usurper filled with preposterous ambitions. His rule etched deeper lines on Ghana's political life than was first apparent after his fall. The man who had for a time a price upon his head in his own country has subsequently been admitted into its pantheon. With his death in exile and reburial in his homeland, his countrymen have moved towards a longer view of the leader who was so much bound up with the emergence of his country's modern identity. Divisions of political opinion in Ghana may well revolve in future round the formative experiences of the first decade of independence. Paradoxically, the party which was built so much around the cult of its founder's personality may yet survive in spirit, if not in name, the death of its hero.

There are Ghanaians who regard the entire Nkrumah episode with distaste, seeing it as an unfortunate lapse from the ideals of liberal representative government which animated the pioneers of national consciousness in colonial West Africa. A few are inclined to pessimism, doubtful whether Ghana can ever hope to regain its lost political traditions without a change of heart amongst its people. Nkrumah all too successfully uncovered a receptivity to demagogy which later politicians will certainly exploit again.[3] For many others, however, the recollections of

Nkrumah's shortcomings are already blunted by a nostalgia for the days of excitement and promise when their small country occupied a prominent position on the African and world stage out of all proportion to its size and importance. If the proliferation of offices under Nkrumah's rule was not particularly productive, it was at least preferable to the unemployment and austerity which has plagued the country in its attempts at reconstruction. And although popular feeling turned against the CPP in its last years, it did succeed for a time in giving hundreds of thousands of ordinary people a sense of identification with a great, national movement. Nothing has subsequently emerged in Ghana's political life to replace the CPP in this repect. The donnish Dr Busia's party, victorious at the polls during the short-lived second Republic, failed to capture popular imagination. It may have been respected — it may arguably have proved more capable than the CPP had it been given more time — but it was never loved, and has perished without much lament.

Some regard the Nkrumah years, not as an aberration but as a movement, however clumsily and ineffectually executed, in the right direction — towards a social state in a united continent. The CPP's public aims still command substantial emotional support. Many of its former supporters began to re-emerge into public life during the second Republic and they are likely to be an important force in the future, particularly if the present military government chose to stand down and let the politicians try again. Their problem will be to ensure that the ideals of their movement, if it is allowed to reclaim historic links with the old CPP will not be corrupted as they were in Nkrumah's day by personal dictatorship.

They will face difficulties. One is that posed by those still strongly influenced by the magnetism of the dead President who believe that it was his lieutenants who betrayed their leader rather than the leader who corrupted the movement. They have the testament of Nkrumah himself, written after his downfall, to support their case. The evidence of Nkrumah's own venality is unlikely to convince them of his responsibility for the canker which spread through the CPP from the top downwards. Even if they admit his blemishes, what political leader is ever impeccable? For all his faults Nkrumah was the symbol of Ghana itself. It was he who gave his countrymen a genuine sense of pride in a common nationality. Such a memory is not easily excised. How can the birth of Ghana command respect if the dead father is execrated? If he is discredited, what is left? How can the grey rule of collective leadership or the remoteness of military or bureaucratic government compare with the myth of the wronged, dead Messiah, the father of his nation? Sentiments like these open up the possibility of a bonapartist road to power for a man possessing personal *élan* and commanding popular support who will claim to be the spiritual successor of Nkrumah.

Another and more immediate difficulty is whether a popular democracy, in which a movement animated by the CPP's ideals of socialism and unity could play a part, will be given another chance — whether Ghana will be allowed to resume the political voyage it embarked upon twenty years ago. A reversion to popular democracy does not, admittedly, seem likely in the near future. The army engineered the first coup in 1966 partly to rectify its own grievances, but also because it regarded itself as the ultimate custodian of a national interest which it felt was being betrayed by the politicians. It was not a rebellion for the sake of power alone. Once the NLC felt that its revolution was secure it handed over to those whom it thought were capable of ruling with more prudence, honesty and efficiency than Nkrumah's men had shown. But the army's act of intervention was itself a major breach of the disintegrating traditions it sought to restore. The magic vessels which had hitherto separated the possession of force from the exercise of power were first broken in 1966. If the army could seize power for the best of motives in that year, then they could do so for worse reasons in the future. The soldiers had been aroused to a fatal sense of their own strength and of the weakness of the civil power. The NLC itself had a foretaste of this ominous development in the unsuccessful 'mini-coup' of April 1967 in which Kotoka lost his life. Almost five years later a second intervention by the soldiers put an end to the painstakingly constructed second Republic. The dangers for the future are obvious. Revolutionary zeal could easily decay into a struggle for spoils, opening up a dismal prospect of long periods of repression, punctuated by bursts of civil strife in which the once promising political inheritance of Ghana would be totally destroyed — a melancholy conclusion to the pursuit of the elusive political kingdom on which Nkrumah embarked.

Notes

Chapter I

1 Kwame Nkrumah, *Ghana: The Autobiography of Kwame Nkrumah* (Nelson, London 1957).

2 Both Garvey and Du Bois were subsequently honoured in Nkrumah's Ghana. Du Bois became editor of the *Encyclopaedia Africana* which Nkrumah started until his death at an advanced age in 1965. Garvey's 'Black Star Line', which was set up in name only to repatriate the New World negroes back to Africa, gave its name to Ghana's own commercial shipping line.

3 The expression 'African Personality' fell into disuse as Nkrumah swung towards 'scientific socialism' after 1961. The term was probably first used by the nineteenth-century Liberian writer and diplomat, Edward Blyden. In 1958 Komla Gbedemah, then a close associate of Nkrumah's, defined it as meaning that 'Africans should be able to stand up to any other person, no matter what his colour or skin; this is not necessarily looking down on others, but we should think ourselves equal.'

4 See James Hooker, *Black Revolutionary* (Pall Mall, London, 1967) for a fuller account of Padmore's

association with Nkrumah. Hooker suggests that Padmore may have shaped Nkrumah's views on pan-Africanism in such a way as to make them unacceptable to other Africans. Certainly the brand of pan-Africanism Nkrumah continued to preach after Padmore's death had more emotional appeal to West Indian and American blacks, especially those living abroad, than it had for African peoples and their leaders.

5 See Dennis Austin, *Politics in Ghana, 1946-1960* (Oxford University Press, 1970) for an admirable account of Ghana's transition from colony to independent statehood.

6 Dr Joseph Boakye Danquah, a prominent Gold Coast lawyer and writer, was born in 1895 and described by an official report in 1948 as 'the doyen amongst Gold Coast politicians'. It was Danquah who revived the name of an eleventh-century West African kingdom, Ghana, as the modern title of the Gold Coast.

7 Ako Adjei was the son of a prominent Ga family. He attended Lincoln and Pennsylvania universities in the United States, and then the London School of Economics. Although he was instrumental in getting Nkrumah his job with the Convention, he did not join Nkrumah's new party until 1953. After serving for a time as Ghana's Foreign Minister he was arrested and imprisoned late in 1962 (see Ch. IV).

8 The members of the working committee who were arrested, tried and exiled from the capital were popularly known as the 'Big Six' — Nkrumah, Edward Akufo Addo, William Ofori Atta, Ako Adjei, Danquah, and Obetsebi Lamptey. The last three eventually found themselves in Nkrumah's prison in conditions far inferior to those they had experienced in 1948. As Danquah later wrote, 'When in 1948 we were

arrested by the British government and sent to the north for detention, they treated us like gentlemen and provided each of us with a furnished bungalow with a garden, together with opportunity for reading and writing.' ('Dr J.B. Danquah: Detention and Death in Nsawam Prison', extracts from evidence, p.116, N.L.C., Accra).

9 'Report of the Commission of Enquiry into the Recent Disturbances in the Gold Coast' (Aitken Watson Report, no.231, Colonial Office, London, June 1948).

10 Several successful libel suits were brought against Nkrumah as owner of the *Evening News*, including one by Dr Danquah. Failing to claim his award, he sent in the bailiffs to seal the newspaper's offices, thus hoping vainly to muzzle it.

11 In fact, most of the members of Nkrumah's first government of 1951 were graduates or from leading Gold Coast families. However, not all stayed the course, and their non-graduate, locally-educated associates, such as Komla Gbedemah, Krobo Edusei, Kofi Baako and John Tettegah emerged as more durable political figures.

12 Dr Busia, whose own Ghana Congress Party, founded in 1952, incorporated the pro-Danquah rump of the Convention, but won only one seat in the 1954 election, did not share the widespread optimistic view of Nkrumah's triumphant progress. Writing in *Parliamentary Affairs* (vol.v, no.4) in 1952, he stated that 'the present constitutional experiment is the child of agitation, and it is to the agitators that power was delivered. With the rejection of the Chiefs and older leaders, with a large number of the best-educated youth in the Civil Service, the field was left clear for demagogues, and seldom has demagogy paid as high dividends as in the Gold Coast today.' Disappointment,

no doubt, sharpened his perception. In exile throughout Nkrumah's later career, he survived to become the first and only Prime Minister of the short-lived second Republic which was overthrown in 1972 after only thirty-one months of life.

13 Nkrumah's official title in the days of the Republic was 'Osagyefo Dr Kwame Nkrumah, Head of the Order of the Black Star, Head of the Order of the Volta, President, and Supreme Commander of the Armed Forces'. 'Osagyefo' was a martial title borrowed from the Ashanti. The title of Doctor came from an honorary degree bestowed upon him by the University of Pennsylvania after his political success. Nkrumah's effigy appeared on the coinage with the superscription 'Conditor Ghanaiensis'. Statues and framed photographs of Nkrumah were common in public places. After his downfall it was said that he was planning to change the capital city's name to 'Nkrumakrom'.

14 Danquah was first detained in 1961. Released in the following year, under a partial amnesty, he was invited to witness the award of a Lenin Peace Prize to Nkrumah. The latter commented sourly that Danquah looked fitter than himself and had obviously been fed upon 'eggs and bacon' during detention. The Director of Prisons was later instructed to feed detainees in future on 'garri, salt and water only'. Danquah was detained again in January 1964, and died in prison a year later. ('Dr Danquah: Detention and Death in Nsawam Prison', p.52)

15 Nkrumah's major publications, apart from his autobiography, were *I Speak of Freedom* (1961), *Africa Must Unite* (1963), *Consciencism* (1964) and *Neo-colonialism: The Last Stage of Imperialism* (1965). Of these books, *Consciencism* was the most curious. It contained twenty-two quasi-mathematical theorems

'proving' the necessity of a union of independent African states.

16 Tibor Szamuely, *Spectator*, no.7158, 11 March 1966.

17 'Report of the Commission of Enquiry. University of Science and Technology, Kumasi' (Manyo Plange Report, N.L.C. 1967, paras. 677-87).

18 K. Nkrumah, *Ghana: The Autobiography*, p.9.

19 *Ghanaian Times*, 28 April 1966. See also 'Report of the Commission to Enquire into the Kwame Nkrumah Properties' (Apaloo Report, N.L.C., 1966). Yankey himself was to be left £10,000 in Nkrumah's will.

20 An interesting example of this kind of mental dissociation was noticed by David Brokensha in his book *Social Change at Larteh, Ghana* (Clarendon Press, Oxford, 1966). He describes the Minister of Health's address to the inaugural meeting of the 'Ghana Psychic and Traditional Healing Association' in April 1962. The Minister spoke first in English, warning his listeners that 'psychic and traditional healing must be divested of all the trappings of fetischism'. Then he spoke in Twi recounting 'many personal experiences he had had with the supernatural and was generally more conciliatory than he had been in English' (p.187).

21 Bing's apologia of these years has been published (*Reap the Whirlwind*, Macgibbon and Kee, London, 1969). In a review of Bing's book, a Ghanaian lecturer in politics wrote that 'one very important reason why Nkrumah failed in Ghana and was alienated not only from the "intellectuals" or the "elite" but, in the last years of his regime from the "masses" as well, was that he relied too much on foreign political advisers, mostly left-wing dissidents at odds with their own societies. These people never understood Ghana.' (Kweku Folson, *Encounter*, 1969).

22 *Off. Jnl. Parl. Debs.*, 15 February 1965, col.1061.

Chapter II

1 There was no widespread public demand in Ghana for the introduction of the Republic before the government's exercise, and even less for the severance of the Commonwealth connection. Nkrumah himself held the appointment as one of the Queen's Privy Counsellors — an appointment which took the edge off his disappointment at the postponement of the Queen's visit to Ghana made necessary by her pregnancy.

2 'White Paper on the Government's Proposals for a Republican Constitution' (Government Printer, Accra, 1960).

3 *Proceedings of the Constituent Assembly*, 15 March 1960.

4 In connection with the 1958 Preventive Detention act, one writer has commented that 'historical antecedents of such executive power need not be traced beyond the disturbances in the Gold Coast in 1948'. See W.M. Harvey, *Law and Social Change in Ghana* (Princeton University Press, Princeton, N.J., 1966, p.28).

5 *Off. Jnl. Parl. Debs.*, 14 July 1958, col.418.

6 The National Assembly (Disqualification) act of 1959 deprived members of parliament ordered into detention of their seats.

7 The first act was tightened up by amending acts in 1962 and 1963 and was replaced by a new Preventive Detention act in 1964 which placed in the President's hands exclusive powers to make or revoke detention orders. Previous detention orders remained in force.

8 Harlley, interview with editorial board of the *Legon Observer*, 17 February 1967.

9 *Ghanaian Times*, 12 July 1966.

10 Ibid., 16 March 1967. Boateng had protested mildly to the President at the practice of detaining people at

police stations without regard to the formalities prescribed by the act. But Nkrumah warned him not to interfere with those held without warrants of arrest, 'because he (Nkrumah) was head of security and knew what people had done'. Boateng claimed that he knew it to be an unpleasant business to detain people. 'I would have resigned, but did not because I was scared stiff of the very powerful act.'

11   Ibid., 27 July 1966.

12   A detailed account of the two opposition leaders' confinement is contained in the 'Report of the Commission appointed to enquire into Conditions prevailing in the Ghana Prisons Service' (N.L.C. 1968). Danquah was suffering from a heart condition, Lamptey from cancer. Both men died in prison.

13   Professor Sir Arthur Lewis, 'Beyond African Dictatorship' in *Encounter*, vol.xxv., no.2, August 1965.

14   In an article on 'Parliament in Republican Ghana' (*Parliamentary Affairs*, vol.16, 1962-63), J.M. Lees wrote that 'one must be prepared to accept that the party had superseded parliament as the centre of debate.' This observation was hardly true for the years up to 1963 — and certainly wasn't true for the remaining lifetime of the Republic. As the party became increasingly moribund and the economic crisis intensified, the Assembly revived as the most important, indeed the only centre of political debate with the sharp edge of rebellion rising to the surface.

15   *Off. Jnl. Parl. Debs.*, 12 May 1964, col.62.

16   See Ch.VIII for a fuller account of this critical debate.

17   'Report of the Commission of Enquiry into Mr Braimah's Resignation and the Allegation arising therefrom' (Korsah Commission, Gold Coast, Government Printer, 1954).

18   Apaloo Report, para. 408.

19 Ibid., paras. 408-17.
20 'Report and Statement by the Accountant General and Report Thereon by Auditor General for year ended 31.12.64' (Accra, 1967, para. 360).
21 Ibid., para. 361.
22 *The Spark*, 28 May 1965.
23 The number of MPs was increased from 114 to 198 in the second parliament. Their basic pay was cut from £1,200 to £854 per year. But many MPs also held other paid posts in the state corporations and the party agencies. Nkrumah was not totally opposed to his MPs receiving money from other sources — providing that these too were within his own control.
24 A debate arising from a motion on Africanization in the civil service in 1963 revealed the rapidly shrinking British component. In 1953 there were 1350 expatriate and 809 indigenous officers; by 1958 289 expatriates and 1984 Ghanaians. By 1962 only 39 expatriate civil servants remained compared with 3294 Ghanaians. (*Off. Jnl. Parl. Debs.*, 1 March 1963, col.102).
25 Occasionally their resentment took a physical form. In March 1961 Francis Tachie Menson, ironically a relative of Sir Charles Tachie Menson, the head of the Civil Service Commission, was sacked as ministerial secretary for losing his temper and striking a civil servant whilst the latter was carrying out his duties. (*Ghanaian Times*, 1 April 1961).
26 'A New Charter for the Civil Service', Government White Paper, 2/60 (Government Printer, Accra, April 1960).
27 Ibid.
28 'Statement by Osagyefo the President at the Seminar for Senior Civil Servants at Winneba', 14 April 1962.
29 Ibid.
30 Ibid.

31 *Evening News*, 12 and 13 December 1963.
32 After the coup Nkrumah wrote that he 'had for long had the gravest doubts about many of those in leading positions in my party. Despite the establishment of the ideological institute at Winneba ... it was clear to me that many in high positions still failed to understand the political and social purposes of the State.' (*Dark Days in Ghana*, p.73).
33 In the *Annual Estimates for 1965* the Office of the President was headed by the secretary to the cabinet, who was also head of the civil service, and was responsible for 'the overall administrative direction, control and co-ordination of those subjects that come under the direction of the President'. These subjects included parliamentary business, legislative policy, ministerial functions, administration of the civil service, the Volta River Authority, regional organizations, higher education, foreign trade, internal security, African affairs, chieftancy matters and the Workers Brigade. The amount of money needed to run the President's Office rose sharply from £15.5 million in 1963-64 to an estimated £23 million in 1965.
34 Adu left Ghana on secondment to become secretary general of the East African Common Services Organization, joining the outflow of Ghanaian top civil servants, including Robert Gardiner and C.H. Chapman, who preferred to work abroad. Adu later wrote of Nkrumah, 'his policies did much to undermine the integrity of the Civil Service which he himself had done so much to inspire in the immediate post-independence period.' (A.L. Adu, *The Civil Service in Commonwealth Africa*, George Allen and Unwin, London, 1968).
35 J.H. Mensah, 'Relevance of Marxian Economics to Development Planning in Ghana', *Economic Bulletin*

of Ghana, vol.9, no.1, 1965. Mensah's independence caused the *Ghanaian Times* in 1964 to accuse him of being a 'quisling' and an 'armchair bourgeois theoretician'.

36 'Public Accounts Committee; Second Report', submitted to the National Assembly, October 1964, paras. 46 and 47.

Chapter III

1 *Toward Socialism: Osagyefo's Message to the Seminar for Regional Commissioners, Regional Secretaries, Party Attachés, District Commissioners, and Senior Officials of the Party's Integral Wings* (Ministry of Information and Broadcasting, Accra, 24 November 1962, p.18).

2 Amongst the Winneba staff were the British communist writers, Pat Sloan and Idris Cox, two Nigerian communists, Bankole Akpata and Samuel Grace Ikoku, and the Hungarian, Tibor Szamuelly, whose uncle had been a leading member of Bela Kun's short-lived communist regime in Hungary in 1919. Szamuelly took advantage of his stay in Ghana to defect to Britain in 1965. After many upsets Ikoku became Commissioner for Trade and Industry for the East-Central Region of Nigeria under General Gowon's administration. After being expelled from Ghana in 1966, he was imprisoned in Nigeria and took advantage of his incarceration to write a book on his Ghana experiences (*Le Ghana de Nkrumah*, see p.269).

3 Addison became a member of the group known as the 'socialist boys' so detested by the conservative wing of the party. He presided over the Ghana-Soviet Friendship Society and the CPPs education committee.

Despite being sacked from the Institute for his inefficiency he crowned his career by getting himself appointed to the party committee set up in 1964 to purge school and university libraries of books deemed to be of a 'capitalist' or 'reactionary' nature.

4 *Evening News*, 1 October 1965.

5 Interview with *Agence Presse France*, 19 May 1965.

6 Writing of Mali and Ghana, the authors of *National Liberation Movements* (Foreign Languages Publishing House, Novosti Press, Moscow, 1965) commented that 'The socialist doctrines in these countries do not constitute elaborate philosophical systems but rather a sum total of contemplated economic and political measures reinforced by a number of ideological principles.' (p.137) What seems to have worried these authors was the 'insufficient development of classes' in Ghana which produced a 'desire to go over to socialism on the basis of the political organization of the whole people' rather than to introduce a dictatorship of the proletariat directed by a party vanguard.

7 Thomas Hodgkin, *Freedom for the Gold Coast* (Union for Democratic Control, London, August 1951).

8 Thomas Hodgkin, 'What Future for Africa?', in *Encounter*, June 1961.

9 Rita Hinden, a fabian socialist, in a critical review of Fenner Brockway's book *African Socialism* (The Bodley Head, London, 1963) wrote with considerable justification that 'the real trouble in African thought today is that it is in many places caught up in a massive process of self-deception, blindly encouraged by men like Fenner Brockway', in *Encounter*, March 1964.

10 J.K. Twum in *Off. Jnl. Parl. Debs.*, 4 June 1962, col. 365.

11 It is not of course only the unsophisticated peoples of Africa who may be impressed by arguments based upon

authority. Thomas Hobbes three centuries ago observed that 'Words are wise men's counters; they do but
reckon by them, but they are the money of fools, that
value them by the authority of an Aristotle, a Cicero,
or a Thomas, or by any other doctor whatsoever if but
a man.' (*Leviathan*, Ch.IV)

12 *Off. Jnl. Parl. Debs.*, 7 February 1966.

13 A detailed account of party and government machinery
is given in the unpublished Ph.D. thesis of Benjamin
Amonoo, *The Politics of Institutional Dualism;
Ghana, 1957-1966* (University of Exeter, 1974).
Amonoo explains the strange combination of anarchy
and authoritarianism in Ghana's political system as due
to an unresolved tension between 'unorthodox'
political necessity as represented by the party's
structures, and 'orthodox' bureaucratic rationality as
exemplified by the regular administration, both operating within an incompletely adapted colonial system.

14 Of the other regional commissioners, Joseph Hagan,
commissioner first for the Central Region and then of
the Eastern Region, had been a storekeeper before
becoming a trade union official. Like Adam, Hagan
was a foundation member of the MPP. E.H.T. Korboe
in charge of the Eastern Region until his transfer in
1965 to the Central Region, had been a cocoa farmer
and a clerk. R.O. Amoaka Atta worked in local
government and rose to become town clerk of the gold
mining town of Obuasi. He was Minister of Labour in
1960 before taking over the Ashanti Region in 1963 and
then the Brong-Ahafo Region the following year. In
1965 he was transferred back to the Ashanti Region.
Hans Kofi Boni, in charge of the Volta Region until
appointment as Minister of Food in 1965, had also been
a school teacher. John Arthur, in charge of the Western
Region, had started as a clerk and moved into trade

union activity in Sekondi-Takoradi. The only regional commissioner to hold a university degree was O. Owusu Afriyie in the Ashanti Region until his appointment as Minister of Labour late in 1962. The control of the provinces was thus rotated between a small group of men of humble backgrounds whose loyalty to their leader was unquestioned and whose immunity to dangerous ideas from the left of the party was very high.

15 *Ghanaian Times*, 11 January 1968.

16 Amonoo (op.cit.) sees the secretaries of the regional commissioners as figures of considerable importance in the running of the regional organizations. They were civil servants, not paid by the party, and were powerful enough sometimes to challenge their chiefs' activities.

17 *Ghanaian Times*, 17 August 1967.

18 Five former regional commissioners were all subsequently discovered by the commissions of enquiry to have acquired assets in excess of their lawful earnings.

19 'Unlike the district commissioners (*sic*) of the colonial era, the district commissioners of the 1960s were mostly people with little or no administrative experience — Standard VII school-leavers whose only qualification was either their total commitment to the CPP or a recommendation from the Regional Commissioner, or both. In some cases the post ... was "purchased" outright.' (Maxwell Owusu, *The Uses and Abuses of Political Power*, University of Chicago Press, Chicago, 1970, p.286). The purchase of office was not always successful. In one case a petty trader, an illiterate with only a rudimentary knowledge of English, paid £400 to J.E. Hagan, Regional Commissioner for the Eastern Region, to be gazetted as a district commissioner. Hagan took the money, but the trader did not get the

post (*Daily Graphic*, 17 January 1967).

20 This was F.K. Buah, D.C. for Twifu Praso in 1964. Buah, an unfrocked priest, was a Tema headmaster and co-author with Basil Davidson of a school history of West Africa.

21 *Ghanaian Times*, 8 March 1963.

22 *Off. Jnl. Parl. Debs.*, 18 May 1964, col.118.

23 Brokensha, op. cit.

24 *Off. Jnl. Parl. Debs.*, 18 May 1964, col.115.

25 Ibid., 20 July 1961, col.497.

26 *Towards Socialism*, p.27.

27 *Ghanaian Times*, 6 March 1963.

28 Owusu, op. cit.

29 Bensah was one of the six ministers asked to surrender properties in excess of the limits laid down by Nkrumah in his 'dawn broadcast'. He did not lose his ministerial rank however and was restored to the government as Minister of Works in the second Parliament of the Republic, August 1965.

30 Sintim Aboagye continued his career as MP for Akim Abuakwa until the coup. Called before a Commission of Enquiry into the affairs of the Kumasi University after the coup, he was alleged by witnesses to be 'a very mean man' who, it was claimed, spent only NC 10 per year on clothing for his three children but spent NC 600 on an ornamental fishpond for his house. 'You politicians are very fond of fishponds' remarked the chairman amidst general laughter. See *Ghanaian Times*, 25 January 1967.

31 Welbeck, a former teacher, joined the CPP at an early date. He was first elected to parliament in 1954. In 1960 he was sent to the Congo (Zaire) as Nkrumah's emissary to Lumumba, but was soon expelled by the Congolese.

32 Peter Barker, *Operation Cold Chop* (Ghana Publishing

Corporation, Accra, 1969), p.57.

33 J.H.A. Watson, 'French-speaking Africa since Independence', address to the Royal Commonwealth Society, London, May 1963.

34 Immanuel Wallerstein, *Africa: The Politics of Independence* (Random House, New York, 1961). See also Professor S.E. Finer's critique of African one party states in *Government and Opposition*, vol.2, no.4, July-October 1967, for a less enthusiastic summing up of the arguments for such regimes.

35 This brilliant band of young American scholars writing on the African party systems in the optimistic days of the early sixties included James S. Coleman, David Apter, Ruth Schachter Morgenthau, William J. Foltz, Frank P. Snyder, Aristide Zolberg and Martin Kilson. They did not agree with each other in all respects, but worked indefatigably on the assumption that African parties were the key to understanding African politics. The armed forces, which almost everywhere possessed an older corporate identity than the political parties, were virtually ignored. In the late sixties, however, many of the regimes they had studied were overthrown by the military. The pendulum of academic fashion swung over to the opposite but equally unbalanced study of military regimes.

36 J.H.A. Watson (op.cit.) for instance maintained that 'all West Africans are good at politics. There is no area of the world which has acquired such a wide range of independence with so little bloodshed, with so little discord, in world history.' Whilst his sentiments were admirable, the events of the last decade hardly support his assertion. The truth is that West Africans are neither 'good' nor 'bad' at politics compared with other peoples. This kind of optimism, whilst widespread, was not universal. Sir Arthur Lewis remarked that the

single party state in Africa was '... the basic stuff of European totalitarianism. The single party representing all the people is the fascist branch; the single party representing only the oppressed is the communist branch. Its adherents in West Africa picked it up during their journeys through Europe.' ('Beyond African Dictatorship', in *Encounter*, vol.xxv, no.2, 1965).

37 *Off. Jnl. Parl. Debs.*, 12 September 1962, cols.202-403. Baako's meretricious arguments in favour of the single party state and in praise of 'democratic centralism' were really based upon a collection of sophisms common enough in the communist world. The essence of Ghana's political system — as understood by the great majority of the population — was powerfully expressed, although somewhat unthinkingly, only a week before by a lady MP, Miss Victoria Nyarko, who described the President as 'A man who has been endowed with supreme power over the lives and destiny of our whole nation; a man who is entrusted with the well-being of every individual of the state. Such a man indeed holds the power of life or death over every single person in Ghana. (*Off. Jnl. Parl. Debs.*, 6 September 1962, col.66).

38 *Ghanaian Times*, 24 January 1964.

39 Baako, *Off. Jnl. Parl. Debs.*, 18 May 1965, col.8.

40 Ibid., col.10.

41 Ibid., col.30.

42 David Apter in *Ghana in Transition* (Athenaeum Press, New York, 1963).

43 Ruth First in *From the Barrel of a Gun* (Penguin, London, 1970).

44 After Nkrumah's fall, two American marxist writers, Bob Fitch and Mary Oppenheim, both erstwhile admirers of his regime, wrote that 'the situation in

Ghana was quite different from the appearance which
we, along with many others, had all too uncritically
accepted as reflecting reality'. ('Ghana: The End of an
Illusion', in *Monthly Review*, New York, vol.18, no.3,
1966).
45 *Ghanaian Times*, 10 March 1966.

Chapter IV

1 *Ghanaian Times* 1 October 1963.
2 Edmund Nee Ocansey, a builder and contractor,
organized the CPP's 'motor despatch' units in its early
years. He bought a printing press for Nkrumah who
used it to print the *Evening News*. Ocansey was rewarded with a succession of deputy ministerial posts for his
loyalty, finally ending his career in parliament as
Minister of Parks and Gardens in 1965. His principal
job in this latter capacity was to tidy up Accra for the
1965 OAU summit meeting.
3 The title Adamafio chose for his student organization
was a calculated piece of flattery of his new master,
since it invoked the title of the earlier 'National Association of Student Organizations' in which Nkrumah
and Padmore had worked after the Pan African
Congress in Manchester in 1945.
4 At his trial in 1963 Adamafio admitted that his uncle,
the MP Robert Abbey, was 'related somehow' to
Obetsebi Lamptey (*Ghanaian Times*, 10 October 1963).
Emmanuel Obetsebi Lamptey was born in Accra in
1902. He studied law in Britain and returned to the
Gold Coast in 1945. A founder member of the UGCC,
he was one of the 'Big Six' arrested after the 1948 disturbances. After his release he served on the Coussey
Commission and later helped to found the Ghana

Congress Party which was absorbed into the United
Party in 1958. In 1961 he went into exile in Togo,
returning to Ghana after Nkrumah's offer of an
amnesty. Later in the year he was arrested and put into
detention where he died of ill-health in January 1963.
('Mr E. Obetsebi Lamptey: Detention and Death in
Nsawam Prison', N.L.C., Accra, 1967).

5 The Jiagge Commission after the coup cleared
Adamafio of any charge of unlawful acquisition of
wealth during his public career.

6 An example of the adulatory way the press reported
Adamafio's activities can be found in the TUC paper,
African Worker (7 March 1960). It referred to
Adamafio and Tettegah as 'these two apostles of
Nkrumaism'.... [who] 'spent sleepless nights planning
and discussing with our Socialist Leader, Teacher and
President of Free Ghana, the raising of the living
standards of the Workers, Farmers and people of
Ghana.'

7 Adamafio, reported in the *Ghanaian Times*, 9 October
1963.

8 Ibid., 2 October 1963.

9 Ibid.

10 Baah was a graduate of an American University and
had been one of the original directors of the party's
private commercial company, NADECO (see Ch. VI)
but had resigned a year later, dissatisfied with the
increasing hostility in certain circles of the CPP
towards indigenous businessmen. He was probably
under no illusions about the nature of NADECO's
operations (see Ch. VI).

11 John Tettegah was a close associate of Adamafio's,
and widely regarded as a leading radical. He was a
native of Ada, a coastal town not far from Gbedemah's
home town of Keta. Tettegah started work as a

stenographer and later became a full-time trade union official, rising to become general secretary of the TUC in 1954.

12 *Off. Jnl. Parl. Debs.*, 23 February 1961, col.197.

13 Ibid., col.199.

14 *Ghanaian Times*, 27 February 1971.

15 Ibid.

16 *Off. Jnl. Parl. Affairs*, 27 February 1961.

17 Ibid., col.273.

18 Ibid., col.273/4. Part VII, Section 29, of the National Assembly Act of 1959, guaranteed a member of parliament a measure of privilege for his speeches in the Assembly. It did not, however, guarantee them immunity from arrest under the Preventive Detention act. By the end of the year (1961) several opposition members were in prison, and others were to follow.

19 The committee was headed by Sir Charles Tachie Menson, the chairman of the Public Service Commission and a relative of Francis Tachie Menson, one of the politicians accused of having extensive business interests. The other two members were the expatriate Auditor-General, Nevile Sabine, and the Solicitor-General, G.C. Mills Odoi, who had links with the Adamafio group.

20 *Off. Jnl. Parl. Debs.*, 24 April 1961 col.134.

21 Ibid., col.137.

22 Tettegah finally got a seat in the Assembly in the enlarged second parliament of the Republic in August 1965.

23 *Off. Jnl. Parl. Debs.*, 24th April 1961, col.137.

24 Ibid., 25th April 1961, col.173.

25 Ibid., col.175/176.

26 Ibid.

27 Ibid.

28 Quaidoo's fate took a better turn after the coup.

Quickly released from detention he resumed his business career early in 1966 and became chairman of the Black Star Line. In May 1969 he re-entered the short political life of the second Republic as a founder member of the unsuccessful Republican Party.

29 *Ghanaian Times*, 27 April 1961.
30 *Off. Jnl. Parl. Debs.*, 25 April 1961, col.180.
31 Gbedemah, interview with editorial board of *Legon Observer*, 19 August 1966.
32 Goka, born in 1921 in the Volta Region, had qualified as a teacher before entering into political life. He was Regional Commissioner of the Volta Region in 1959-60 before becoming Minister of Trade in 1960. Goka was later dismissed from the front bench but was soon re-instated.
33 The government's handling of the budget proposals before parliament was extraordinarily clumsy. The opposition member, Joe Appiah, accused the Finance Minister of laying before the House an order, without a date or a proper signature, exempting cocoa farmers from payment of income tax. It was, Appiah claimed, and the Speaker ruled, invalid. 'Yet the Honourable Member (Goka) got up with a piece of paper which he pretended was an Executive Instrument duly and properly signed.' (*Off. Jnl. Parl. Debs.*, 11 July 1961, col.206).
Almost as damaging to the government's reputation as the proposals themselves were the rumours circulating at this time about the new impositions. One rumour had it that Savings Bank deposits were going to be taken over by the government, which led to a rush of withdrawals. Another rumour suggested that the National Development Bonds were not going to be repaid. Unfortunately for the farmers, this latter

rumour turned out to be true (see Ch. VII).

34 *Off. Jnl. Parl. Debs.*, 10 July 1961, col.184.

35 Ibid., col.165/166.

36 *Ghanaian Times*, 25 August 1961.

37 Ibid., 7 September 1961.

38 St Clair Drake and Alexander Leslie, 'Government versus the Unions; the Sekondi-Takoradi Strike of 1961' in Gwen Carter (ed.), *Politics in Africa: Seven Cases* (New York, Harcourt, Brace & World, 1966).

39 Adamafio soon afterwards denied having used the term 'despicable rats' a phrase which brought him great public odium. But at his trial in 1963 he admitted that he had in fact 'used the description to refer to those leading the workers to a political strike'.

40 'Statement by the Government on the Recent Conspiracy' (Ministry of Information and Broadcasting, Accra, 11 December 1961), p.14.

41 In Nsawam prison Dr Danquah met Napoleon Grant for the second time. Danquah noted Grant's account of his interview with Nkrumah. 'Mr Grant has a vivid account of how all sorts of things were suggested to his mind...he affirms categorically that there is no truth whatsoever in the assertion that he told the President or the cabinet that some foreign merchants had passed £10,000 through me to the workers at Sekondi-Takoradi to organise a strike against the Government's budget.' ('Dr Danquah: Detention and Death', p.80).

42 'Statement by Osagyefo the President' (Ghana Information Services release, 29 September 1961). The limits laid down by the President were (a) not more than two houses of a combined value of £20,000 (b) not more than two cars (c) plots of land (other than those covered by (a) of a total value greater than £500.

43 Gbedemah later claimed that his own business interests at the time were connected with a poultry farm at Adidome which he had offered to sell to the state in April, but the offer had been refused.

44 As a result of the government's desire to find a sinister, external agent behind the strike, relations with Britain were at a low ebb during these months. The government's white paper on the 'recent conspiracy' argued that a series of articles on the budget published in the London *Times* in July was evidence of foreign 'interference' in Ghana's internal affairs. Some London journalists were summarily deported for reporting the strike.

On 20 September, the *Ghanaian Times* accused the British government of 'History's Number One Murder' of causing the death of Dag Hammarskjold in a plane crash in Northern Rhodesia. When the British government protested, the Ghana government replied that, in Ghana, the press was 'free' to publish what it liked.

45 Nkrumah was easily convinced after the strike that the presence of British officers on secondment to the Ghana forces might be an impediment to the Ghana government's freedom to deal with any future internal upheaval. In fact, the opposite was the case. This point had been made almost two years before, when one observer wrote that:

It is an immense advantage for Dr Nkrumah to have loyal British officers in key positions throughout the army, civil service and police. As a result he can feel confident that the instruments of state will not be turned against him. This, in turn, enables the government to take risks which it would never feel free to do, if potentially unreliable Africans held the posts. The British presence, in short, introduces an unnatural element of stability which makes it

possible for the government to be more blatantly
authoritarian than it would otherwise dare to be.
(Peregrine Worsthorne 'Trouble in the Air: A letter
from Ghana', in *Encounter*, May 1959).

46 *Off. Jnl. Parl. Debs.*, 16 October 1961, col.41.

47 Baako seems to have suffered from epileptic attacks.

48 *Off. Jnl. Parl. Debs.*, 16 October 1961, col.61.

49 The letter was published in the *Ghanaian Times* on 28
December 1961. All that it evoked from Bing was a
non-committal *envoi* to his former colleague, telling him
that 'anyone who is in the service of the state must give
his whole loyalty to the state'.

50 Gbedemah, of course, had gone into exile. E.K.
Dadson never recovered his former status and W.A.
Wiafe was shortly to be detained. But Kojo Botsio
showed remarkable powers of suvival and despite a setback in February 1962 when he was dropped from the
Cabinet again, ended up in 1965-66 as chairman of the
State Planning Commission, leading the cabinet in
order of precedence. Ayeh Kumi became the President's ex-officio 'financial consultant', and Yeboah
was made a regional commissioner. Of those required
to surrender properties to the state in September 1961,
Inkumsah, de Graft Dickson, Korboe, E.K. Bensah and
J.E. Hagan all subsequently maintained — and even
advanced — their positions in the government, Krobo
Edusei, despite incurring the President's disfavour,
proved very durable, although dropped from the last
government in 1965-66.

51 The police showed more zeal than discrimination
immediately after the bombing. Several hundred
villagers were rounded up and about ninety remained in
detention long after the incident. (*Ghanaian Times*, 12
May 1964 and 17 August 1967).

52 Adamafio was with Nkrumah when the latter visited

the Lenin Mausoleum in Red Square. He was reported to have said — out of Nkrumah's hearing — 'They are just like Nkrumah and myself. Nkrumah is like Lenin I am like Stalin.'

53 *Ghanaian Times*, 4 and 10 October 1963.
54 *Off. Jnl. Parl. Debs.*, 6 September 1962, col.61.
55 Ibid., 7 September 1962, col.103.
56 Tettegah has not subsequently been so fortunate. Late in 1973 he and Kojo Botsio were arrested on a charge of plotting against the second military government and both were sentenced to death, although their sentence has subsequently been commuted to long terms of imprisonment.
57 *Off. Jnl. Parl. Debs.*, 7 September 1962, col.140. Boateng survived, despite his immense unpopularity with certain of his colleagues, to continue as a cabinet minister.
58 Sir Arku Korsah was not, however, dismissed from the judicial service, but he resigned from it a few days later, as did his fellow judge in the trial, Mr Justice Van Lare. The third judge presiding over Adamafio's first trial, Mr Justice Akuffo Addo, remained in the judicial service until he was dismissed a few months later. Akuffo Addo became the President of the short-lived second Republic in 1969.
59 *Ghanaian Times*, 13 October 1963.
60 Ametewee chased the President into the kitchens but was stunned by a rebounding swing door before being overpowered by his astonished colleagues. Nkrumah afterwards had himself photographed pinioning the hapless constable to the ground as if at the moment of capture. It is possible that Ametewee, an Ewe, was prompted by a dark, secret grievance of his own, although it is possible to argue, on purely circumstantial grounds, that he was persuaded to act as he did by

certain of his superior officers who could promise him protection if he succeeded.

Chapter V

1 The balance of Ghana's external reserves stood at £171 million in December 1957. Two years earlier they had peaked at £208 million (*Quarterly Digest of Statistics*, Central Bureau of Statistics, Accra).

2 See Walter Birmingham, I. Neustadt and E.N. Omaboe, *A Study of Contemporary Ghana*, vol.1 (*The Economy of Ghana*), table 6.12., p.141 (George Allen and Unwin, London 1966). This remarkable statistic, based upon a comparison between the money wage index and the cost of living index, was a most damaging indictment from official sources of twelve years of continuous CPP rule. At the beginning of 1960 the government announced a seventeen per cent increase in the statutory minimum daily wage of unskilled labourers, bringing it to six shillings and sixpence. But the benefits did not last long. A year later the July budget increased indirect taxation and prices, and by the end of 1962 real wages were down to their 1952 level and declined alarmingly in subsequent years.

3 Peak prices per ton on the New York commodity exchange occured in May and June 1954, when levels of £556 and £557 were reached. From 1954 until 1957 the average price per ton did not fall below £200 and was usually higher. From 1961 onwards prices fell to around £100 per ton (*Quarterly Digest of Statistics*).

4 In *Dark Days in Ghana* Nkrumah stated that 'the forcing down of the price of cocoa was part of their (Britain and the United States) policy of preparing the economic ground for political action in the form of a

"coup" and a change of government'. But the depression in cocoa was world-wide and affected other producers, such as the Ivory Coast, Nigeria and Colombia, towards which western interests were allegedly well-disposed.

5 Nkrumah never successfully related his national economic policies to his political aims. If he had succeeded in transforming Ghana, other African leaders would have been tempted to follow a similar brand of economic nationalism, increasing rather than diminishing the obstacles to unity. On the other hand, Ghana's economic difficulties were soon noticed by other states and reinforced their distaste for Nkrumah's policies.

6 There are signs of a more self-critical attitude amongst economists towards the claims of their profession. Speaking at the American Economic Association in December 1971, Professor Milton Friedman said 'we economists have done vast harm — to society at large and to our profession in particular — by claiming more than we can deliver. We have thereby encouraged politicians to make extravagant promises, inculcate unrealistic expectations in the public at large, and promoted discontent with reasonably satisfactory results because they fall short of our economists' promised land.' (*The Times*, London, 3 March 1972).

7 Prof. A. Lewis, *Report on Industrialisation and the Gold Coast* (Accra, Government Printer, 1954).

8 Ibid.

9 Kaldor had advised the governments of India, Chile, Ceylon and Mexico before arriving in Ghana. After leaving Ghana he was invited to British Guiana where he helped to draw up a similar budget to the one imposed in Ghana in 1961. The political effects were much the same, leading to a general strike in

Georgetown in February 1962. Leaving British Guiana Kaldor served in Turkey and Iran before joining Harold Wilson's 'Hungarian empire' of economic advisers, Thomas Balogh and Michael Posner, between 1964 and 1968.

10 One of these professors was Dr Joseph Bognar from Hungary whose influence was to supersede that of Dr Kaldor as economic adviser to Nkrumah. Bognar, whose political links were with the communist-front Smallholders Party, had been a mayor of Budapest and Minister of Internal and External Trade respectively, between 1948 and 1956.

11 'Foreword to the Seven Year Development Plan' (Office of the Planning Commission, Accra, March 1964).

12 *Off. Jnl. Parl. Debs.*, 11 March 1964 (President's Address to the National Assembly).

13 The number of state corporations continued to increase every year until the coup of 1966. In March of that year, fifty-three state enterprises and twelve joint state-private ventures were in existence, covering a wide range of activities ('Accountant-General's Report, 1967', para. 181). After the coup about half the state corporations were put under the control of a new body, the Ghana Industrial Holdings Corporations, whilst the other half were made into joint state-private enterprises, or dissolved altogether.

14 *West Africa*, 7 April 1965, p.419.

15 Ghana's external balances had toppled alarmingly from £148.6 million in 1960 to £73.7 million in 1961, £42.6 million in 1963. No figures are given for the state of the reserves in 1964-5 (see *Quarterly Digest of Statistics*, Central Bureau of Statistics, Accra).

16 The phrase belongs to Dr Naseem Ahmad in 'Deficit Financing, Inflation and Capital Formation: The

Ghanaian Experience 1960-65' (Department of Economics, University of Ghana, Legon, and Ife-Institut für Wirtschaftforschung, Munchen, p.13). He ascribed the root cause of the severe economic crisis of 1966 to ' ... the fact that domestic output by and large failed to respond to the expansionary impulses generated by deficit financing in the government sector, partly due to the peculiar structure of the economy, and partly due to the very nature and direction of government investment outlays.'

17 White Paper on the Progress of the Seven Year Development Plan (Accra, 1965).

18 Birmingham, Neustadt and Omamboe (op. cit., vol.1), p.170. See also *West Africa*, 9 October 1965, p.317. A statement put out by the Minister of Finance at the time of the 1965 Budget revealed significant differences between the performance of the state enterprises and the joint public-private enterprises. 'In contrast with wholly state-owned enterprises, balance sheets of the joint enterprises reveal that they are able to keep costs at a minimum. Wages and salary bills are moderate and overheads are low while plant is utilised to fullest capacity. The managements were generally more efficient ...'

19 'Report of the Financial Statement by the Accountant-General' and 'Report Thereon by the Auditor-General for the Year ended 30.9.73.' (Accra, Government Printing Dept. 1964. para. 227).

20 Ibid., para. 236.

21 A statement issued by the Ministry of Finance at the time of the 1965 budget warned that even those accounts submitted had to be regarded with caution. Managements were 'sometimes quite ignorant of developments affecting their enterprises' (see *West Africa*, 9 October 1965, p.317).

22 'First Report of the Public Accounts Committee, 22nd May, 1964', para. 8.

23 Ibid., para. 185. This might have been a veiled way of referring to payments corruptly demanded of the manager. It is interesting, however, that it should have been thought acceptable as an excuse.

24 See the following chapter for a fuller account of Djin's career.

25 Ahmad, op. cit., points out that of the twenty manu- facturing enterprises in 1964, 'only ten were working at half, or more than half, of their optimum capacities. In one case (the Paper Bag Division of the Paper Conver- sion Corp. at Takoradi) the rate of utilization was as low as 3.5%.' (p.116).

26 *Off. Jnl. Parl. Debs.*, 12 January 1965, col.10.

27 *Off. Jnl. Parl. Debs.*, 27 August 1965, col.128.

28 Ahmad, op. cit. In 1958-59 the gross domestic product showed a rate of increase of 6.3%; in 1960-61, 5%; in 1962-63, 4%; in 1964, 2.1%; and in 1965 of 1.4%. Ahmad pointed out that 'any increase that did occur in the gross domestic product was increasingly absorbed by a persistent rise in the population.' (p.112). Ghana's average annual rate of population increase in these years was between 2.6% and 2.8%.

29 As inflation gathered pace and as the overseas havens were closed by exchange regulations, those with capital sank it into house building. Frequently their money ran out before their properties were completed. Half- finished houses were a common sight in Accra and its suburbs. The boom in building was one element in the spurious air of prosperity which impressed visitors to Ghana in these years.

30 'Report of the Commission of Enquiry into Irregulari- ties and Malpractices in the grant of Import Licences' (Ollennu Report, 1967, para. 59-60).

31 Ollennu Report, para. 370.
32 Ibid., para. 371.
33 Mary Korentang, one of the twelve lady MP's, was the customary 'wife' of Nkrumah until 1956, when he got rid of her to marry Madame Fathia.
34 Remarking on the confusion arising out of the government's decision in 1964 to make the financial year fit the calendar year, ostensibly to help the seven year plan, the Auditor-General's report commented that 'It is obvious that these frequent changes in accounting periods, far from facilitating comparisons, introduced a great deal of confusion and were nothing more than desperate attempts by the government to postpone the day of reckoning since it was becoming increasingly difficult for them to balance the budget.' ('Report and Financial Statement by the Accountant-General' and 'Report Thereon by the Auditor-General for the Year ended 31.12.64.') (Ministry of Information and Broadcasting, Accra, 1967, part 1, para. 2).
35 E.N. Omaboe, a graduate of the London School of Economics, became the government's chief statistician and co-author of *A Study of Contemporary Ghana* (1966). After the 1966 coup he became chairman of the Economic Committee of the National Liberation Council.
36 Watson Report, op. cit. para. 23.
37 Economic Survey, 1964.
38 'Report and Financial Statement by the Accountant-General and Report Thereon by the Auditor-General for the year ended 30.9.63.' (Government Printer, 1964, para. 29).
39 The government's chief statistician during these years later revealed that 'the true size of the country's external debts was not known, simply because no single agency had a complete inventory of our external debt

obligations.' (E.N. Omaboe, 'The State of Ghana's Economy', Address to the 5th Annual 'Bu Bere' School, Kumasi, 30 August 1967).

40 Many of the projects were 'white elephants' of little economic value. However, such white elephants seem to be inseparable from state intervention in richer countries than Ghana. One could instance the nuclear energy programme, Concorde, Maplin, the Channel Tunnel contemplated or initiated by successive British governments.

41 *Off. Jnl. Parl. Debs.*, 29 May 1964, col.305.

42 *Ghanaian Times*, 11 June 1966.

43 Ibid.

44 In February 1972, it was reported that Colonel Achampong had repudiated debts of nearly 95 million dollars, about one third of the debts still left over from Nkrumah's reign. In addition, his National Redemption Council disowned any debt agreements negotiated since the coup of February 1966. Clearly, whatever the Council sets out to redeem, Ghana's overseas debts were not amongst them. Fortunately for Ghana, cocoa prices have rallied strongly in recent years, giving the government more room to manouevre.

Chapter VI

1 See J.S. Coleman, *Nigeria: Background to Nationalism in Modern Nigeria* (University of California Press, Berkeley, 1948, revised ed. 1953) and John Caldwell 'The New Urban Elite in Ghana' in *Population and Family Change in Africa* (Australian National University Press, 1968). Coleman found that the 'new classes emerging from the western impact ... have not only moved into the upper strata ... they have also displaced

the upper strata in traditional societies ... It is doubtful whether in the modern world such rapid vertical mobility has been equalled.' Caldwell found that 'the élite of Ghana's cities is essentially an administrative élite'. Like the Fanti 'middle class' of the nineteenth century which flourished under the patronage of the colonial establishment, the new urban middle class of Ghana derive their income and status primarily from government service rather than private business.

2 Nkrumah remarked in his autobiography (op. cit., p. 70) that '...it became a standing joke with one of the members (of the Convention) that I was quite indifferent to money and never understood the value of it.'

3 'Report of the Commission to Enquire into the Kwame Nkrumah Properties' (Apaloo Report, N.L.C., Accra, 1966).

4 Apaloo Report, para. 99.

5 Ibid., para. 438.

6 This might have been the lady referred to in Nkrumah's autobiography (p.109) who adopted his name and at a rally in the early fifties slashed her own face and smeared herself with blood to show that no sacrifice was too great for the party.

7 Chief Biney had emigrated to Lagos before the war and prospered as a cargo handling agent. In gratitude for Biney's help to Nkrumah in the past (he provided him with his passage money to the USA) Biney's company was given charge over the Tema harbour stevedoring operations on Nkrumah's directions against the advice of his cabinet (see 'Report of Commission of Enquiry into ... the Ghana Cargo Handling Company', Accra, 1968).

8 Interview with editorial staff of the *Legon Observer*, 19 August 1966. Peduase Lodge was the venue of the

abortive peace talks between representatives of the Nigerian and Biafran sides in January 1967.

9 'Report of the Commission of Enquiry into the Affairs of NADECO Ltd ' (Azu Crabbe Report N.L.C., 1966, para. 198).

10 See the following chapter for an account of the Cocoa Purchasing Company.

11 Government White Paper on the Azu Crabbe Report, para. 2.

12 Edusei's talent for playing to the gallery did not desert him even after the abrupt reversal of his fortunes. The Azu Crabbe Report commented that 'In the midst of conflicting evidence it is a matter of great satisfaction to us that the whole issue should be thrown into bold relief by the evidence of Krobo Edusei ... who ... was the star witness of this enquiry. He was at times theatrical and often loquacious, but we are satisfied he was a witness of truth.' (para. 31)

13 Azu Crabbe Report, para. 29.

14 Andoh and other collectors were brought to trial in May 1967. During his evidence Andoh revealed that NADECO kept five different bank accounts. The ex-President only allowed one of these to be subjected to outside audit as required under corporation law. (*Ghanaian Times* 24 May 1967).

15 W.M.Q. Halm, born in 1902, educated in Freetown and the United States, he belonged to the 'upper crust' of the colonial Gold Coast bridging the gap between the old society and independent Ghana. A member of the British Council, he also became Chairman of the Ghana Industrial Development Corporation, President of the Black Star Line, and sat on the boards of various educational and charitable institutions. He joined the CPP in 1950 and was imprisoned under the emergency regulations.

16 In Ghana Year Book for 1962, Ayeh Kumi is credited with the Queen's Coronation Medal for Public Services, the Order of Merit (Egypt), the Collar of the Grand Officer of the Order of the Star of Ethiopia, the Order of Istiqlal (Tunisia), and the Freiheer von Stein Badge of the Land of Hesse.

17 Statement by Mr E. Ayeh Kumi, in the *Rebirth of Ghana* (Accra, 1966), p. 42.

18 'Public Accounts Committee Report', submitted to the National Assembly, 31 July 1961, para. 4.

19 Ibid., Appendix 'A', p.10.

20 Leventis provided the CPP with its fleet of distinctively coloured propaganda cars which did so much to make the party known in the countryside.

21 Apaloo Report, quoted para. 203.

22 Ibid., paras. 231-3.

23 Ibid., para. 212.

24 Ibid., para. 230. See also Jiagge Report, p. 196-9. Ayeh Kumi informed the Jiagge Commission that he opened an account with the Swiss Credit Bank in Zurich on behalf of Nkrumah on the latter's instructions. Part of the £750,000 was settled on Nkrumah's son, Gorkeh.

25 *Ghanaian Times*, 23 June 1966. After Gbedemah broke with Nkrumah in October 1961, and went into exile, a publication entitled *The Truth about Komla Gbedemah* appeared overseas stating that Gbedemah was living on the interest of £10 million which he had allegedly stolen during his years as Minister of Finance. This allegation originated from the murky recesses of the Publicity Secretariat and was designed to discredit Gbedemah's campaign against Nkrumah in foreign circles. The Jiagge Commission after the coup found no truth in the allegation — but did find that Gbedemah had 'unlawfully acquired' assets valued at £17,000 during his public career.

26　Azu Crabbe Report, para. 112.

27　*Ghanaian Times*, 26 April 1966.

28　*Off. Rept. Parl. Debs.*, 11 March 1964. In essence this was an open acknowledgment that Ghanaians were being subjected to double taxation — the official kind, and an unofficial kind for the benefit of the ruling party. Only two years previously Nkrumah had warned the Kumasi City Council that the collection of 'unauthorized' commissions had to stop — at least, in Kumasi. By 1964, however, the commission system had quietly become an accepted part of life.

29　A comprehensive and detailed list of the funds distributed by NADECO is given in the Azu Crabbe Report.

30　Azu Crabbe Report, para. 168. (Quotation taken from a letter to the Guinea Press from the Secretary to the Cabinet.)

31　Apaloo Report, para. 170. The water in question was in fact Malvern water, a taste for which Nkrumah had acquired from Queen Elizabeth.

32　Ibid., para. 171.

33　Ibid., para. 159.

34　Interview in *Legon Observer*, vol.1., no.4, April 1966. Gbedemah was questioned after the coup about differences between himself and Nkrumah. On the subject of the 1961 budget which Gbedemah was preparing when it was taken out of his hands he said 'He (Nkrumah) wanted £2 million included in the budget ... over which Parliament would have no control. As Minister of Finance I refused to create a new Fund, and I lost my post on that.'

35　*Off. Jnl. Parl. Debs.*, 25 April 1961, col.181.

36　'Report of the Committee of Enquiry into Mr Braimah's Resignation, etc.' (Government Printer, Accra, 1954). Edusei, then Minister of Justice, was reduced to the backbenches and only regained his ministerial rank in July 1956, as a reward for his support during the Ashanti crisis.

37 *Ghanaian Times*, 8 April 1967.

38 Ibid., April 7th, 1967.

39 *Ghanaian Times*, 7 April 1967.

40 Hardwood timbers provide a valuable export for Ghana. Most of the felled timber comes from the Ashanti region and production is divided between small local producers and foreign companies leasing concessions. Until 1960 producers were free to produce, sell and export as they liked, subject only to payment of export duty. In 1960 the government set up a Timber Marketing Board to handle the transport, storage and shipping of the timber. It was not a success, and timber exports declined considerably. Associations of small, local operators tried in vain to get the Board's directors to change their policies. In desperation they turned to Edusei who was successful in getting the Board dissolved. For the generally disastrous effects of government interference with the timber trade, see the 'Report of the Commission of Enquiry into the Affairs of the Timber Marketing Board etc.' (The Blay Report, N.L.C., Accra, 1968).

41 *Ghanaian Times*, 9 May 1967.

42 After the coup Edusei was examined by the Jiagge commission and ordered to refund a total of £307,000 alleged to have been unlawfully acquired. Edusei was subsequently brought to trial, convicted, and given a sentence of imprisonment with hard labour.

43 In 1965 the Commissioner of Police, John Harlley, and his deputy Anthony Deku, considered the possibility of arresting Nkrumah himself under the provisions of this act (see Ch. VIII).

44 *Towards Socialism*, p.7.

45 *The Spark*, 15 February 1963.

46 A typical example of the manner in which the radicals
   dealt with lesser miscreants can be drawn from the column of the anonymous guardian of public morality of the
   Evening News, 'Patu-Bufoso' (the Owl). In the issue of 29
   April 1965, he wished to know 'if that arch-mercenary
   Adjaye Kwame, who falsely claims himself to be the
   brother of the Father of the Nation, does not know that
   the public is aware that Kwame Nkrumah has no brother.
   And if he will stop telling people that he is a security officer
   and refund Musuli villagers £10 which he had collected in
   connection with that bogus day nursery?'
47 *Off. Jnl. Parl. Debs.*, 13 May 1964, col.66.
48 'Rebirth of Ghana: Statement of Mr. E. Ayeh Kumi,
   Economic Adviser to the Ex-President' (Accra, 1966,
   pp.42-3).
49 'Report of the Commission of Enquiry into Alleged
   Irregularities and Malpractices in connection with the
   Issue of Import Licences'. Akainyah Report (Accra, 14
   February 1964).
50 *Off. Jnl. Parl. Debs.*, 13 May 1964, col.66.
51 'Report of the Commission of Enquiry into Irregularities and Malpractices in the Grant of Import Licences'
   (Ollennu Commission: Proceedings, p. 21, para. 147).
52 Akainyah Report, para. 51(a).
53 See Chapter VIII.
54 On the contrary, many of the witnesses who gave
   evidence before the Akainyah and Abraham Commissions were victimized or threatened with deportation.
   Obed Mensah, a Ghanaian trader who testified before
   Akainyah was blacklisted by Andrew Djin, the Minister
   of Trade, despite Akainyah's private representations
   on his behalf. It was only when Djin was replaced by
   Akainyah's friend, Kwesi Armah, that Mensah was
   finally awarded an import licence (Ollennu Commission: Proceedings paras. 538-9).

55 Ibid., para. 46.
56 Ibid. para. 40.
57 Ollennu Report (proc.) op. cit. para. 45.
58 The 'Report on the Second year of the Seven Year (1965) Plan' commented that the expansion of industry had been severely handicapped by 'difficulties in the administration of the import licensing system ... a particularly unfavourable aspect of the situation has been the waste of capital and the loss of potential output when major pieces of capital equipment have been unable to operate owing to an absence of small, but vital spare parts. All sectors of the economy seem to exhibit this feature ... Many industries have had periods of slowdown or even complete stoppage in production.'
59 Ollennu Report (proc.) para. 55.
60 Ibid., para. 57.
61 *Ollennu Commission*, (Proceedings) op. cit. para. 160-7.
62 Ibid., para. 172.
63 Ibid., para. 188.
64 Djin was finally dropped from the government in July, although he retained his seat in Parliament. The *Jiagge Report* (*vol. vi*) subsequently found that, although his properties were acquired from his lawful income, his action in upgrading his own company for increased import licences was 'most improper'. Djin seemed to the Commission to be 'not a prosperous businessman'. He appeared to have spent money as fast as he made it, and his income as stated on his income tax returns was regarded as unreliable.
65 *Ollennu Commission*: (*Proceedings*) para. 472. Mrs Akainyah declined to give any evidence before the Commission. She was later tried before a court of law in July 1968 and sentenced to six years' imprisonment.

66 Mr A.E. Inkumsah, born in Sekondi in 1900, was a pharmacist by profession. He was a foundation member of the CPP and was made Minister of Labour after the 1951 elections.

67 *Ollennu Commission*: (*Proceedings*] para. 741.

68 Ibid., para. 673.

69 After the 1966 coup the N.L.C. set out to examine the assets and activities of specified persons associated with the Nkrumah regime. Their number ran into several hundreds and the work had to be divided between three commissions of enquiry (the *Jiagge, Sowah* and *Manyo Plange* reports, N.L.C. 1966-1968).

70 Kwasi Amoaka Atta — not to be confused with Robert Amoaka Atta — entered parliament first in 1964 for Kade constituency after the murder of the previous member. He was immediately made Minister of Finance and proved to be one of Nkrumah's happier appointments. He had had a banking career and served in New York and Tel Aviv. The Sowah report said of him 'We cannot but observe that he had through all the years the opportunity for self-enrichment (but) in our view he displayed in his banking career those qualities which are expected from men of trust. It is to the greatest credit that he never abused this position.' (Sowah Report, vol.1, p.64)

Chapter VII

1 Employment in the private sector declined steadily over these years, from 149,000 in 1959 to 114,000 in 1965, reflecting the malaise from which private enterprise suffered under the government's economic policies. This decline was offset by a rise in the public sector associated with the creation of a host of state

corporations (figures from *Labour Statistics 1965*, Central Bureau of Statistics, Accra, 1966, Series III, No.10, table 8, p.11).

2 The 'Annual Report of the Labour Department' for 1960-61 referred to a few minor disputes resulting in stoppage of work (table X, p.95) but omits entirely any reference to the strike of September 1961.

3 *The Ghanaian Worker*. The Annual Report for 1960-61 gives a membership of 328,000 for the sixteen recognized unions.

4 The government of Dr Busia during the second republic summarily deported tens of thousands of these African 'aliens' in a desperate attempt to alleviate unemployment. Mass deportation was not an option open to Nkrumah, however, because of his pan-African policies.

5 The Auditor-General's report for the year ended 1963 revealed that the audited accounts of the Brigade had not been released for some time, because the National Organizer had refused to sign them. By June 1963, the Brigade had received grants totalling over eight and a half million pounds. (paras. 219-23).

6 'Report of the Commission appointed to enquire into the Functions, Operation and Administration of the Workers Brigade' (Kom Commission, Accra, 1966, para. 250 and Appendix X).

7 Quoted in the Kom Commission (Minority Report), para. 23.

8 Kom Commission (Majority Report), paras. 288 and 291.

9 Ibid., paras. 347-354, 1967.

10 Ibid., para. 40.

11 *Off. Jnl. Parl. Debs.*, 8 September 1965, col.555.

12 Ibid.

13 The Kom Commission discovered, to its annoyance, that all copies of the Ewah Report had disappeared

without trace. It was, however, able to compile a list of brigadiers and officers from whom sums of public money were to be recovered. On this list, the largest amounts due were from Ababio's successor and his deputy. Like some of their junior staff, they had cultivated the art of drawing the salaries of 'ghost brigadiers' — dead or non-existent members of the Brigade — whose names swelled its pay-roll. This practice was made easier because no one at the Brigade's headquarters had any precise idea of the Brigade's strength.

14 *Off. Jnl. Parl. Debs.*, 12 September 1962, col.221.

15 Ibid., 22 May 1964, col.205.

16 After the 1966 coup the Workers Brigade was given a reprieve, after extensive purges of its administration. Urban unemployment remained one of the gravest problems facing the new regime.

17 1960 *Census of Population. Advance Report* revealed that of the total labour force of over 2.7 million, sixty-two per cent were wholly engaged in agriculture and forestry. The proportion partly dependent upon agriculture must be added to this component. Many counted as engaged in commerce — particularly women — were basically dependent upon an agricultural breadwinner.

18 See Polly Hill, *The Gold Coast Farmer: A Preliminary Survey* (O.U.P. London, 1956) for a succinct account of the traditional organization of agriculture in the cocoa growing areas.

19 Economic Survey, 1963, para. 204.

20 Ibid., para.204.

21 The most common form of non-household labour is the 'abusa' labourer, sometimes called the 'caretaker'. He is paid a one third share of the crop value, the other two thirds going to the employing farmer and the stool

respectively (see Polly Hill, op.cit.). There are, however, many other different kinds of arrangement by which the individual farmer can supplement his household labour.

22 For many years the most important company was Cadbury Brothers, the Quaker firm based in Bournville, England. Cadburys refused to purchase cocoa from the forced labour plantations of Portuguese and Spanish Africa, switching their imports in the late nineteenth century to the Gold Coast. After prohibition was introduced in the United States cocoa drinking was extensively advocated as a night-cap for the tired citizen. Moral principle and profit in the cocoa trade thus worked hand in hand.

23 'Ghana: Seven Year Development Plan', Accra, 1963, p.54.

24 P.T. Bauer, *West African Trade* (Routledge & Kegan Paul, London, 1954), p.316.

25 'Report of the Committee of Enquiry on the Local Purchasing of Cocoa' (De Graft Johnson Report, N.L.C. 1967 Appendix xvii, p.151). After the coup the overseas companies were invited to re-enter the purchasing field but refused.

26 The story of the Cocoa Purchasing Company — which Edusei once referred to as the 'atomic bomb' of the CPP — is contained in the official report which led to its dissolution ('Report of the Commission of Enquiry into the Affairs of the Cocoa Purchasing Company', Jibowu Report, Accra, 1956). Although never as disliked by the farmers as the later Council, the CPC was found to be riddled with irregular practices and to have been in fact an 'unofficial' wing of the ruling party, using its powers to favour the party's friends and intimidate its enemies.

27 De Graft Johnson Report, p.45, para. 174.

28 R.O. Amoaka Atta had been a timekeeper and steno-
    grapher with one of the Ashanti gold mining
    companies. He was elected to parliament in 1954 and
    three years later became Regional Commissioner in
    Ashanti for a few months before becoming Minister of
    Labour and Co-operatives in July 1960.
29 *Off. Jnl. Parl. Debs.*, 17 May 1961, cols. 680-6.
30 Ibid., 23 February 1961, cols. 206-7.
31 Ibid., col. 216.
32 Ibid., col. 223.
33 De Graft Johnson Report, paras, 11 and 15.
34 *Off. Jnl. Parl. Debs.*, 12 March 1965, col.1371. A
    special audit of the UGFCC accounts by the Auditor
    General in 1967 concluded that it 'operated neither as a
    registered friendly society, nor as a registered limited
    liability company ... It suffered a total liability of
    about £1,401,000 in two years on agricultural produc-
    tion operation alone' (*Ghanaian Times*, 31 May 1967).
35 De Graft Johnson Report, para. 33.
36 *Off. Jnl. Parl. Debs.*, 18 June 1963, col.39.
37 De Graft Johnson Report, para. 52. The 'Secretary-
    Receiver' was the title given to the Council's licensed
    buying agents.
38 Ibid., paras. 41-3.
39 Ibid., para. 55.
40 Ibid., para. 65.
41 *Off. Jnl. Parl. Debs.*, 18 May, 1964. Answer by deputy
    Minister of Finance to private member's question.
42 A.W. Osei, one of the few surviving opposition mem-
    bers, described the manner by which the Council
    secured the farmers' 'agreement' 'Whenever there is a
    conference, the UGFCC calls only the officials to meet,
    and the Council asks these officials to convey the
    decision they take at the meeting to the farmers. At the
    meeting the head of the Council just gets up and says

'we are going to do this and that.' (*Off. Jnl. Parl. Debs.*, 28 October 1963, col.353)

43 De Graft Johnson Report, para. 118.

44 *Quarterly Digest of Statistics*, (Central Bureau of Statistics, vol.xiv, table 55).

45 Lord Hailey, *An African Survey* (1956 edition).

46 'First Report and Accounts: Gold Coast Agricultural Development Corporation' (Accra, 1957).

47 Rene Dumont, *False Start in Africa* (English edition, Sphere Books, London, 1962), p.49. For a fuller discussion of the special problems of tropical Africa, see also Pierre Gourou, *The Tropical World* (Longmans Green, London, 1966 edition).

48 'First Biennal Report: State Farms Corporation' (Ministry of Information and Broadcasting, Accra, 1965).

49 'Ghana: Seven Year Development Plan: Report 1963-64 to 1969-70', p. 75.

50 *Off. Jnl. Parl. Debs.*, 16 March 1964, col.160.

51 The first biennal Report of the State Farms Corporation admitted that 'in certain areas where the majority of farmers fully and willingly surrendered their lands to the Corporation, there have been one or two people who, after giving their consent, have risen up in arms against the officers.' The Report then observed, somewhat inconsistently, that 'This resistance was very prevalent in certain parts of the Eastern and Central Regions.'

52 Dr J. Gordon, *State Farms in Ghana*, Case study 120, Symposium on Change in Agriculture, University of Reading, 1968.

53 The State Farms Corporation failed to produce reliable statistics of its own operations. An attempt was made by the University of Ghana to assess independently the performance of the Corporation in *Background to*

Agricultural Policy (Proceedings of a seminar organized by the Faculty of Agriculture, University of Ghana, April, 1969).

54 'Ghana: Seven Year Development Plan: Report for the Second Plan Year 1965', p.19.

55 'On a nation-wide basis they were still, at the time of the 1966 coup, unable to meet their operating costs, much less contribute any return on the initial capital invested.' (Marvin P. Miracle and Ann Seidman, *State Farms in Ghana*, Land Tenure Center, University of Wisconsin, L.T.C. no.43, March 1968).

56 J. Gordon, op. cit., p.6.

57 During a debate in August 1965, the chairman of the Corporation admitted that this kind of interference was widespread. He told of how 'a district commissioner went to a farm and suggested that he should be supplied with 100 tubers of yam a week. People in high positions sometimes come to our farms and instead of buying a few pounds of rice, they buy bags of it. I know that many of these men have large families but you will agree with me, Sir, that in Ghana no family, however large, can consume 100 tubers of yam in a week.' (*Off. Jnl. Parl. Debs.*, 27 August 1965, col.107).

58 'Auditor General's Report on the Accounts of Ghana, 1966-67', paras.242-3.

59 Miracle and Seidman, op. cit.

Chapter VIII

1 'A Bright Future for All', Sessional Address by Osagyefo Dr Kwame Nkrumah, 12 January 1965, Accra.

2 Sir Patrick left Accra in 1967 after forty years service in Ghana. The radicals' hostility to him was not shared by

others. The *Ghanaian Times* wrote that 'He was a disciplinarian of the highest order ... sometimes when irritated, he would shout and bang his fist on the table, but beneath all lies a tender heart and an ardent desire to see that things are done properly.' In April 1965, having successfully weathered the passbook storm, Sir Patrick, in an interview for the *Daily Graphic*, admitted the GNTC's difficulties, but ascribed a major share of the blame to the 'improper shipment methods' used by the trade pact countries who supplied his corporation with an increasing proportion of its goods. The result was confusion and delay in clearing goods through the customs.

3 *Off. Jnl. Parl. Debs.*, 20 May 1965, col.101. Kusi, who had resigned from the CPP in 1954 and rejoined in 1964, was shortly afterwards dropped from the second parliament for this and many other impertinences.

4 *Evening News*, 15 July 1965.

5 *Off. Rept. Parl. Debs.*, 26 August 1965.

6 'Report of the Commission of Enquiry into Trade Malpractices in Ghana' (Abraham Report, 30 August 1965). The members of the commission, in addition to Abraham, were the deputy Attorney General, J.K. Abbensetts, Kwodwo Addison and Kweku Akwei of the party's radical wing, and two lady members of parliament, Lucy Seidel and Lily Appiah.

7 Ibid., para.66.

8 *Off. Jnl. Parl. Debs.*, 30 August 1965.

9 *Off. Jnl. Parl. Debs*, 30 August 1965, cols.206-10. Iddrissu's reference was to paras. 76-93 of the Akainyah report (op. cit.). His earlier reference was about Ambrose Yankey, junior, who was arrested by Special Branch detectives as he collected a £2,000 bribe paid over to him by some Lebanese merchants. Yankey senior remonstrated with Ben Fordjuor, the head of

Special Branch, but Fordjuor refused to release him. Yankey then forcibly removed his son from police custody and Fordjuor promptly re-arrested him. Yankey then went to Nkrumah who demanded that his son be released. But the magistrate had already remanded him and the President ordered the case to be dropped on security grounds. Fordjuor, until then an ardent Nkrumaist, was dropped from Special Branch.

10 The committee was drawn largely from amongst the new members of parliament, the 'socialist boys' and ideologues, who had little regard for parliamentary conventions and the autonomy of its debates.

11 The 1960 constitution said nothing about the constitutional position of the CPP. The 1964 Act had made the CPP the only constitutionally permitted party, but said nothing about the nature of its relationship to the National Assembly.

12 *Off. Jnl. Parl. Debs.*, 7 September 1965, col.490. The last reference was to Komla Gbedemah whose execution in this manner was suggested in the press in 1962.

13 *Off. Jnl. Parl. Debs.*, 7 September 1965, col.526.

14 Iddrissu's motion was put to the Assembly and agreed. Those who actually spoke in favour, or revealed themselves in sympathy with its author, numbered twenty one. They were from a variety of backgrounds, but all belonged to the backbenches.

15 The only account of the Peduase Lodge meeting is in Samuel Grace Ikoku's *Le Ghana de Nkrumah* (Francois Maspero, Cahiers Libres, 197-8, Paris, 1971). Ikoku, writing from the position of the far left, identified Baako as the villain of Nkrumah's last years, the principal instigator of Adamafio's fall and of the 'cult of personality' which continued to surround Nkrumah.

16 Military coups took place in Algeria in June 1965, in

Dahomey in November, in the Congo (Zaire) and in
Nigeria, the Central African Republic and Upper Volta
early in 1966.

17 *Off. Jnl. Parl. Debs.*, 1 February 1966, cols.2 and 3.
18 Nkrumah later wrote that 'In Ghana the embassies of
the United States, Britain and West Germany were all
implicated in the plot to overthrow my government. It
is alleged that the US ambassador, Franklin Williams,
offered the traitors 13 million dollars to carry out a
coup d'état.' (*Dark Days in Ghana*, p.49). Naturally
the CIA was also alleged to have been involved. The
absence of evidence, however, did not dismay
Nkrumah's sympathizers; it was, rather, itself evidence
of a cunningly concealed plot. As for the allegation
against Britain, Nkrumah had broken off diplomatic
relations in January 1966, over the Labour government's handling of the Rhodesian question. To suggest
that the Labour government could topple Nkrumah
with ease but could do nothing about the rebellious
colonists of Rhodesia would make nonsense of the
history of independent Ghana over the preceding nine
years, and rob Nkrumah of any claim to have been an
authentic African leader.
19 *Off. Jnl. Parl. Debs.*, 4 February 1966, col.40.
20 David Wood, *The Armed Forces of the African States*,
Adelphi Papers, No.27, April 1966, (Institute of
Strategic Studies, London).
21 *Ghanaian Times*, 11 November 1963.
22 Captain Benjamin Awhaitey was convicted early in
1959 for failing to report a coup allegedly being
organized by two opposition MPs. Bing later wrote that
'the events which this trial disclosed were ... a dress
rehearsal of the military coup which was to take place
seven years later' (*Reap the Whirlwind*, p.239). No
evidence, however, was ever produced to show that any

other officers were involved. The government was determined to play up the incident for all it was worth to justify the Preventive Detention act passed earlier in the year. The commission it set up to examine the circumstances surrounding the affair could not reach an unanimous conclusion as to whether there had been a conspiracy or not, or if there had been, whether Awhaitey was a party to it. ('Enquiry into the Matters disclosed at the Trial of Captain Benjamin Awhaitey ... before a Court Martial convened at Gifford Camp, Accra', the Granville Sharp Report, Government Printer, Accra, 1959).

23 Alexander wrote to Colonel Ankrah outlining his objections. 'It is most unwise for several reasons. Firstly it splits up the training and the outlook of the officers into two camps, and that can breed neither contentment or efficiency. Secondly, I consider that such action may in the long run prove dangerous to the President himself.' (H.T. Alexander, *On the African Tightrope*, Pall Mall, London, 1965, p.147). In the event, only about eighty cadets left for Russia. On their return they were usually attached to the Presidential Guard under a presidential 'certificate of urgency' overruling the army's advice that most of them should be discharged as unsuitable for service. The Russians refused to inform the Ghana army of the content of the cadets' training course. (Brig. A.K. Ocran, *A Myth is Broken*, Longmans Green, London, 1968, p.13).

24 The 'Presidential Detail Department' to which Ambrose Yankey's intelligence unit was attached, supervised the 1,500 strong presidential Regiment and in 1965 was busy raising and equipping a second such regiment. It also looked after the secret training camps for training African guerillas under Russian and Chinese supervision for activities in other black African

states. (*Nkrumah's Subversion in Africa*, N.L.C., Accra, 1967, p. iv).

25 Ocran, op. cit.

26 A detailed account of the secret camps and Nkrumah's security services was published by the N.L.C. after the coup (*Nkrumah's Subversion in Africa* and *Nkrumah's Deception of Africa*, 1967). For all the money spent on such activities they were remarkably unsuccessful. Complaints amongst the trainees and the local population about the behaviour of the advisers were common. Few of the guerrillas succeeded in returning to their own countries. The Bureau itself was not very efficient, and in July 1965 its director was dismissed and confined as a mental patient in the military hospital.

27 About 260 police stations existed throughout the country of which about eighty were equipped with motor vehicles and the police radio. The armoured car section, set up in 1958, had 'already proved its operational value in several trouble spots, and has been a marked deterrent to subversive elements during election campaigns'. ('Ghana Police Service: Annual Report for the Year ended 31st December', 1959, Accra, p.14).

28 *Dark Days in Ghana*, p.40.

29 'Dr. Danquah: Detention and Death in Nsawam Prison', p. 54.

30 Kotoka was an Ewe from Fiahoo. Starting his adult life as a school teacher, he first enlisted in 1947, rising rapidly to company sergeant major. He was sent to the officer training school at Eaton Hall in Britain and commissioned in 1954. In the Congo crisis he saw action in Leopoldville and Luluabourg with the second battalion. Returning home he was promoted lieutenant-colonel late in 1961 and given command of the second battalion, this time in Katanga. After the coup he served on the National Liberation Council, but was

killed in the 'mini-coup' in April 1967.

31 After the coup General Ankrah observed that 'when a regime reaches a stage where the top secrets of its intelligence are laid open to the scrutiny of foreign advisers from one bloc, when the head of that regime considers his personal security incomplete without the assistance of experts drawn exclusively from that bloc, then of course, adherence to the principles of "non-alignment" is surely reduced to a farce.' (Major General Ankrah, 'Aspirations of our Nation, N.L.C. 24 March 1966')

32 After the coup it was discovered that their arrest was imminent and that cells had been allocated for them in Nsawam prison.

33 Bentum and Iddrissu were the only two members of parliament not arrested after the coup. Two days afterwards Bentum was made acting secretary general of the TUC.

34 Indeed, Afrifa claimed that independently of Deku and Kotoka he had conceived a plan for a coup in 1964 when stationed at Elmina, but nothing came of this plan. Afrifa had taken little trouble to conceal his antipathy towards the CPP whilst in training at Sandhurst. (Afrifa, *The Ghana Coup*, Frank Cass, London, 1966).

35 *Off. Jnl. Parl. Deb.*, 7 February 1966.

36 Ocran's view was that 'I did not consider myself ready for a coup by then, and to be fair, I had no idea that anyone else was planning a coup. (Ocran, op. cit., p.50-4).

37 Afrifa wrote 'Since November 1965 we had been in a high state of readiness to move into Rhodesia at short notice. We exploited this situation to deceive the intelligence situation.'

38 In addition to the books by Brig. Ocran and Col.

Afrifa, both of which deal in some detail with the actual seizure of power, there is also an entertaining work by the Rev. Peter Barker, *Operation Cold Chop* (Ghana Publishing Corporation, 1969). Prof. Ofusu Appiah's eulogy on the life of Kotoka is also worth consulting (*The Life of Lt. General E.K. Kotoka,* Waterville Press, Accra, 1972).

39 Peter Barker's book (op. cit.) recounts that when an excited American told the Ambassador Hotel group of the firing going on in the vicinity of Flagstaff House, one chief said, 'if there is so much fire and firing all over the place, why don't we call in the Fire Brigade?'

Chapter IX

1 The nineteen members of the Constitutional Commission included two former CPP members of parliament, Bentum and Braimah, members of the former opposition parties, members of the young, university-educated group connected with the *Legon Observer*, and other public men. No soldiers or police officers sat on the Commission.

2 Robert Pinkney who has chronicled the first period of military rule (*Ghana under Military Rule, 1966-69*, Methuen, London, 1972) judged Dr Busia's victory as due to a widespread desire to prevent the return to power of those who had ruled before 1966. Certainly the parties led by some of Nkrumah's former lieutenants, such as Gbedemah and Quaidoo, who had broken with their master before his fall, made a poor showing.

3 Professor Ofusu Appiah, who never bothered to conceal his distaste for Nkrumah and his regime, commended that 'we are a noisy people and we admire noise-makers, and noise-makers generally do not make

deep thinkers.' Of the future, he concluded gloomily that 'the discipline needed amongst the educated classes in Ghana to establish an efficient and honest administration does not exist.' (*Legon Observer*, 14 October 1968).

Select Bibliography

I Books on Ghana's Political History, 1945-1972

Afrifa, A.A., *The Ghana Coup*, Cass, London, 1966.
Alexander, H.T., *On the African Tightrope*, Pall Mall, London, 1965.
Apter, D., *Ghana in Transition*, second revised edition, Princeton University Press, Princeton, N.J., 1972.
Austin, D.G., *Politics in Ghana, 1946-1960*, revised edition, Chatham House by Oxford University Press, London, 1970.
Austin, D.G. and Luckham, R. (eds), *Politicians and Soldiers in Ghana*, Cass, London, 1975.
Barker, P., *Operation Cold Chop*, Ghana Publishing Corporation, Accra, 1969.
Bing, G., *Reap the Whirlwind*, McGibbon and Kee, London, 1968.
Birmingham, W., Neustadt, I. and Omoboe, E.N., *A Study of Contemporary Ghana,* vol.1 *The Economy of Ghana,* vol.2 *The Social Structure,* George Allen and Unwin, London, 1966.
Bourret, F.M., *Ghana: The Road to Independence 1919-1957*, Oxford University Press, London, 1960.
Bretton, H., *The Rise and Fall of Kwame Nkrumah*, Pall Mall, London, 1966.
Davidson, B., *Black Star: A View of the Life and Times of Kwame Nkrumah*, Allen Lane, London, 1973.
Dowse, R.E., *Modernisation in Ghana and the USSR: A Comparative Study*, Routledge, London, 1969.

Dunn, J. and Robertson, A.F., *Independence and Opportunity: Political Change in Ahafo*, Cambridge University Press, London, 1974.

Fitch, R. and Oppenheimer, M., *Ghana: The End of an Illusion*, Monthly Review Press, New York, 1966.

Genoud, R., *Nationalism and Economic Development in Ghana*, Praeger, New York, 1969.

Harvey, W.B., *Law and Social Change in Ghana*, Oxford University Press, London, 1966.

Ikoku, S.G., *Le Ghana de Nkrumah*, Francois Maspero, Cahiers Libres, Paris, 1971.

Marais, Genoveva, *Kwame Nkrumah as I Knew Him*, Janay Publishing Company, Chichester, 1972.

Nkrumah, K., *Ghana: The Autobiography of Kwame Nkrumah*, Nelson, London, 1957.

Ofusu Appia, L.H., *The Life of Lieut. Gen. E.K. Kotoka*, Waterville Publishing House, Accra, 1972.

Omari, T.P., *Kwame Nkrumah: The Anatomy of an African Dictatorship*, C. Hurst, London, 1970.

Owusu, M., *The Uses and Abuses of Political Power*, University of Chicago Press, Chicago, 1970.

Peil, Margaret, *The Ghanaian Factory Worker: Industrial Man in Africa*, Cambridge University Press, London, 1972.

Pinkney, R., *Ghana Under Military Rule, 1966-1969*, Methuen, London, 1972.

Rubin, L. and Murray, P., *The Constitution and Government of Ghana*, Sweet and Maxwell, London, 1961.

Thompson, W.S., *Ghana's Foreign Policy*, Princeton University Press, Princeton, N.J., 1969.

Woronoff, J., *West African Wager: Houphouët versus Nkrumah*, Scarecrow Press, London, 1973.

II. A Selection of Nkrumah's Publications

I Speak of Freedom: A Statement of African Ideology, Heinemann, London, 1961.

Africa Must Unite, Heinemann, London, 1963.

Some Essential Features of Nkrumaism, Lawrence and Wishart, London, 1964.

Consciencism, Nelson, London, 1965.

Neo-colonialism, The Last Stage of Imperialism, International Publishing Company, New York, 1965.

Axioms of Kwame Nkrumah, Panaf Publications, 1967.

Dark Days in Ghana, Lawrence and Wishart, London, 1968.

Statement by Osagyefo, the President, at the Seminar for Civil Servants at Winneba, 14 April 1962, Ministry of Information and Broadcasting, Accra, 1962.

Towards Socialism: Osagyefo's Message to the Seminar for Regional Commissioners, Regional Secretaries, Party Attachés, District Commissioners and Senior Officials of the Party's Integral Wings, and the Seminar for Members of Parliament, 1962, Ministry of Information and Broadcasting, Accra, 1962.

III. Ghana: Official Publications, 1960-1965

Statement by the Government on the Recent Conspiracy, December 1961 (White Paper 7/61), Ministry of Information and Broadcasting, Accra, 1962.

Report of the Commission of Enquiry into Alleged Irregularities and Malpractices in connection with the Issue of Import Licences (Akainyah Report), Ministry of Information and Broadcasting, Accra, 1964.

Report of the Commission of Enquiry into Trade Malpractices in Ghana (Abraham Report), Ministry of

Information and Broadcasting, 1965.

Industrial Census Report, 1962 (Central Bureau of Statistics), State Publishing Corporation, 1965.

Industrial Statistics, 1962-64 (Central Bureau of Statistics), State Publishing Corporation, 1965.

Economic Surveys, 1960-65, Ministry of Information and Broadcasting, Accra.

Reports and Financial Statements by the Auditor General for the years ending 30 September 1961-64, Ministry of Information and Broadcasting, Accra.

Reports of the Public Accounts Committee of the National Assembly, 1961-65, Ministry of Information and Broadcasting, Accra.

Seven Year Development Plan for National Reconstruction and Development, Office of the Planning Commission, 1964.

The Ghana Gazette, 1960-65.

IV. National Liberation Council, 1966-69, Official Reports of Commissions and Committees of Enquiry

Commission appointed under the Commission of Enquiry Act, 1964, to enquire into the Kwame Nkrumah Properties (Apaloo Report), 1966.

Commission of Enquiry on the Commercial Activities of the Erstwhile Publicity Secretariat (Ribeiro Ayeh Report), 1966.

Commission appointed to enquire into the Functions, Operation and Administration of the Workers Brigade (Kom Commission — Majority and Minority Reports), 1966.

Committee of Enquiry on the Local Purchasing of Cocoa (De Graft Johnson Report), 1967.

Commission of Enquiry into Student Disturbances and

Alleged Irregularities and Malpractices in the Administration of the University of Science and Technology, Kumasi (Manyo Plange Report), 1967.

Commission of Enquiry into Irregularities and Malpractices in the Granting of Import Licences (Ollennu Report), 1967.

Commission on the Structure and Remuneration of the Public Services in Ghana (Mills Odoi Report), 1967.

Commission appointed to Enquire into the Manner of Operation of the State Housing Corporation (Effah Report), 1968.

Commission appointed to enquire into the Manner of Operation of the State Distilleries Corporation (Taylor Report), 1968.

Commission of Enquiry into the Circumstances surrounding the Establishment of the Ghana Cargo Handling Corporation (Koranteng Addow Report), 1968.

Proposals of the Constitutional Commission for a Constitution for Ghana, 1968.

Commission appointed to enquire into Conditions prevailing in the Ghana Prison Service, 1968.

Commission of Enquiry into the Affairs of the Timber Marketing Board (Blay Report), 1968.

Commission of Enquiry into the Affairs of the National Development Corporation (NADECO Ltd) (Azu Crabbe Report), 1968.

Commissions of Enquiry into the Assets of Specified Persons (Jiagge, Sowah and Manyo Plange Reports), 1966-1968.

Other NLC Publications

A New Era in Ghana, Ministry of Information, Accra, 1966.

Rebirth of Ghana, Ministry of Information, Accra, 1966.
A Year in Review, Broadcast on first anniversary of 1966 coup by Lieut.-Gen. A.A. Ankrah, Chairman, National Liberation Council, 1967.
Nkrumah's Deception of Africa, Ministry of Information, Accra, July 1967.
Nkrumah's Subversion in Africa, Ministry of Information, Accra, November 1967.
Ghana's Economy and Aid Requirements in 1967.

V. Newspapers and Periodicals

Africa Research Bulletin, London.
Daily Graphic, Accra.
Evening News, Accra.
Ghanaian Times, Accra.
Ghana Year Book, 1960-, Accra.
Legon Observer, University of Ghana.
The Spark, Accra.
West Africa, London.
West African Directory, London.

VI. Articles

Ahmad, N. 'Deficit Financing, Inflation and Capital Formation: The Ghanaian Experiment, 1960-65', University of Ghana, Department of Economics, 1966-67.
Austin, D.B. 'The Ghana Case', in *Politics of Demilitarisation*, collected seminar papers, Institute of Commonwealth Studies, London, 1966.
Austin, D.G. 'Opposition in Ghana, 1947-67', in *Government and Opposition*, vol.2, no.4, July-October 1967.

Austin, D.G. Six articles on Ghana's 1969 general election in *West Africa*, August-September 1969.

Blunt, M.E. 'State Enterprise in Nigeria and Ghana. The End of an Era?', in *African Affairs*, vol.69, no.274, 1971.

Busia, K.A. 'Prospects for Parliamentary Democracy in the Gold Coast', in *Parliamentary Affairs*, Journal of the Hansard Society, vol.5, no.4, autumn, 1952.

Finer, S.E. 'One Party Regimes in Africa: Reconsiderations', in *Government and Opposition*, vol.2, no.4, July-October 1967.

Folson, K. 'Nkrumah's Ghana', in *Encounter*, July 1969.

Goldsworthy, D. 'Ghana's Second Republic: a Post-Mortem', in *African Affairs*, vol.72, no.286, January 1973.

Gordon, J. 'State Farms in Ghana' in symposium on change in agriculture, occasional papers, University of Reading, 1968.

Grayson, L.E. 'Role of Suppliers' Credits in the Industrialisation of Ghana', in *Economic Development and Cultural Change*, vol.21, no.3, April 1973.

Hodge, P. 'The Ghana Workers Brigade', in *British Journal of Sociology*, vol.15, 1964.

Hodgkin, T. and Huxley, E. 'Two Views: What Future for Africa?', in *Encounter*, June 1961.

Hodgkin, T. 'The Nkrumah Myths', in *Venture*, vol.18, no.5, 1969; and letter to *The Times*, London, 5 March 1966.

Ingham, B.M. 'The Ghana Cocoa Farmers. Income-Expenditure Relationships', in *Journal of Development Studies*, April 1973.

Kraus, J. 'On the Politics of Nationalism and Social Change in Ghana', in *Journal of Modern African Studies*, vol.7, no.1, 1969.

Lawson, R. 'The Distributive System in Ghana', a review

article in *Journal of Development Studies*, January 1967.

Lees, J.M. 'Parliament in Republican Ghana', in *Parliamentary Affairs*, vol. 16, 1962-63.

Legum, C. 'Death of Kwame Nkrumah' in *African Contemporary Record*, 1972-73.

Lewis, W.A. 'Beyond African Dictatorship', in *Encounter*, August 1965.

MacRae, D. 'Past and Future of Nkrumahism', in *Government and Opposition*, vol.1, no.4, July-September 1966.

Mensah, J.H. 'Relevance of Marxian Economics to Development Planning in Ghana', in *Economic Bulletin of Ghana*, vol.9, no.1, 1965.

Peaslee, H.J. 'Constitution of the Republic of Ghana', in *Constitution of the Nations*, vol.1, Africa, 1965.

Price, B.M. 'A Theoretical Approach to Military Rule in the New States. Reference Group Theory and the Ghana Case', in *World Politics*, vol.23, no.3, April 1971.

Rathbone, R. 'Businessmen in Politics: Party Struggle in Ghana, 1949-57', in *Journal of Development Studies*, April 1973.

Shaloff, S. 'Sedition Proceedings in the Gold Coast, 1933-39', in *African Affairs*, vol.71, no.283, April 1972.

Staniland, M. 'The Manipulation of Tradition: "Politics" in Northern Ghana', in *Journal of Development Studies*, April 1973.

Szereszowski, R. 'The Process of Growth in Ghana', in *Journal of Development Studies*, January 1965.

Werlin, H.H. 'Consequences of Corruption: the Ghanaian Experience', in *Political Science Quarterly*, March 1973.

Worsthorne, P. 'Trouble in the Air: A Letter from Ghana' in *Encounter*, May 1959.

Worsley, P. 'One Party Democracy in West Africa', in *The Listener*, 4 August 1960.

VII. Dissertations and Theses

Kofi Kafe, J. *Ghana: An Annotated Bibliography of Academic Theses, 1920-70, in the Commonwealth, the Republic of Ireland and the United States of America*, G.K. Hall and Co, Boston, 1974.

Amonoo, B. *The Politics of Institutional Dualism: Ghana, 1957-66,* Ph.D., University of Exeter, 1973.

Peasah, J. *The Ghana Civil Service, 1945-60*, M.Phil., London, 1970.

Saffu, E.O. *Politics in a Military Régime: The Ghana Case, 1966-69*, D.Phil., Oxford, 1973.

Tiger, L.S. *Bureaucracy in Ghana: The Civil Service,* Ph.D., London, 1965.

Twumasi, E.Y. *Aspects of Politics in Ghana, 1929-39: A Study of the Relationship between Discontent and the Development of Nationalism*, D.Phil. Oxford, 1972.

Winstanley, M. *Ghana since 1966: The N.L.C. in Power*, M.Sc., Kano, 1969.

Sources

Composing a history of Ghana's first Republic presents the writer with a wide variety of sources. Most of the important political figures of the time are still alive. At first sight this would seem an inestimable advantage to the historian who is able to cull their memories. But living people change their minds. Their memories, by design or natural decay, become selective and their assessment of the events in which they have played a part has to pay regard to future contingencies. The tide of fortune which first carried them high and then dashed them down may yet turn again in their favour, and it is safer to rely upon the record of statements and activities of such public men when they were in the plentitude of their power than to invite them to recall those same years during the period of reflection allowed to them after their fall.

Official papers of government — cabinet minutes, memoranda and the like — together with the minute books and files of the ruling party must also be treated with caution. They are unlikely to be the repositories of secrets revealing the inner springs of political life. For the most part they are in any case largely inaccessible and unpublished and are likely to remain so. But the party and its 'integral wings' were notoriously inefficient organizations. From the few glimpses of their internal records which have been made available, it seems that these faithfully reflect this inefficiency. A further reservation about these sources stems from the very nature of the polity Nkrumah created. No man can see clearly into the mind of another, even in the most open and disciplined of associations. Where power lies in the hands of one man there is always an area of invisibility about his motives, no matter how sharp the observer's focus. The fate of his people rested upon decisions taken by Nkrumah himself — sometimes for curious reasons known only to himself, and perhaps to a few men behind the scenes who generally found it prudent to keep quiet. Some evidence has since leaked out, but some is likely to remain forever hidden. The apparatus of state — civil servants, cabinet and central committee — was expected to endorse the leader's decisions rather than to inform or challenge them. When Nkrumah changed his mind they were expected to follow suit. But although Nkrumah's decisions were supreme, if not always welcome to his advisers, they were by no means rigorously and comprehensively executed. Few men who wield supreme power can ensure that their commands are always carried out to the letter. Much of what was done — and undone — under the Republic was entrusted to Nkrumah's lieutenants who themselves decided how to enforce the leader's directives within intimate circles of their friends and kinsmen on the backstairs of political life.

There are nevertheless copious and reliable sources about the effects of the government's policies, and about conditions within the ruling party. One of these, neglected perhaps because its very accessibility runs counter to academics' instinctive preference for arcana, lies in the debates of the National Assembly. The Assembly became the only national forum within Ghana. Within its walls ministers at odds with each other and with restless back-benchers were thrown together face to face. Things were said in the heat of debate which proved far more revealing about the mood of the country than anything to be found in the party's literature or in the speeches of the President. Fortunately the Assembly's proceedings were ably and fully recorded by its clerks and stenographers.

Ghana's press during this period is also useful, although in a different way. The leading ideological journal, *The Spark* — so-called after Lenin's famous newspaper — was aimed primarily at a pan-African readership and did not circulate widely within Ghana itself. Nevertheless it contains articles inspired or possibly written by Nkrumah himself. The two main popular newspapers controlled by the Convention Peoples Party — the *Ghanaian Times* and the *Evening News* — had the difficult task of mobilizing popular opinion in support of the government's policies in a country of high illiteracy. A popular press continued to exist outside the party's direct control, but only precariously in view of the party's intolerance of open dissent. But the party press was not simply an instrument of propaganda on behalf of the party as a whole. It was under the control of a faction within the party and spent a great deal of energy attacking its rivals. There was a contrapuntal theme running throughout the lifetime of the Republic made up by the radicals who controlled the press attacking the party's old guard, and being attacked in turn by the old guard within the Assembly. The sparks which fly off from these two points of friction throw a considerable amount of illumination upon the internal politics of the CPP.

Other sources of evidence are to be found from the official, published reports produced by various government agencies and departments. The Bureau of Statistics, the Accountant General's office, the Auditor General's department from time to time issued hard statistical evidence of the economic and financial consequences of Nkrumah's policies, limited only by the slender resources these agencies could command. Their findings were surprisingly frank and detailed, serving as raw material for the investigations of the public accounts committee of the National Assembly. With these sources it is possible to build up a very detailed picture of the last five years of Nkrumah's Ghana.

Other parts of the jigsaw can be filled in from the detailed work accomplished by a number of capable authors upon specialized subjects of life in Ghana. Other works, autobiographical in nature, have appeared from time to time in recent years from those who worked for Nkrumah, as well as against him, at various stages of their careers. Rather surprisingly, but perhaps for the reasons of caution already mentioned, no autobiography has yet appeared from any of Nkrumah's principal lieutenants, although reports suggest that Komla Gbedemah may be preparing his memoirs for publication. The obvious danger of such works, despite their undoubted value, is that they may serve as apologies for their authors' past activities rather than as dispassionate sources of information.

Finally, there are the reports of the various commissions of enquiry set up by the National Liberation Council after Nkrumah's downfall to investigate in detail various aspects of his regime. These commissions were not kangeroo courts or vengeful popular tribunals. They were set up under the provisions of Nkrumah's own Commissions of Enquiry act of 1964 and followed established legal procedures. Law officers and public men, involved neither with Nkrumah's government nor with the successful conspirators against it, presided over them. All sessions were conducted in public and those brought before the commissioners were allowed proper legal prepresentation. The commissions dealt with a variety of issues, but the largest single task which they undertook was an investigation into the personal assets of former ministers and party officials of the Republic, including those of Nkrumah himself, who were suspected of having abused their offices for personal profit. The commissioners' *modus operandi* was a simple one although in detail much of the evidence was inevitably tortuous and confusing. The defendants had their entire income from their public careers and from any other sources shown to be legitimately acquired totted up. The totals were then set against the actual value of their assets at the time of the coup. After making an appropriate deduction on the income side to allow for personal savings, any surplus which could not be satisfactorily accounted for was deemed to have been unlawfully acquired. On the basis of the commissioners' conclusions the new government then decided to take whatever steps it thought appropriate to recover such holdings, and whether further action in the regular criminal courts was desirable.

Most of those arraigned before the commissioners proved co-operative. Very few struck defiant or unrepentant attitudes. There seems to have been a strong desire amongst members of the former ruling party to make a clean breast of things, as if they saw their best hope for the future in a total break with the past. For a short time the old standards of public rectitude reasserted themselves in Ghana's public life, and the former politicians behaved on the whole like chastened schoolboys taking their medicine bravely from the headmaster.

Much of the evidence uncovered by the commissions was unreliable in detail, resting often upon nothing stronger than verbal allegations which the commissioners felt obliged to accept with caution. Nor was the picture of bribery and corruption revealed before them a totally accurate one. The cash bribes for which no receipts were ever taken and which never found their way into a bank account could not be recorded. But the exercise as a whole seems in terms of its comprehensiveness and detail to be unique in recent African history and is unlikely ever to be undertaken again on such a scale. As a source of information about the realities of political life in Ghana's first Republic the commissions' findings are invaluable.

Index

Nkrumah, F.K., (*contd.*)
CPP, 78; relations with his party, 80-1, 91-3, 95-100; 'dawn broadcast' 1961, 106-8; arbiter of party disputes, 114; relations with Gbedemah, 117-18; visit to communist states, 118; handling of 1961 strike, 121-7; assassination attempts on, 133-5, 139; economic opinions and strategy, 142-4, 145-50, 174, *319*; Volta project, 159-60; relations with businessmen, 161-4; and Drevici contract, 171-3; personal wealth, 177-83; connection with NADECO, 184-6; and Leventis deal, 187-8; use of contingency fund, 195-6; policy on agriculture, 246-7; authority questioned in parliament and party, 262-8; policy towards army, 273-7; his fall, 287-9; place in Ghana's history, 290-2, *297, 341*; on his overthrow, *341*
'Nkrumaism', 18, 63
Nsawam prison, 136
Ntosuah, D.K., 81
Nyerere, Julius, 62

Ocran, Brig. A.K., 274, 283, *342, 344*
Ocran, Robert, 163-4
Ofori Atta, K.O., 88
Ofori Atta, W.A., 39, 258
Ofusu Appiah, Prof., *345-6*
Okoh, Enoch, 43, 54, 117, 164, 215, 285
Ollennu report, 216, *322*
Omaboe, E.N., 102, 166, *323, 324*
Osei, A.W., 43, *336*
Osei Bonsu, K.G., 200
Owusu Afriyie, O., 258, *306*
Owusu, Maxwell, 75, *306*
Owusu Sechere, 136, 207-8
Owusu, Victor, 28-9, 120-1

Padmore, George, 9-11, 22, 97, 184, *294-5*

Pan-African congress, Manchester, 8, 9
Phillips, J.V.L., 215
Police Service, 139, 277, *315, 343*
Powell, Miss E., 101
Powerful Bulley, E.K., 72
Presidential commissions, 118, 285
Presidential election, 1960, 29
Presidential Guard unit, 223, 274, 278, 284, *342*
Preventive detention, introduction of, 30-1; numbers detained, 33; effects of, 34-5, 129, *299, 300, 312*
Private business sector, 149, 160-4, *321, 332*
Provencal, H.T.S., 119
Public accounts committee (*see also* National Assembly), 42, 156, 166, 186

Quaidoo, Patrick, 93, 111-14, *312-13, 345*
Quartey, Kwatelai, 97-8

Referendum on single party state, 1964, 86
Regional Commissioners, 68-71, 75-6, *305-6*
Repressive legislation, 35-6, 128-9
Republican constitution, 28, *299*
Ricz, Madam Fathia, 180, 188, *323*
Rodianov, M., Soviet ambassador, 62

Sakyi, K.A., 208
Sandys, Duncan, 127
Sarkodee Addo, 254
Savundra, Dr E., 41
'scientific socialism', 18, 19, 21, 67, *309*
Second republic: constitution of (1968), 289, *345*
Seidel, Lucy, 180, *339*
Seidu, A., 72

For Product Safety Concerns and Information please contact our EU
representative GPSR@taylorandfrancis.com
Taylor & Francis Verlag GmbH, Kaufingerstraße 24, 80331 München, Germany

www.ingramcontent.com/pod-product-compliance
Lightning Source LLC
Chambersburg PA
CBHW060136280326
41932CB00012B/1540